Birth, Death and the Afterlife
Remembering Who You *Really* Are

... in a world filled with food, booze and a gazillion other distractions...

In a world filled with food, booze and a gazillion other distractions, Birth, Death and the Afterlife offers innovative approaches to living fully, peacefully, and loving unconditionally.

"No matter where you are on your spiritual path, Birth, Death and the Afterlife meets you there and guides you to your next level of self-discovery. Designed for spiritual seekers of all types, it includes case studies and stories that awaken, enlighten and empower.
—**Nancy Fischer,**
Author, Choices: Escaping the Illusion of Being a Victim

"A wonderful book. Very comfortable and very deep. It's like having both your best friend and spiritual teacher sitting next to you on your couch, teaching you, reminding you of who you are and what's important in your life."
—**Robert Peterson,**
Author, Out of Body Experiences

"In my work both as a lawyer and a psychic, I have met with hundreds of people struggling with fears, addictions, and blocks, many of which stem from past life issues. Birth, Death and the Afterlife brings marvelous relief by teaching you how to remember your divine self and reclaim your personal power."
—**Kathryn Harwig,**
Author, The Return of Intuition and seven other books

Dr. Kettler escorts you on the journeys of others, using fine-tuned regressive hypnotherapy skills, to discover unremembered memory segments in the soul's life-cycle that validate your human and spiritual existence. It illuminates hypnotherapists, potential clients, and the general readership in multiple areas of personal growth and transformation."
—**Allen S. Chips, PhD, DCH,**
President, NATH, Author, Killing Your Cancer Without Killing Yourself and other hypnotherapy textbooks

Birth, Death and the Afterlife
Remembering Who You *Really* Are

Madonna J. Kettler, PhD

BALBOA
PRESS
A DIVISION OF HAY HOUSE

Copyright © 2012 Madonna J. Kettler, PhD

All rights reserved. No part of this book may be used or reproduced by any means, graphic, electronic, or mechanical, including photocopying, recording, taping or by any information storage retrieval system without the written permission of the publisher except in the case of brief quotations embodied in critical articles and reviews.

Balboa Press books may be ordered through booksellers or by contacting:

Balboa Press
A Division of Hay House
1663 Liberty Drive
Bloomington, IN 47403
www.balboapress.com
1-(877) 407-4847

Because of the dynamic nature of the Internet, any web addresses or links contained in this book may have changed since publication and may no longer be valid. The views expressed in this work are solely those of the author and do not necessarily reflect the views of the publisher, and the publisher hereby disclaims any responsibility for them.

The author of this book does not dispense medical advice or prescribe the use of any technique as a form of treatment for physical, emotional, or medical problems without the advice of a physician, either directly or indirectly. The intent of the author is only to offer information of a general nature to help you in your quest for emotional and spiritual well-being. In the event you use any of the information in this book for yourself, which is your constitutional right, the author and the publisher assume no responsibility for your actions.

Any people depicted in stock imagery provided by Thinkstock are models, and such images are being used for illustrative purposes only.
Certain stock imagery © Thinkstock.

ISBN: 978-1-4525-5898-1 (sc)
ISBN: 978-1-4525-5899-8 (e)
ISBN: 978-1-4525-5900-1 (hc)

Library of Congress Control Number: 2012917474

This material is not intended to be a substitute for medical treatment, but is inspired, complementary information designed to enhance a full and vibrant life. It is intended to be educational and not for diagnosis, prescription, or treatment of any health disorder whatsoever. This information should not replace consultation with a competent healthcare professional. The content of this book is intended to be used as an adjunct to a rational and responsible healthcare program prescribed by a professional healthcare practitioner. The author and publisher are in no way liable for any misuse of the material.

Cover art by Nathan W. Guice

Spirit-Directives artist Nathan W. Guice

Printed in the United States of America

Balboa Press rev. date: 9/25/2012

To my family:

On Earth
Above
Below
Around
and
Within

Table of Contents

Preface		ix
Acknowledgements		xv
One (Poem)		xvii
1.	Addictions, Distractions, Fears and Blocks	1
2.	Balance in Relationships	7
3.	Marching to the Beat of a Different Drummer ◆ Being Creative	19
4.	Destiny and Fate ◆ Building a Stable Foundation	41
5.	Choosing Freedom From ◆ Moving into the Unconventional ◆ Change IS	52
6.	Filters and the Unseen ◆ Dreams ◆ Acceptance of What Is	77
7.	The Power of Words ◆ Seeking Deeper Truths – Inner Reflection ◆ Deception and Perception	103
8.	Forgiveness and Happiness ◆ Worthiness ◆ Manifesting and Empowerment	114
9.	Universal Love ◆ Releasing Fear ◆ Living Consciously and Loving Unconditionally	122
10.	We are Eternal, Divine Beings ◆ Self-Empowerment ◆ Respect	135
11.	Thankfulness and Gratitude ◆ Do Be-ing	143
12.	Celebrating our True Selves	161
13.	Courageous New Beginnings ◆ Be In Love	179
14.	Love Research	195
15.	The I AM WOWED™ Program	200
16.	Grace, the Tao, and NOW ◆ Remembering who we *Really* Are	207
Supplemental Information—Contributing Authors		216
Art/Creativity		217
Brain State Technologies		218
Chakra Clearing		220

Chiropractic	221
Crystals and Rocks	224
EFT (Emotional Freedom Technique)	225
Energetic Resonance Encoding (ERE)	227
Feng-Shui	228
Healing/Energy Work	229
Healing Breath	229
Reiki	230
Health Coach, Life Coaching, Integrative Coaching	231
Do you need a Health Coach?	231
Why Explore Integrative Coaching?	233
Hypnosis and Hypnotherapy	234
Journaling	237
Life Between Lives Spiritual Regression	238
Massage Therapy	240
Meditation	241
Mindful Mediation for Depression	241
Empowerment Through Meditation	242
Mediumship	244
Numerology	246
Oracle Decks	248
Healing with Cards	248
Past Life Regression	250
Reflexology	252
Empowerment With Shamanism	253
Soul Clearing	254
Traditional Chinese Medicine (including Acupuncture)	256
Volunteerism	258
Appendix A Contributing Authors' Contact Information	260
Appendix B Original Creations for Sale	264
About the Author	267

Preface

A small group of women had been guided to come together for a spiritual journey in the Black Hills, having heard countless stories about people coming to the butte to meet spirit animals and receive messages from the ancestors. We were looking forward to our own spiritual experiences, as each was drawn to a different spot to meditate for the day. After dragging my despairingly out-of-shape body to a special spot on Bear Butte in the Black Hills of South Dakota, I carefully and deliberately arrange my sacred objects around me. I placed my blanket on the loose rock, burned some sacred sage to "set the intention and clear the space," all in anticipation of receiving Divine Guidance on where to go or what to do next in my life.

Anticipation high, I began the process of going within. The rocky slope I was called to was uncomfortable at best, the day steamy hot, but I was determined to get some guidance!

Within a few minutes, I was deep in meditation, oblivious to the wind and burning sun.

Nothing.

I chanted awhile. Breathed deeply, going deeper within than I'd ever experienced before.

More nothing.

Then, after two more hours, I felt a connection… I connected with the wind as it spoke to me, and was filled with a sense of oneness as I *finally* heard three words, very clearly.

Be In Love.

The feeling of oneness quickly passed. Did I make this up? Are you kidding me? I drove 800 miles to hear three friggin words?

I tried again but after two more hours of listening and breathing, I knew I was done for now. After gathering up my goods, I gingerly descended down the steep, slippery butte.

On the drive back to Minnesota everyone shared the information they received and the personal experiences they had. Mine seemed to pale in comparison, yet wasn't I learning to *not* compare, and to be grateful for whatever experience I had?

Okay. I'll try.

At the time, I had no idea the impact these three wind-driven words would have! They have become me. They are emblazoned in my heart, in everything I do and *am*.

Those three words started me down a path of remembering instead of the destructive path I had been on the first forty years of my life. They were the impetus for the years of research I have done, and are the primary reason I pursued this book—to share and to assist you in remembering that we are love.

There's no one way to Be In Love. Be-ing in love is simply an energy field, an is-ness, an experience. It is not do-ing. Love is not an emotional, affectionate, sexual, or overt gesture. To Be In Love is to remember your Divine Essence.

Most certainly, love is different for each of us. There is energy in love that is different for everyone, yet the same. This book will assist you by sharing a variety of personal stories and case studies on how the contributors came to a place of Love; how they removed blocks, addictions, distraction and fears in order to acquire inner peace, live their full potential and remember their true, Divine Selves (Love).

Life can be a grand, joyous experience or a persistent, all-encompassing struggle. Most of you reading this already know we don't die, and that we are spiritual beings having a human/Earth experience, not the reverse. Yet many of us may not know how to optimize this Earth experience. In the following chapters you will be guided on how to remember your Divine Self in every moment. Through the sharing of the following case studies, life experiences, and dedicated research results, you will discover *your* way to remembering. Jung said, "When the unconscious becomes conscious, change happens." The past twenty years of my life have been about just that—remembering—first remembering who I really am, then assisting others in this wonderful recall, through hypnosis, meditation and a myriad of other holistic practices.

I personally have benefited greatly from hypnotherapy, hypnosis, meditation, energy healings and most of the holistic modalities covered in this book. I also have created various techniques and methods that help me and others achieve a deeper sense of Self. As you will see in the following chapters, when we remember our Divine Self (as opposed to the egoic, human self), everything changes. This transformative process can take as short or as long as you desire. It's all up to you.

Life truly is a journey that never ends. We don't die, we don't even really "cross over," we simply *change our vibration*. Only our physical body returns to dust. Our spirit, soul and Divine Self goes on forever. And Earth is not the only school! In the following chapters you will discover there are unlimited ways for us to evolve, not just on Earth. In this book, many beautiful souls share *their* current truths and profound experiences in order that you may come to realize what *your* truths are. As Shirley MacLaine said in *Sage-ing While Age-ing*; "I've come to believe it's all true." Discovering my personal truths and choosing to march to the beat of a different drummer has not been easy, but it *has been worth it*.

What we experience as truth is determined through our personal filters. The same experience may be perceived differently by someone else. What is most important is that we ultimately find our way back to Love. That is our life purpose and our mission, should we choose to accept it: *Be In Love*.

While this book may feel like a "how to" dialogue, I'd like to suggest that as you read, you *observe how you are feeling* relative to the case studies and others' experiences, then *check with your intuition* to see what could work for YOU. My dad used to say, "Everybody's different, otherwise it would be a pretty boring world." A friend of one of my sisters, an 80-year old Benedictine Sister of German descent used to say, in her very strong, German brogue, "Everybody different, everybody right."

There are many ways to remember our Divine Selves. It's up to us to discover what works best for us.

In Chapter 1 we discuss how addictions, distractions, blocks and fears can keep us from remembering. I used to feel I was pretty much done with releasing fears and addictions and the forgiveness work attached to that, only to discover that as *long as I'm breathing, I'm not done!*

Chapters 2 through 13 spotlight the different topics covered in the I AM WOWED™ (I AM Worthy of Whatever Empowerment Desired) Program. In each of these chapters I reveal several of the forty-four Spirit-

Directives related to that chapter's focus. These Spirit-Directives are also uniquely appropriate to two weeks of the Program. Also included is a case study or personal story related to how an individual overcame a specific issue in order to *remember who they really are*.

Chapter 14 outlines the results of the research done in relation to the I AM WOWED™ Program and summarizes how, through the use of self-hypnosis, movement and sometimes regression therapy, the participants were more able to love themselves unconditionally.

Chapter 15 gives an in-depth description of the I AM WOWED™ Program and outlines how it can help people manifest whatever they desire into their own lives. This is the program that all of my research has been about. It has helped participants release weight, remove creative blocks, promote their business, and move through a variety of blocks and fears that had plagued them for years and sometimes lifetimes.

In Chapter 16, the Epilogue, all my research, personal education, and recent channeled guidance are combined to summarize just what remembering who we really are means.

After the Epilogue there is a section entitled "Supplemental Information" which includes a variety of contributing authors sharing how their holistic modality can assist in the process of permanently releasing anything that no longer serves us. There are articles on acupuncture, shamanism, hypnotism, art/creativity, and meditation, to mention a few. These modalities have helped me and many others in finding our Dharma! Some of the contributors were also participants in the Love Research. All of the contributors share what has worked for them, and their contact information is included in Appendix A.

Originally, the title of this book was "*Rescripting Your Life: Living Fully in a World Filled with Food, Booze, and a Gazillion Other Distractions.*" Over the course of many years, as research and inspirations came and went, it occurred to me that my Creator wouldn't ask me to rescript my life, so why am I asking this of me? My Creator loves me unconditionally. The great sages say for us to remember who we really are is the most important message of our time. Once we remember who we really are, everything changes. We change from unconscious to conscious beings that can love ourselves and all beings unconditionally, and we realize our connection to All That Is.

So I changed the title, because the most important message of our time *is* the most important message in this book—to remember who we REALLY ARE—Divine, Spiritual Beings who are loved unconditionally, no matter what. We are all connected; we are all one. Love.

Bartholomew, an energy that was channeled through Mary Margaret Moore, says that we came to Earth to experience the full range of emotions and to become master of those emotions. He says that mastery comes when we realize we can choose our responses, we can choose which thoughts we accept and bring into our life. He suggests that most of the thoughts we typically accept have to do with the misguided notions that we are not loveable, not worthy, there is something wrong with us, and that we have to do something in order to be loveable. He suggests, as do I, that we begin today, to love ourselves, *no matter what*. We can do this by repeating the mantra over and over again until we *get it*—I AM LOVED, I AM LOVE, I LOVE. This progression begins with the realization: *I am loved,"* moves us to a state of be-ing in love with *"I am love,"* and then we come to a place of sharing our love through the last two words, *"I love."* Any blocks or thoughts we may encounter deep within that may cause us to believe we are anything less than pure love, *can be released*. This book will guide you to your fullest potential—LOVE.

There are many books that affirm this. *A New Earth* by Eckhart Tolle, the works of Dr. Michael Newton and The Newton Institute, Dr. Wayne Dyer, Marianne Williamson, the Kryon channelings, Steve Rother and The Group, as well as Bartholomew, Gary Zukav, Louise Hay, to mention only a few. Over and over we are told that we are Divine Spiritual Beings, yet we tend to forget and fall into old, destructive patterns. *Birth, Death and the Afterlife* is about embracing all we are and accepting ourselves, unconditionally, in every moment.

I have continually had the *opportunity* to work through the challenges of a plethora of addictions, distractions, fears, and blocks, beginning at a very young age. Now it feels right for me to share how many have come to love themselves in the most magnificent manner—at least MOST of the time! For me it began with that first contact on Bear Butte.

We are all "a work in progress." We are loved unconditionally by our Creator, and we are asked by our Creator to love ourselves as He/She loves us. This is a self*less* love, not a self*ish* love. When we get this, life IS love, life IS an adventure!

In the following chapters I will share many of my own and others' stories and experiences. My truths come from these and other experiences, as well as my intuition, extensive research, and education—but they are MY truths. As you read this book, enjoy, listen to *your* intuition, try not to take anything personally, and if the words don't feel quite right for you, *change them* to words that work for you! My intention here is to help you find your truths as I and others have found ours, and to assist you in remembering… who you REALLY are.

LOVE.

With deepest affection and gratitude,
Madonna Joeletta Kettler
Silver City, NM 2012

Acknowledgements

The creation of this book involved the patience, fortitude, and commitment of many people, including those who volunteered their case studies, the Love Research group, an infinite number of beings who contributed their knowledge and expertise, as well as friends and family, who supported me, knowingly and unknowingly, throughout this nearly 10-year process.

It was wonderful working with my editors, Lily Rivertree, Rebecca Blackman, Karen Lauseng, and Donna Clayton Walter—your expertise allowed the words to transform into readable and enjoyable text! Many thanks to the artistic contributor, Nathan Guice (cover art and Spirit-Directives creator), whose artwork continually inspires me. And to everyone else involved with the publishing and printing of this book—the clients, book contributors, friends—thank you all so very, very much. Without all of you this project would never have been completed. I am also eternally grateful to every dimension of myself for finishing this project! *There were times…!*

Finally, thanks to those Above, Below, and Within, my Spirit Helpers, Ancestors, and the God in every thing, for guiding my fingers, thoughts, and inspirations. It continues to be an honor to serve, in any capacity, the Greater Good.

Namasté

One

by Madonna J. Kettler, PhD
Inspired on a *VERY* windy day on Port St. Joe Beach, Florida

The Wind
    Holds my head up
    Straightens my hair
    Sometimes reduces my movements to cartoonish slow motion.
The Wind
    Stops my breath
    It is itself breath
    It calms my spirit and clears my soul.

The Water
    Has a rhythm
    Has a sound
    That changes, based upon Wind and Earth.
The Water soothes
And the Water crashes against the Earth.
The Water sustains everything –
And over-sustains at times.
The Water cools and warms.
Has its own rhythm, guided by Wind and Earth.

The Earth
    Holds a story,
    Shares her wisdom, holds me in her womb.
She nurtures and supports me.
She sings to me, disorients me, fools me into thinking she is angry (sometimes rightly so?)
She allows Wind to alter her figure,
And Water to divide her into seemingly separate personalities,
But she fools us in that as well.
When she moves, those around her take heed: she is noticed.
And she loves, and loves, and loves.
She regards Water and Wind as her champions.
And the kinship of these three is Spirit.
Is God.
Is who WE are.
One.

Chapter 1
Addictions, Distractions, Fears and Blocks

Addictions

We are an addiction-driven society. Anything we do can easily become habitual—not just alcohol or drugs or sex, but TV, gaming, relationships, food, computers, health, work, you name it, has the potential to become addictive behavior. Eckhart Tolle calls compulsive thinking an addiction. So if anything can become addictive, what specifically characterizes an addiction?

We are addicted to something when we no longer feel we have a choice in using or doing it. We are powerless over it. The addictive behavior also gives us a false sense of pleasure that invariably turns into pain. An addiction can be a habit that causes us stress, a craving that overwhelms any logical thinking, an obsession that can alienate us from friends, family, and most importantly, our Divine Self. A person is addicted to alcohol when they cannot stop at one drink, or when one drink leads to another, *no matter what the initial intention was*. The drinking ultimately takes the person past the false sense of pleasure to pain when they realize, once again, they could not stop when they wanted to. Likewise, watching television is not an addiction until we have it on 24/7 or cannot get by without watching a certain program or if it causes friction in a relationship. Food is not usually addictive but can become so when a person constantly thinks about it, or consistently eats more than desired. Then it may be time to look at their relationship with food. Even giving of self, when taken to the extreme, could be classified as an addiction, when it causes us to neglect our health, family, or spirit, and is not centered in loving service to others.

Whatever causes us to think from our ego can potentially lead to or become an addiction. Anything we do and think can turn into an addiction of some sort, or at least a distraction, that can keep us caught in a hamster cage. Addictions can keep us from remembering who we really are and work very well in stifling or diminishing any light we hold. They are a huge block in our spiritual as well as physical, emotional, and mental growth, which makes them, in my mind, the number one contributor to all the chaos, depression, fear, and anger that can disrupt our lives.

Distractions

Distractions, when discussed in this book, are generally considered to be a lesser form of addiction. While a distraction may not cause you the distress and pain an addiction might, it certainly could cause you to delay, postpone, or in some way deter you from the path you'd like to be taking. A distraction causes you to divert from your original intention, interrupt a program you had started, or disrupt your thought process without actually taking you completely away from it.

In most cases, a distraction won't negatively affect others (or yourself) as an addiction usually does, but it still has all the qualities that could cause distress or lead you down a road you would rather not experience. For example, an addiction to gaming would consume most of your waking hours while if you were distracted by gaming, it would merely cause you to interrupt what you were doing or divert you from your original goal for that day while still allowing you to eventually get back to whatever you were intending to do. In addition to that, a distraction could even have the potential to be healthy, whereas an addiction is most often seen as something negative that keeps you from… (fill in the blank.) A distraction could be a vacation or leisure activity that draws you away from an addiction like work. Alcohol as a distraction would be perhaps having a drink instead of taking the walk you intended to, or from a different perspective, having a drink when a friend drops over and temporarily postpone mowing the lawn for the time being.

Fears

Fears are anything that prevents you from living peacefully. They can present themselves as worry, suspicion, or doubt, and can move you into anxiety if strong enough. We all know what fears can do, but perhaps what we do not realize is how detrimental they can be to our peacefulness. A fear, like anything else, can be very small or it can be overwhelming. Lately it seems many of us have been consumed with fear—especially if we choose to listen to what our government or news media are saying about most anything. (I have pretty much eliminated watching the news and most TV for just this reason.)

Fears can mask themselves as other things like the notion of being careful, not taking any chances, taking precautions when in fact we are being *too* careful, afraid to take *any* chance, or being *overly* cautious in a variety of circumstances. For example, it may be a good idea to not drive in Los Angeles during rush hour if you are afraid of traffic, but if your job requires it, it would be healthy to either overcome that fear or find an alternative way to get to work. Likewise, fear of rattlesnakes may be a healthy fear, yet if just the thought of them causes anxiety, it may be healthy to look at the root of that fear.

In my earlier years I was overwhelmed by fear: fear of not getting married, then fear of losing my husband, fear of not having a job, fear of losing the house, fear of having children, fear of not being able to have children, fear of losing the children for any reason, fear of anything that deviated from my Midwestern perspective of "normal." Through diligent personal work and with the help of other holistic practitioners, I have released the greater portion of these fears as well as a healthy amount of the addictions and distractions that had consumed my life. Oh, I still have a few that crop up from time to time, but as the saying goes, "If I'm still breathing, I'm not done."

Blocks

Blocks are anything that prevents you from doing, being, feeling, intuiting, seeing, hearing, tasting, experiencing, or manifesting your desires. Emotions such as anger, rage, sadness, grief, despair or terror, and negative thinking or stubbornness are just a few examples of what can create blocks.

Addictions, distractions, and fears are all blocks, but not all blocks are addictions, distractions or fears. You usually know when you experience a block, because your intentions do not manifest or you feel completely stuck.

There are many, many ways to release fears, distractions, addictions and blocks, including the I AM WOWED™ Program, discussed in Chapter 15, and other holistic practices, some of which are described in "Supplemental Information" in the back of this book. There are many paths that can lead you toward your best life. Through a variety of holistic practices that focus on releasing anything we no longer desire to have in our lives, then introducing other practices like meditation, fitness, mindfulness, and focusing on whatever brings us to a place of peace within, anything is possible. When we regularly remember the God that is within each of us, life becomes a phenomenal experience that allows us to have "aha" moments on a regular basis. Life gets easier and easier as we let go of excess baggage and replace it with peace. Addictions, distractions, fears, and blocks are opportunities for each of us to awaken—until we GET IT, and realize our True Selves.

Perseverance pays off. Back in the early 1990s, while studying psychic development and hands-on healing and prior to taking hypnotherapy training, a dear friend "gently" suggested I might benefit from a regular practice of meditation. I was terrified to try it for fear I would not succeed. Eventually I gave in and faced my fear. I knew that studies showed how regular meditation could help in so many ways, so I caved. When my teacher at the time, Echo Bodine, would lead us in meditation she would ask us to go to a special place, or fly with the angels. I would "leave" and when she would ask us to return from wherever we were, my spirit would "clunk" back into my body, oblivious to whatever it may have experienced. It was as if I was asleep but not asleep. Echo told me not to worry about this because she said my spirit needed to do other things. She stated emphatically that my experience was just as valid and important as everyone else's, but I didn't feel my experiences were good enough. I wanted to remember what had happened, like the other students did! I wanted *more*.

With the help of a drumming tape I learned to clear my mind and listen.

After three or four weeks of daily practice, on a cold, blustery winter day in Minnesota, I had my first profound meditation experience. My eyes were closed and I had been meditating for about ten minutes. My mind was clear; I was almost in a state of sleep, which often times happens when I meditate. All of a sudden I felt a light. It was like the sun had come out from behind a cloud. I opened my eyes just a bit to see if that was what happened, but it was still dismal outside. No sun. I quickly closed my eyes again, and immediately felt a wash of whiteness enfolding me, followed by a blissful feeling of peace and unconditional love; it was ecstasy!

"What is this?" I asked in my mind's eye.

"Metatron," was the immediate response.

I picked up the pen I had next to me, and wrote down the word before I resumed reveling in the experience.

When it was over I smoothed my aura, grounded myself and came back to reality. I called a friend to ask what a Metatron was. She thought it might be one of the higher realms of angels, but wasn't certain. I had never heard of anyone called Metatron in my Christian upbringing.

Similar experiences happened quite often during the next few weeks. Whenever I would ask Metatron to come in, I would get the same feeling of whiteness, light, and unconditional love and this certainly motivated me to keep up the practice. Later, when I began teaching meditation, I would ask Metatron to come so my students could experience the same feeling and sure enough, some of them would say they had experienced either light or a wisp of air, or they would open their eyes to see if someone had turned on the light! Everyone described it as "unconditional love and white light." After the meditation I would tell them my story and that I had silently asked Metatron to come for a visit.

A few months had passed since that first experience and I had certainly released the fear (block) about not succeeding, at least relating to meditation. However, I still did not know who the heck Metatron was. At the end of a particularly rough day, I was sobbing and feeling sorry for myself. I angrily queried to nobody in particular, "Why do I get these messages and have these wonderful experiences yet still do not know who the heck you are?"

Then I heard a voice that instructed me to pick up a book someone had given me that described the hierarchy of angels. (No accident that it was right where I was seated.) I had put off reading it because I'm not one for "hierarchy." I opened the book, read no more than one paragraph, turned the page, and there was Metatron! It described him as being from the higher realms of angels who is known in the Jewish Kabbalah for bringing "unconditional love and white light." Exactly as I had experienced him!

In the following chapters I discuss some of the most predominant issues clients have presented with over the years. I outline how each case study removed obstacles (addictions, distractions, blocks or fears) that had plagued them for years and even lifetimes. Through the practice of hypnosis, hypnotherapy, and/or life-between-lives spiritual regression, every client, *in their own way and through their own perceptive filters*, discovered something that was previously unconscious to them. Upon this revelation, they remembered their true, Divine Self. This knowledge allowed them a new perspective, allowed them to live more fully and peacefully, which is our Divine birthright. Releasing fears *is* worthwhile. When you surrender to the greater good, you free yourself from the things that keep you from realizing who you REALLY are. You are worth it.

Chapter 2
Balance in Relationships

The first time I heard the three inspired words, "Be In Love" I vaguely grasped the depth of the phrase. Be In Love? When we returned from our day of meditation and I discovered everyone else had received a variety of detailed, inspired messages while all I got was "Be In Love," I was disappointed. I wanted more! However, as months and years passed, I began to feel grateful for having received these powerful yet simple words, because of the continually positive impact they have had on my life. I call this phrase the Primary Spirit-Directive and it is why we are here. It is about building a balanced relationship with the self, so we can then experience healthy, balanced relationships with others and with our community.

Be In Love…

BE

Not DO, but BE. If you are like me, this takes a lot of practice. I was at ease with DOing, but I had to constantly practice BEing in order to slow the thoughts, the ideas, and the chattering "monkey mind." DOing is from ego, BEing is from Spirit.

IN

Not out, but IN. To be IN the now, is to be IN a place of peace and IN a place of acceptance. Not what was or will be, but what IS. An acceptance of what is, IN the moment, IN the present, IN the now, IN our Divine Center.

LOVE

Love is absolute acceptance of what IS. Love is the experience of inner peace, acceptance, honor, gratitude, and non-judgment. It is not selfish love but self-less love, ego-less love, as our Creator loves us. It is being at peace in our mind, body and spirit. It is being grateful for our body, exactly as it is. It brings us gratitude for every thing and every emotion, every challenge, every adventure. Love involves surrender—not merely in the sense of relinquishing something, but in acknowledging that "Not my will" (ego) "but Thine" (egoless) "be done" (Luke: 24:22). Life is a process of ebb and flow. While meditating, walking, practicing Yoga, singing, laughing or playing, I am in the flow of love. With LOVE, I was able to shift the forty year habit of pushing up the river (sometimes without a paddle!) to flowing with the direction of the river. When we are in the moment, present and aware of what is, our life can change from struggle to peace, from drama to joy. My primary Spirit-Directive is Be In Love, and it was *exactly* what I needed to hear, even though I may not have known it back then. It has become the base from where I make my choices. It is who I AM.

In the years that followed the gift of this message, there were other Spirit-Directives that came during meditation, or just as inspirations while walking. I have summarized them into forty-four specific words or phrases that bring us closer to the Primary Spirit-Directive. These messages are meant to be used as daily guidance, as tools to self-empowerment. Each of them can move us closer to a consistent experience of love. Some of them may overlap or feel repetitive, but they all intertwine so that we *get it*.

Before we begin, here are a few questions for you:

- Are you *aware* that you are loved, unconditionally, by your Creator?
- Do you understand what unconditionally means? It means NO MATTER WHAT.
- Have you stilled your mind for at least five to ten minutes today? If not, please do so. Just *try* it! Then practice…
- Have you forgiven someone (including yourself) for

WHATEVER? (i.e.; not stilling your mind, doing too much or too little, judging another or yourself...)
- Are you grateful for this moment? For breath? For life? For pain and sorrow? For it ALL—are you grateful? Practice...
- Are you peaceful within? Are you able to slow down and appreciate each moment—no matter what? Practice...
- Will you release any fears, thanking them for what they have taught you, then gifting yourself with whatever that fear has blocked from you?
- Will you allow loving and supporting relationships into your life—healthy relationships, beginning with yourself and then with others?
- And finally, remember—you are a Divine Being who chose this temporary Earth suit—your human body—to grow, learn and enjoy.

In this Divine moment, why don't you initiate your Self into what we will call "The Order of Unconditional Love." This allows you to be free from anything (judgment, fear, anxiety, impatience, anger...) that held you back. Free to be...

The Spirit-Directives for this chapter are:

Set a Foundation

It is time to plant roots in some thing or project you have started, or to begin a project you may have been putting off. JUST DO IT. The pyramids of Egypt represent a very firm foundation that has been around for a LONG time—focus on the steadfast energy of the pyramids—how firmly they are anchored into Mother Earth, and relate this to your own life, to where you are being called to set a foundation. Then begin to write that book, or take steps towards healing your relationships, volunteer at a local nonprofit, create a center, whatever feels right and appropriate to you. Follow your bliss! Now is the time to take one step forward into this new beginning.

Positive Intent

Writing or stating some of your highest intentions in a positive manner is integral to manifesting. Any intentions you have, put on paper. An intention can also be a goal—write them in a positive manner—an optimistic, simple manner. Focus on being optimistic, and state your intentions in a positive way. The glass IS half full! When you state what you need in a positive manner, *with pure intent*, you will get whatever help is needed. However, don't sit and wait for it to happen; trust that it is happening *as you take steps toward your intentions*.

Commit (to yourself)

It's time for you to come into your power—to accept and commit to your highest calling. This commitment will allow you to move into a higher level of consciousness, whatever that means for YOU. If you are reading these words, it is time for you to commit to yourself in order to help you move into the next level of consciousness. This could mean a commitment to meditate, journal, write… (fill in the blank). Commit to whatever feels right and appropriate for you.

Believe

Throughout our lives we constantly are asked to trust and believe in someone or something. This may be something you have not allowed yourself to believe previously, or something or someone you have not understood. Believing sometimes calls for releasing judgment, shame, blame, or guilt in order to allow a new perception into your life. Belief sets a firm foundation, yet in this current energy, beliefs are changing, being repeatedly challenged, and new beliefs are replacing the old. This is a time of change and transformation for the Earth and all her beings—believe this is so, and allow the process that waits to unfold. Allow your beliefs to change and transform you into a life that is free from anything you no longer need. Write down three beliefs you are currently questioning, meditate and/or discuss them with others until you once again have a firm understanding of what they mean to you. Then if they no longer feel right or appropriate for you, release them and make room for new ones!

Be Amazed

This is your message to look at the wonder and beauty in every thing, and trust that your Spirit Helpers are with you always. Look around you this month and notice the sun, the colors around you, hug a tree or walk in nature and be amazed. Be amazed at the beauty of every thing and take note of where or how you are supported. Focus on all the things in your life and in nature that are amazing. Look around and be amazed at what is outside as well as what is within YOU. Begin to remember your true Self, and be amazed!

Each of the above Spirit-Directives is integral to building a balanced, healthy relationship with ourselves and others. By following the guidance in each Directive, we set the stage for peace-filled success. If we choose to deny ourselves or continue to judge ourselves, how can we expect others to love and accept us?

It is crucial that we take care of ourselves in ALL our relationships! The following Case Study shows how two past life regressions and six weeks of Earth time can take lifetimes of abuse and perceived unworthiness and transform it into a fulfilled relationship with the self and the release of a relationship that was not serving either person.

Case Study

For this Case Study I am sharing the exact letter that was sent to me, printed with author's permission:

"Dear Madonna:

I would like to share with you my deep, heartfelt gratitude for your work and how it has touched my life.

I came to you for two past-life regressions. In both of these, I had the opportunity to go back to other lives with my current husband. The main theme of these lives was our initial attraction and love that turned out to be his abuse.

I was so grateful to know who he is—he has been my teacher. He has brought me the opportunity to remember that I AM peaceful and I come here to share that peace and healing in my world. The past lives mirrored my current life with him. There was one exception to this however. In the past lives he had "gotten the better of me." I did not learn and break free. The first life, he killed me and then himself. The second, I killed him. In this life I DID break free—I am free! The cycle has ended and we don't need to revisit the same issues again in any future lives. I know in my heart this is true.

It was six weeks after my second session with you that we finally separated. It has taken me a decade to come to this, but only six weeks to put an end to it all. How miraculous this truly is for me!

So if there is ever a time or place when doubt enters your mind or you feel unsure about your skills or if you are on the right path, simply remember my words and KNOW that your work and spirit has been instrumental in healing my life. I have put to rest issues that have spanned over hundreds of years and many lifetimes. It continually amazes me too—you'd think that after being with someone for a decade there would be a period of anger or feelings of loss. There is nothing here now but restored peace! I feel no loss or emptiness. I do not grieve. I carry no anger or grudges toward this man who I really believe is doing the very best he can do. Thank you very much, Madonna.

P.S. The weight has been melting off of me without effort since the separation. I am down two sizes and it continues to come off. It didn't have anything to do with diet or exercise, like I thought. I had been stuffing my true self in order to survive in the relationship."

In the four hours of her two sessions, this client was able to leave an abusive relationship that had plagued both of them over many lifetimes. During the two sessions she discovered why she was in the relationship, which empowered her to do what was necessary to balance any karma related to the volatile situation. During her regression session she was able to revisit their contract, realize the vicious circle they had become entangled in, and release all past, present and future karma. She then was easily able to move into a healthy relationship with herself and others, which continues to this day. When she consciously remembered who she REALLY was, everything shifted and she was free to be.

Here is an update to her story, written nearly 15 years after her sessions, in response to my request:

"Dear Madonna:

It was never my intention nor did I realize what I was getting myself, my innocent child and future children into when I entered into an abusive relationship. I didn't wake up one day and consciously decide to seek out and enter into an abusive relationship. Yet I did.

I can see now how my upbringing of neglect and the chaos of living in an alcoholic family planted seeds and supported my woundedness and discontent. It was all I knew. It was my normal. My life prepared me for the experience of a victim. A victimizer cannot victimize without a victim. A fully wise and

Birth, Death and the Afterlife

grounded person wouldn't know how to attract a victimizer. And a victim can't attract a wise and grounded person. I came to understand that one powerful way to know myself is to look at my relationships; they are always direct reflections of what is inside.

Pain is a clear signal of being out of flow of the Divine. Pain is the mechanism by which we have an opportunity to take a look. The body works the same way. If there is a wound, it hurts so that we can look at it and correct it. Life is this simple; resolve the pain and follow the Divine flow of 'yes.'

There is always a solution. There is always another way. I learned that I've lost completely if I think there is no other option. When I embrace the possibility that there is another way and that things can get better, it simply shows up.

My life is dramatically different from the life I left behind more than 14 years ago. I can hardly believe that I am the same person that was involved with and married to the man I married. Yet I'm not the same. At the time, I made a vow to my babies before they were born that they would have a father, until I later realized how harmful staying would be. I was in a burning building; staying would mean complete destruction for us all. Still I couldn't find my way out. Part of the abuse included financial abuse designed so I couldn't leave. But I did. The experience felt like jumping from a burning building to a sinking ship. When I made the right move and left, the Divine sent help. People appeared from nowhere to help support us.

At the time, my daughters were 19, 8 and 6. Although sadly the 19-year old still has not healed and has continued to demonstrate the trauma she lived growing up with him, the 8 and 6-year old girls grew up almost unscathed. The abuse cycle is broken with them. My middle daughter, now 21, has chosen a very loving man who is present and supportive and nurturing. It's a wonderful and joyful experience to see her engaged in a healthy relationship!

I recognize that life flows best and I am my most successful when I follow my Divine 'yes.' My 'yes' guided me to past life therapy when I was ready, and it helped me finally get out of abuse. My 'yes' supported my choice of healthy living, free from abuse even when I didn't know how to make it happen, and even when I didn't know how I would support my children and me.

I realize that I'm no good to anyone if I'm miserable and wounded. I am the only one responsible for embracing joy or pain. I can only give what I have, nothing more and nothing less. I am grateful for him because he helped me find myself. I grew up wounded and he was a perfect mirror, the perfect reflection to help me remember my Divinity. Life is truly lived by first noticing what shows up in the present moment, knowing I always have choice, and embracing my 'yes.' Most importantly, remembering that only love is real; anything else is illusion."

If we are in a rut, no matter how deep, we can still choose something different. We always have options, as this case study shows. Life is what we make of it, and once we realize this and let go of what is no longer working for us, we naturally "flow with the go" and become an active, enthusiastic participant in the game of life.

Chapter 3
Marching to the Beat of a Different Drummer • Being Creative

When we are planning our upcoming life with some of our soul group and Spirit Helpers on the "Other Side," there are quite a few things to consider. When we are not human, we seem to forget what it's like to *be* human, just like we forget what it's like to be in spirit while on Earth! Because of this (and for other reasons) we sometimes choose some pretty extreme, outlandish challenges here on this Earth School!

Before incarnating, we often decide who our parents will be, where we will be born, what day we will arrive, possibly who our siblings will be (if we have any), what type of body and brain we will have, with whom we will be in relationship and what our major purpose or intention is for this life. Sometimes our purpose, or destiny, is vague. Other times it can be very specific. For instance, a soul may choose to learn unconditional love, which can be experienced in many ways—through an abusive parent, sibling or spouse, or perhaps through choosing a disfigured body. There are a great many ways we can learn to love ourselves and others unconditionally.

Some souls get extremely creative in the interlife-planning process while others choose a more traditional role for their life on Earth. Our Spirit Helpers are usually active in the planning process, yet they do not force us into any decision. We never, in my experience and in the experience of my clients, have to follow through 100% with our plan, and we are never judged (by a vengeful God or our Spirit Helpers) for not following through. However, we often may judge *ourselves* for some of our choices. Nevertheless, when we reincarnate, we promptly forget whatever plans were made. This is where free will kicks in. We can (and do) go off track, give up, decide we cannot follow through and come around again, planning it differently. In some cases, we choose to take our life because we simply can not handle what we chose to learn. Sometimes one of our soul group goes off track and forces us to readjust our life, which can cause much angst for others involved with the plan. Luckily, there are always options to help us achieve what we had mapped out, and just like any school, when we are ready (and willing), we move to the next level of experience that is appropriate for our personal evolution.

If we create or plan for our upcoming incarnation, then it would follow that our spirits continue to create, even while in our Earth suits. Thoughts are things. In fact, it is the primary mode of communication while in the Spirit world. Therefore, since *we are always spiritual beings*, we continually create with our thoughts.

In *The Four Agreements*, Don Miguel Ruiz talks about being impeccable with our word. I would say it is extremely important because these words are our thoughts! Our thoughts create the words therefore our thoughts create. So, to be impeccable with our creation skills and with our thoughts is of primary importance. We are what we think about, and the more positive our thoughts are, the more positive our life becomes. We have moved into an age where we can create instantaneously and even though we may not have it all figured out yet, we are in that place now, where it is more possible than ever before in recorded history. (Or at least we are more *aware* of this fact!) I repeat, *we have the ability to create instantaneously with our thoughts*. Feel free to take a look at not only what you planned and created before you incarnated, but also what you currently are creating in every moment. What are you thinking? What are you creating, both consciously and unconsciously? How are you feeling in this moment? Being creative is innate in every one of us, so if you feel blocked in relation to your creativity, the case study at the end of this chapter may help you to understand, a little more, about that creation process. It may help you to release any blocks that could be holding you back from creating that which *you* desire in your life.

What we do affects everyone and every thing. Because we are all connected, yet uniquely different from each other, the more we honor and respect ourselves, the more we honor and respect everyone else, the more we come into a loving and peaceful relationship with all things. As mentioned earlier, when I would complain or grumble about someone who had hurt me or a situation that had caused me to be frustrated, my Dad would look at me with great kindness and gently say, "We're all different. If everyone was the same, it'd be a pretty boring world."

Sigh. You're right, Dad.

So honor yourself for marching to the beat of your individual drum. Honor others for marching to the beat of their individual drums. If we all played the same drum..........

The Spirit-Directives that follow will assist in your creation process:

Conscious Choices

You are being called to become more aware of every thing and everyone, and make choices that are based in this conscious awareness. There may be things you have done unconsciously in the past, and this card reveals to you that it's time to become more aware of everything in your life. The purple border represents the higher consciousness awareness also—become more aware of your Higher Self and the choices you make that involve your Spirit Helpers. This Spirit-Directive is calling you to be more aware in every moment, and to make conscious choices beginning today, that affirm that awareness of who you really are and why you are here.

Birth, Death and the Afterlife

Change and Movement

There will be dramatic change in your near future. You will either move through something that has been blocked or you will change the way you are doing something. This card is a card to call and accept the change and movement happening in your life, for it is all moving you toward your highest intentions. The green border (on the original card) indicates getting help from nature during this period. The one thing we can be sure of in life is *change*. This time in your life there may be more than the average amount, and it will be easier for you to move through it, into that next phase of your life, if you use the energies of nature—the sun, the Earth and water. Allow those parts of creation to be your helpers through this time of change and movement.

Blocks

There may be something that is holding you back in some way. It could be an addiction, which would be strongest of these three, a block, or a distraction. It could be something you are aware or unaware of. This Spirit-Directive indicates that it's time for you to let go of anything that is holding you back. Meditate on the picture, the long wall, yet with the help of wind and sky and your intention, there is movement through that block, a permanent release of that distraction or addiction. We are in a time where anything that holds us back is not acceptable. We are making conscious choices now, to move through—gently yet diligently—in order to release whatever is holding us back. This allows us to move into where we are destined to be. The original card has an aqua border which represents purifying water—it's time to do whatever is necessary in order to fulfill your intentions.

You are What You Think

This Spirit-Directive is about self-empowerment, expecting you to love yourself unconditionally in whatever you are thinking, doing and saying. Look at all the pictures within this picture and see how this can bring you to a place of *conscious awareness*, in every moment, *of what you are thinking*—because that IS what you ARE in that moment. This Spirit-Directive is asking you to BE all you can be in every moment, and letting go of anything that is not serving that pure intention. It is a calling for you to BE IN LOVE! If you are not feeling positive thoughts, "FAKE IT UNTIL YOU MAKE IT"—IT WORKS! Focus on the pictures within the picture, and place these in your conscious and unconscious mind. This is truly the most empowering card in this deck—BE IT! IT IS SO!

Focus

    It's time to focus more on what is really important to you. This could be your life purpose, it could be a role you were asked to take. You are being asked to focus in, hone in on what is most important to you at this time, so that you can be the leader you are. While meditating on the picture, focus on her third eye and allow it to open your third eye to being you to higher consciousness, and lead you to your highest calling. Focus on the positive and anything is possible.

Nature

   This Spirit-Directive suggests that you to observe and be more aware of nature, the colors of nature, the sounds of nature, how you feel in nature, the animals or creatures coming to you, the signs nature is giving you. Every aspect of nature is calling to you. This means it's a good time to get out in nature. When you are outside, breathe the fresh air, be in the moment of peaceful and natural feelings. Notice the wind and how it may speak to you. Notice anything happening around you. Nature is calling to you. Notice how nature simply IS. Observe the beauty and peace of nature, and being it into your day with gratitude.

Case Study

   "Charles" was someone who couldn't figure out why he was SO scattered in his current incarnation. He also had several questions relating to past lives where he may have been killed for various reasons. Among other things, he wanted to know where the voices came from that told him to 'tell the people about the God creation,' whether or not to write a specific book, and whether his current life experiences were preplanned or not.

His Past Life Regression (PLR) follows, and is transcribed here:

MK: Just share whatever you're getting, whatever you are aware of.
C: There's a dark purple presence.
MK: Is it with you, in back of you, surrounding you?
C: It seems to be the atmosphere right now. It was the first sense of just the environment... and I'm just waiting to see if I am aware of any details.
MK: Some times that presence or the purple could just separate, like lift a veil or it could take form. Everybody's experience is different. Just take your time and just kind of be in that energy, and just share whatever you're getting. Often times you just get thoughts of what it is too. Just share whatever you're getting.
C: OK that's pretty much gone away. I guess it was just a transition. And now it is more like a brownish white type feeling... or atmosphere.
MK: Oftentimes this happens to help you see you are having an experience and then more things come in. It's kind of like a little introduction.
C: Everything's unfocused, but there were patches of green. So I don't know if that's because I'm not focusing, or that's just the energy from the surroundings that I'm picking up on. I'll just relax and let it come to me. It's almost like patches of red. It's from blood...or a wound...or something like that.
MK: OK. See if you can move into it. I'm going to gently tap your wrist. And just go deeper into it. Knowing just like we talked about, you can always detach from it if it's too traumatic. You can always become the observer. Go deeper into this experience, into this memory. I'm going to count from one to three, when I say three you will be immersed in that memory. You'll be very aware what it's all about, 1-2-3... What are you aware of?
C: Well the thought is, abdomen wound.
MK: Does it feel like you are male or female?
C: Ah, Male.
MK: About how old?

C: Um, 50.
MK: Is it day or night?
C: It's ah, dusk.
MK: What are you wearing?
C: Brown leather.
MK: Are there others around, or are you alone?
C: I'm not aware of others.
MK: OK. Sometimes you don't need to be aware of them. But sometimes they are or aren't there.
C: They might be over there. (points to about 10 o'clock) At a distance.
MK: OK, now just like an old time movie, I'm going to move the scene ahead and just whatever you're getting, whatever's happening.
C: Well there are boulders. There's at least one boulder right there. (I point to about eleven o'clock position. The boulder is about 10 feet away from me as I am lying on the ground.) It's a large boulder, probably eight feet high. I think I've been left to die, because I know I'm gonna die. There's nothing they can do to help.
MK: What are you dying from?
C: A spear to the abdomen.
MK: I'd like you to move to the time in that life then when your spirit left your body. And you can be the observer, you don't have to re-experience any of the pain. And just share whatever is happening.
C: I pulled out and I have long black hair, straggly long black hair. White necklace. Beads.
MK: What is your name? First thought.
C: Sounds like THUMP. (laughs)
MK: OK. You'll get more information on that if it's important. Sometimes the name just isn't important, sometimes it is.
C: There's also a feeling right here, (touches upper left chest, shoulder) I don't know why.
MK: Is that where the spear was from that life?
C: Originally the spear came in here (points to lower left abdomen)

but I also have a feeling there too, I don't know why. (touches upper left shoulder area)

MK: OK. You'll understand that more too.

C: It just showed up.

MK: Very good, very good. As your spirit is leaving your body, what was that life about, what's happening?

C: I have a lot of peaceful satisfaction about that life, but no details yet, but that was the first feeling that just came. Very peaceful satisfaction, with no remorse. (pause) It was a good life. Even though it ended that way, it doesn't matter.

MK: Were you married in that life?

C: Yes, and one child who is an adult now. A boy, a man.

MK: Is there anything else for you to remember or know about this life, that past life, that would help you in your current life, that would help you to understand more who you are?

C: Be satisfied with life's experiences and don't be hard and judging, knowing that there is eternal value from it. It's not lost.

MK: OK… what did you do in that life?

C: (Sees his two ears, both 3 times larger than they really were) I listened to other people. That was the primary service. Because when you asked that question, the ears immediately lit up… and they (the ears) were the ones that did the work.

MK: OK, is there anything else to remember from that life? Or you may get more information later on from this session, but any thing else for you to remember from that life?

C: Be happy with… being connected with the Earth.

MK: OK, now just like I said, if there's more information, you'll get it later, when it's safe and it flashes from dreams, or whatever. But I'm going to count from one to three now. When I say three, you're going to be in another life or an experience that will help you answer some of your questions help you to remember who you really are, 1-2-3…

C: White energy in front of me, over to the left, about 10 feet away. I need to move to that energy and go into it. First of all, sandy and gritty and then, ah, the bones on the back of a dinosaur, I am aware of those, were sticking up in a row, off to my left, and they were dark, they were big, I don't know if they are or not, but that is what it reminds me of. It's the real thing or it's a painting.... of that. The white energy, when I got into it, ah, formed like the shape of a dinosaur energy type mass. No detail, just the intelligence or energy of that. It's almost like I was communing with it or talking with it. The life that I'm in was able to commune with that essence, with that soul. The dinosaur soul, I talked with the dinosaur by connecting with its residual energy. Maybe it was residual in the bone and I had the capability of communing with that life that lived in those bones.

MK: Okay.

C: I could go from place to place and tap into energy and history in my travels. I could time travel and I would go to a place and become aware of something that was old and I would connect with it, and it would come alive. I don't know if that was normal, or if that was a shaman or whatever… but it's something I did… and the uhm, the energy, the stomach energy is way too open in that life. It's out of balance. It's way too open, too sensitive to other peoples pains, the empathic was just too strong. Seems like I should have been able to control it, but I didn't. For some reason it's like it was blown open, almost 18 inches in diameter, the whole stomach area, energy receptivities. Then something happened to the neck. I don't know if maybe the neck was cut and I died, or I think that was it. I'm aware of that too. Something like a stone knife, a sharp stone knife. It wasn't metal.

MK: Waiting to move into the next… what was that life all about then?

C: It was a lot of traveling and a lot of connecting with the different areas that I went to. The physical areas and the artifacts and the ancient history, some of it thousands of years old. I don't think I shared that information with anybody, it just seems like I did it as a personal passion, or a personal drive. For some reason I was a loner, I don't know why. I was a loner. I was a traveler. Living off the land.

(long pause)… Another injury to the left shoulder that I'm aware of.

MK: In that same life?

C: Yes. And that injury preceded the… the throat being cut. I think with that injury I knew I wasn't going to survive so I, I speeded up the death by cutting my own throat, cause the left shoulder and upper, oh, almost into the heart almost, a big hole. I knew I wasn't gonna survive from that.

MK: Were you male or female in this?

C: Ah, male.

MK: What kind of country, what was the country that you, you said you traveled a lot, in what areas?

C: Well there was a lot of rugged, rocky areas, and mountains and streams and forests.

MK: What did you learn from that life then, what was that all about?

C: I could survive on the land, by myself, and connect with memories that are in artifacts, in bones, in rocks, trees, streams. Everywhere you go, you connect and receive information and memories of what took place. Nothing's really hidden, it's always there.

MK: And just like you did before now, I'm going to count from one to three, and when I say three you'll be in another past life or current life experience that will help you understand yourself more clearly, and perhaps answer some of the questions you've written. Gently tapping your wrist, moving to another life, 1-2-3…

C: Blue. Ocean. Blue sky. Warm. On a boat, in the ocean. Big boat. Brown wood. Sails. Part of the crew.

MK: How old are you?

C: Late twenties, early thirties.

MK: Male or female.

C: Male. White t-shirt, ragged, old. Beard. Blondish long scraggly hair. Wind-burnt skin from the wind and sun exposure. Thin, skinny body. Not very healthy. Not very good food, diet. Takes a toll on the body. It's not a happy environment with the crew. It's rough, demanding. Gotta keep your place. Do what you're told.

MK: Do you notice a flag on the ship? Any kind of a flag?

C: There's a light blue flag. Something written on it. It's more like a drawing or a pattern. It's a solid blue, light blue, almost like a baby blue. And a white thing in the lower left hand corner, white star pattern, then in the upper, well in the middle there's a black background. Such an old flag, this thing is really weathered and beat.

MK: You'll remember what it is, and if it is important you will be able to draw it later. Or just remember what it is like.

C: OK.

MK: You can get where this is from. Where is the ship from? Do you know?

C: Ah, Barbados.

MK: OK. And what does it do? What are you doing on the ship?

C: Ah, well they needed hands with the sails. So I work on the deck with the sails. I carry, you know, I'm a manual laborer. So I do a lot of manual labor. When we gotta load or unload the ship. I do that.

MK: Are you married in this life?

C: No. There's a girlfriend in the port that I've known over the years. We're not married.

MK: OK. Move to a scene that will help you understand that life more and how it relates and helps in your current life. Just move into it. You're getting very good at this.

C: Well this one was all about learning to go with the flow and just try and enjoy life, even though it... there's a lot of work involved and sometimes there's not much fun, but learn to just work with the crew and not to be judgmental but .. and not to be afraid. If you die, you die, so what, it doesn't matter. Just being along for the ride and the experience is what it is all about in this life. And I did have a lot of experiences. There's like a black cloud over the left eye. I don't know if that was a brain tumor or if that was a blow to the head, but I think I lost my left eye vision. And I just died.

MK: About how old?

C: Maybe close to forty or in the forties, I don't know.

MK: As you spirit is leaving your body from that life, what is going on? What's happening?

C: I'm going straight up from the ship. I was out to sea and went straight up. And the ship was underneath me and it got smaller and smaller and I just went straight up into the sky. And then the Earth got smaller and I just went away.

MK: Where did you go?

C: Straight up into the sky into heaven. Starry skies away from the Earth.

MK: Where are you now.

C: I almost shot as fast as a rocket. Wow.

MK: Where do you go now?

C: Well I'm with my guide. He and I are old buddies.

MK: What's the name, what is the name of your guide?

C: Bee… Beez. Hmmm…there's like a B and a Z. More like Beez. (laughs)… Hi Beez! Good to see you again old buddy.

MK: What does Beez have to say for you, show you?

C: Well he's… he's happy. He agrees with me, yeah that was a good life. That was a fun life. Learned a lot. It's stuff I needed to learn. Needed to learn to just relax, go with the flow and not be so doggone judgmental. And just let it go. Let it unfold. Not try and figure things out all the time. Just go with the flow… And that was a good one. He says I always tended to try to figure things out too much. That's not what life's all about. It's not about trying to figure it all out. It's not always necessary. And that's the same thing I'm working on in this life. I haven't really let go into that space enough. I get too worried. Always too judgmental, trying to figure it out, thinking I'm not gonna do the right thing and I'm gonna be brought up short and punished for that and that's old, old teachings from the surrounding life. They really aren't true at all. But they impacted me. And Beez has a strange shape. He's ah… he doesn't have a body shape, he's fat in the middle and skinny on both ends and he's bluish gray. And that's my perception of his energy right now, but of course that isn't who he really is. It's what I'm aware of at this moment. And he's a real happy guy. I'm

Birth, Death and the Afterlife

glad I got a happy.... and a lot of the happiness comes from his center, his belly. And he's in front of me to the right a little bit.

MK: Would he help you answer some questions, or will he take you to some other lives or what is he there for right now?

C: He's a companion so I'm not by myself. And he reflects back and forth my thoughts. He confirms or helps to direct and if I get off the path with the thoughts he, he's gentle in nudging me in different ways of thinking, because I'll go down a path like a worry wart and he'll nudge me back into the thoughts that are more beneficial.

MK: Was he the thought you had, the voice when you thought, you heard to become a minister?

C: Um, ah, yeah that was Beez.

MK: Why did he, why did he share, why did he do that for you?

C: I needed the experience.

End of PLR

One month later, the client presented for his Life-Between-Lives session. Rather than verbatim, his LBL is summarized by both of us.

Client Summarization

"During the session I saw a soul shredder. The best way to explain what I saw and felt as the meaning and purpose of this soul shredder is as follows.

I used to work for Alcoa R&D in Merwin, PA, in 1974 and I became aware of the process of electrical galvanization to color the aluminum, where a negative electrode was clipped onto the aluminum part and a positive charge was placed on the liquid bath that the aluminum part was dipped or soaked into. Different chemicals would make the aluminum turn different colors, depending on what you wanted to achieve. This process of coloring the Aluminum electrically is called ANODIZING.

Anyway the soul shredder that I saw shined like aluminum that had been colored a metallic orange color. It was round and rotated on a horizontal shaft. So the rotating was vertical like a bicycle tire rotates in the vertical plane. There were several plates stacked together with the central plate with the largest diameter and the outer plates with smaller diameters. I felt like I and others had walked into this soul shredder to be cut up into smaller parts.

This was an experiment that we as a group had agreed upon to go through knowing that it might be fatal.

When I saw the soul shredder, only the top half was visible and the lower half was in the ground or floor of wherever it was located.

When I left the body of the fellow (me) who was living with a group or tribe that I did not belong to, I went to sit down in the spirit world in a state of utter exhaustion. I was able to pull away and view myself (my soul body) from a distance of about 20 ft. When I looked at my soul spirit body it looked like a marble stone chess piece with a flat head and round flat sides on the head. The arms and legs were short gray and stone cold and didn't move.

I was sitting within a non-physical energetic space created by the shape that an inverted bowl makes if you turn a large mixing bowl upside down and set it on the table or kitchen counter top.

I could see through the semi-spherical wall of this energetic shape and could see that it was made of energy and created a space for me to rest after the last incarnation. Maybe it was a place of protection, solitude, rest and recuperation, reflection, etc.

I became aware of another person, not my guide, but an observer caretaker of some kind. He had his hands raised and placed on his hips and was thinking to himself, "I don't understand why anybody would do this to themselves." (Meaning that he/she wondered why we did the experiment of shredding our soul into small pieces and go through such a dangerous event.)

During the LBL session when nothing was happening and it came to a standstill, it was suggested that I rise up and leave the semi-spherical space and see what happens next.

I rose up and the viewing vantage point for my observation was not within my soul body but from a distance so I could watch it like a movie. I rose straight up and penetrated the energetic wall. Then three or four white entities swooped in and converged to meet me.

They all became one at one point. Their movement left a white wispy trail like a jet leaves in the sky, except each trail in this case was wide and flat and showed a movement from high down to low in a curving arch flight path.

When I focused on the point where all three or four converged, it changed into a green looking dragon head with a long snout. I saw the right eye facing me. I didn't see the left eye because it was on the other side of the head.

As I focused on the eye it was in the flat shape of a triangle, and then as I focused closer I went into the eye and discovered the eye was a doorway passage and it had red misty energy that was lit up like a light that glowed red.

I then floated down this passageway within the red mist and right now I am not remembering what happened next. I think I need to listen to the recorded session to refresh my memory.

I want to say that I next entered another body or lifetime in the physical.

I remember describing during the LBL session that for many lives after this soul shredding experiment, I had to force myself into many lives to get life back into my soul. I had to push my face into the physical body like shoving my face into mud, and re-energize myself, re-ground myself with life. I had become so separated from others and this was a way to re-socialize myself back into the group of humanity. I have always explained to myself that because I had been raped and beaten at age five or six, I had kept myself at a distance in most relationships in this life. But maybe it was the soul shredding experiment that has left an imprint on my soul of being isolated from others.

Before the LBL session began I expressed several goals and questions that I wanted answered. One was to understand why in this life I am living in now that began on July 28, 1948 I am so distant from my birth family members and why I am so distant from my family that I created with my first marriage.

On one level I want to live in active relationships, but on another level I want to be by myself and only live in relationship with my second wife.

So I feel that by being shown the lifetime of exiting a body that is low on energy and alone after having begun the experiment of shredding the soul, maybe this is an answer to why I am isolated in this life and not living in relationship to my family.

That life was not my most previous life (to this current 1948 one), but it may be the first life of the soul shredding experiment.

I also wanted to know why I am so interested in alien abductions in this life. Is that interest just a diversion, or is it something important for me to study and be aware of? In particular the information coming from/through Marshall Vian Summers about the other worldly collectives who are currently making an intervention to take the Earths natural resources and take away our human freedoms.

In one of the two death scenes that I remembered during this LBL session, I was paralyzed from the waist down and couldn't move my legs. I propped my upper torso up with my arms and was attempting to turn to the left and then died and just left my body. I don't remember if that was the scene where I next entered the semi-spherical space or if this was at the time of the second death.

I was shocked and disappointed that I didn't go see my soul group, council, library, body selection room, etc. Instead I was shown that I chose to participate in a dangerous experiment of soul shredding.

I am wondering if maybe I had chosen to participate in this dangerous soul shredding experiment because in a previous life I had participated in something evil where I had hurt or tortured or killed many other people, and then upon entering the spirit world I chose along with the others who as a group had done these horrendous things we decided to do the soul shredding experiment as a form of punishment. Maybe I was part of a group that had done something to hurt other peoples' souls.

I am feeling that there is more to be revealed to me that I would not be happy to know about myself, but I do want to know now, during this incarnation. I don't want to live in denial and ignorance of my past actions. I want to use the CDs with self inductions on them to be by myself and explore more on my own and discover what I did prior to this soul shredding experiment. And then when that discovery is done, go and meet up with my soul group, council, the library, body selection room. and other places."

In Charles' two sessions, he had quite a bit more revealed to him than expected, much of which he really didn't think he wanted to know! However, it did explain some of the challenges he had faced in his current life, and it has helped him understand some of those challenges more clearly. The idea of "soul shredding" was new to both of us prior to this session, and from the sounds of it, was something even his Spirit Helpers questioned. However, these revelations assisted him in a better understanding of why he often felt distant, ungrounded, and separate.

As in any PLR or LBL experience, the client will be processing the unconscious memories that were brought to the conscious for weeks, months, and even years after the actual session. We don't always get clear answers, and sometimes it is difficult to interpret what is being revealed, but I have found that we consistently get what we are ready for, what our Higher Self agrees to share, and what is most important to our continued Earth life—NOT necessarily what the client presented for in the session OR what the facilitator expects to happen. Often times the client will contact me years later, saying, "NOW I understand what that session was about," or "I wasn't ready to understand what I heard and saw until now." These sessions are far more divinely guided than just having a session to see what happens! If a memory is not important, or if it would be too horrendous for that person to remember it, the Spirit Helpers will be there to block that information. There have been times when I have tried and tried, without success, to guide a client into a past life and they remember nothing—they go directly into an experience that is right and appropriate for their journey. I have quit trying so hard, unless the client is determined to experience this; however, once the client releases their expectation and "flows with the go," it is *amazing* what their experience can be, as you will see in future chapters!

8-14-2011 follow-up from Charles:

"My wife and I just completed a 16-day road trip to visit all of her family and mine. I was able to relax and enjoy seeing all of my family. I was not self-judgmental. I had fewer blocks to awareness of others and my own feelings. I feel this is because of the PLR and LBL work."

Chapter 4
Destiny and Fate • Building a Stable Foundation

Destiny. What does it mean? Are some things fated while others are accidental?

Our destiny is the foundation upon which our lives are built. It is our anchor, our very core being-ness, and it supports the foundation that we created on the Other Side. The life that follows is a result of our destiny, and is the free will portion of the Earth experience. Some examples of destinies could be: healer, teacher/sage, minister/priest, parent, artist, consciousness shifter, service provider, volunteer, lover, saboteur, visionary, pioneer, or victim. Our destiny can change from life to life, depending upon our life plan. In one life we may be fated to play the role of victim while in the next, the healer, and still next, the saboteur. We may come around many lifetimes in order to accomplish one goal. And sometimes we are simply here to BE, like an extra in a movie. This may not be *considered* a grand part, but certainly *is* essential, because if those extras were not present, there would be no movie.

Once we realize our destiny, we must figure out *how* to fulfill it. The *how* is much broader than the *what*. For instance, if our destiny is to be a consciousness shifter, how would we reach that end? Some ways would be by meditation with intent to shift the consciousness, writing a book, or sharing ways to live more peacefully through speaking. Let's say your destiny was to help or be of service to others. You could volunteer at a local shelter or nonprofit, or even start your own nonprofit as your personal way of helping. *How* we fulfill our destiny is the free will attached to the destiny we choose.

When we are planning our lives, it is usually with the assistance of some very wise beings I call Spirit Helpers and others may call the "Council," or "Elders," or our Guide(s). When it comes to fulfilling our destiny, they are *helpers*, but the final decision is *ours*.

Do we get sidetracked from fulfilling our destiny? In my experience, there have been very few clients who were way off track from what they had planned. One example would be "Dolly," who felt her mother had agreed to teach her about unconditional love in this life, but had gone overboard on how she fulfilled her part of their pact by severely abusing her, leaving her much more to work through than they had originally planned. This caused much hardship in her life and she felt it was taking her twice the effort and time to heal, forgive, and come to a place where she was able to love herself unconditionally, much less the perpetrators of the atrocities. Nonetheless, once "Dolly" discovered she *had* in fact stayed within her plan and that her mother had gone off track, she was able to work through it, heal, and move toward the fulfillment of her own destiny.

Another example of getting off track is if you were destined to live a long life of service to others, but someone started using drugs again, got in their car, and killed you in an auto accident. This HAS happened, but these cases have been rare. When they do happen, however, "cosmic adjustments" are made, and the natural order of the Universe is restored. For example, if the person being of service was delivering meals to the elderly and after the accident was in a wheelchair, she/he would change the manner in which they were of service. The fulfillment of their destiny may take a little more effort on a few people's parts, but we always get help from the Universe in these instances.

Still one more way a person can get off track from their destiny is what I call "stinking thinking." This is when the ego gets out of hand, grabs onto our thought processes, and runs rampant as it twists our thinking until we lose our sense of knowing and peace

<u>Three Levels of Thought</u>

One of the more common issues my clients deal with is the negative thought process that accompanies this obsessive "stinking thinking." Thoughts like, "If they only knew the real me they wouldn't like me:

they would think I'm bad/stupid/rude; they wouldn't be my friend," etc. Sometimes the thoughts come in (and are accepted) that we are not worthy, or that we are bad for whatever reason, or that we are *not enough* (which is one of the *most common* thought/feelings we have). We are told these things by parents, or religion, and on TV. We are overwhelmed by the media telling us we are not enough—not tall enough, good enough, rich enough, thin enough, young enough, smart enough. And for whatever reason, we accept them into our consciousness.

Over the years, I have developed a theory called the Three Levels of Thought that addresses these disturbing, untrue thoughts.

In the First Level of Thought, our logical, fully conscious, 3-D mind, is aware of the good deeds we've done. We usually know ourselves as kind and caring, or *at least* as a decent human being. We are able to listen to our guidance both internal and etheric, and everything seems to flow as we live out our destiny.

In the Second Level of Thought, the unconscious thoughts enter. Some names for these thoughts are the "monkey mind," the ego, or "stinking thinking." I often call it the "Yeah, but" level of thinking. This is when we consciously are aware that we are a kind and caring person, but the ego, or saboteur, keeps saying, "Yeah, but…" We keep trying and trying and trying to follow our heart's desire, yet *something so deep we can't seem to get at it* holds us captive and life becomes the illusive butterfly.

Finally, there is the Third Level of Thought, where our deepest self resides. This is our connection to Source/God/Creator, and it is where we *know* we are love and we *remember* that we are loved unconditionally. In the Third Level of Thought we are in the present moment and in a profound state of inner peace.

These three levels of thought can intermingle, and if the second level of thought ever dominates the other levels, it can wreak havoc to a work schedule, cause us to doubt ourselves, judge others, or push us into a state of chaos. Below is one example. To relate this to your life, just change some of the words.

Example: You have the thought of doing something creative that you have never attempted before, like pursuing a lifelong desire to write a play.

Level 1 – Conscious:

Your thoughts are: "I can do this. Everyone tells me I can do this and the book says I can accomplish this and I can do it! I'm smart enough, I have enough education and talent for it. They do it in the movies, and my best friend, an artist, wrote one and tells me I have it in me to do this as well. I can and will write this play! This is part of why I'm here on Earth!"

Level 2 – Unconscious:

The above thoughts alternate with: "What makes me think I can do this? I've never really accomplished anything like this before. I only TOLD people I could do it. It only got PARTLY written last time, and with LOTS of help and I was SCARED SILLY. I still have not shown it to anyone because it's NOT GOOD ENOUGH for anyone to produce. If people only knew how I REALLY feel about this, that I'm REALLY not that smart, what I REALLY think of my abilities, they wouldn't be telling me to go ahead with it. Who the heck do I think I am, anyway? I'M NOT WORTHY of any of this stuff, I only pretend I am. Other people do way better writing than I ever could. If they only knew…"

Level 3 – Soul/God/Creator:

Your thoughts combine with deep *feeling*, and are something like, "It really doesn't matter what happens, it is about the experience. It's all about love. Go for it if you truly desire this, because everything is perfect, including you. It is your choice whether or not to write this play. You can do it if you wish, but there is no judgment if you choose to not write. If you do choose, you know you have all the help and resources you need, because this is who you are and could be a large part of why you are here—to be creative. So if this *just feels right* to pursue this play, and it makes you excited to even think about it, it's probably right in line with your destiny…"

As the three levels begin arguing with each other, feelings of frustration, exasperation, depression, and dismay can take over and, usually, next to nothing gets accomplished.

One way to balance these thoughts and get back on track is to listen to a specifically designed, self-hypnosis CD for about 30 days, as you change the self-defeating thoughts into the ones *you* choose to accept. This clears out any negative thinking and allows your positive thoughts to assist you in creating more balance and peace within. When your conscious thoughts are in sync with your deepest internal thoughts and feelings, your core self, you regularly experience a deeper connection to the God within, and your creative potential is unlimited! You clear the way to fulfilling your destiny!

Yes, we plan our lives before we are born and we have free will to change our mind while incarnated. Many clients I have seen had their lives changed by other people who didn't follow through with the interlife plan. For instance, in the interlife, two souls (who had been man and wife in a previous life) planned for one to be the father, another to be the son, and for the father to be physically abusive to the son in their next incarnation. This was so the son could learn forgiveness, because in their previous incarnation the son (male partner) had been unwilling to forgive the father (female partner) for indiscretions she had committed in their prior life's marriage. All this was mutually agreed upon in the interlife, yet once the father had incarnated, he ended up severely abusing the son, both physically *and* sexually. The power the father felt in his new life overshadowed the agreement and he went off track from the agreed upon destiny. Free will allowed him to do this, and the son, after realizing what had happened, accepted that he had more of a challenge than planned, and resolved to fulfill his destiny whether or not his father stayed on track.

Are you still with me? Another possible scenario for this would be if the father simply *couldn't* go through with the plan and committed suicide instead. If he could not fulfill his part of the pre-birth agreement, his son would have to learn about forgiveness another way. In this case history, an uncle stepped in and sexually abused the son. The father's suicide, together with the sexual abuse from the uncle, allowed the son to learn (per the client) much more than originally planned. So the original pre-birth agreement changed, yet the client was not only able to fulfill his destiny—he surpassed it!

When we can believe or at least accept the possibility that we chose the life we are living, it can help us to be grateful for everything, even what we experience as "horrible events." It's our choice as to how we approach the challenges that can hold us back from fulfilling our plan. It has been my experience that the more we listen to our deepest, Highest, God-connected Self, the easier it is to remember who we really are and stay on task with why we are here.

The Spirit-Directives for this chapter are:

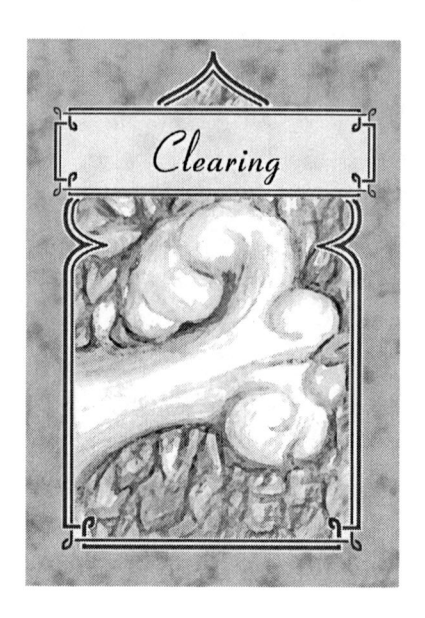

Clearing

You are being asked to clear something from your life. It could be people, places, or things that are not healthy for where you are currently. It could be foods or habits you have formed that are asking to be cleared out. It could be negative thoughts that no longer serve you. This card indicates it's time to push through anything and clear yourself, body, mind, or spirit. Meditate on the energy of this card—the clearing will be helped through nature and your intentions. Notice the energy pushing through, and set your intention to push through and clear excess out of your life. You are worth it!

Gratitude

It is time for you to express gratitude every day. There are many things in life to be grateful for, and this card indicates the importance of expressing gratitude more often. When you look at the image on the card, notice the energy that gratitude sends out. The more grateful you are, the more your energy sends that gratefulness out, which helps others to fee and be more grateful. The gratitude that you express affects everyone and every thing. It allows you to appreciate yourself and others, and life in general, more every day.

Inner Peace

What does inner peace mean to you? If you drew this card, you are being asked to focus on peace within. Do today whatever brings you to a state of inner peace. This could mean there is a message trying to get through that cannot because you are too busy. Or it could mean that your body, mind, and spirit are yearning for at least one day or more of complete inner peace. Find and do whatever it takes to create peace within.

Relax

With this card, you are being asked to take time and relax. Not today only—every day, a little bit. By relaxing you become more aware of your Spirit Helpers, you allow your body to unwind and be open to whatever it needs to know or do in the moment. Meditate on the picture now, take a few deep breaths and notice the peacefulness, the serenity of the water, imagine the greens and blues of Earth and sky. Notice how your body is feeling while looking at the picture. Bring that peacefulness into your day, and then into the next day and the next, until it becomes second nature for you. This is also a call for you to let go of any stress and allow yourself to be peace.

When I had my first Life Between Lives Regression session while taking the LBL training in Virginia Beach, Virginia, the most profound part was when I went to the body selection room and realized I had chosen to live a very, very long life. In this experience I had three choices. For the first choice I received the image of a young fetus and had the *feeling* I would die quite young. For the second choice I saw an image of a stereotypical Pocahontas, or Native American woman, and felt I had "been there, done that" many times and was choosing something different this time. The third choice was an image of my current self, only the body was very fit and a little leaner. With the image came a strong, deep knowing that I probably would live a long, long life, and the thought immediately came, to start taking better care of my body, because it needed to live a *healthy*, long life—not just a *long* life. This knowledge was the impetus for me to "get on the stick" and get my body in better physical shape.

The first 40 years of my life were very stressful in one way or another because of the physical stress from being raised on the farm, the strict work ethic attached to that, my perceptions, and the need to have pretty constant drama. Another form of stress came from my addictions, including alcohol, food, sugar, thinking, stressing—you name it! *Everything* caused drama during this time, and therefore had an element of stress in one form or another.

In my early 40s, once my "conscious spiritual journey" began, the importance of listening to *every* part of my being became the priority. I could no longer deny how profoundly I had ignored the physical, mental, and emotional self! I learned that stress causes inflammation, and in *my* body, most, if not all of the physical, mental, and emotional challenges, were a result of that inflammation. This began my commitment to health, which continues to this day.

I believe the stressful life I had been living was the root cause of the inflammation. I had years of fears and phobias that were not addressed but rather were "fed," alcoholism that was "fed," food addictions that were "fed." There were lots of "stinking thinking" addictions (brain patterns) that were "fed" and got completely out of control at one point. Finally, there were work ethic patterns that were over the top as a result of the accepted thought that what I did was "never enough." All of these thoughts, practices, and negative feelings caused inflammation that was out of control… all in line with *my* destiny!

For over 20 years now, this life have been focused on reducing the inflamed thinking and making better choices that feed the body, mind, *and* spirit in a positive and loving way. As I replace addictive or inflamed thinking and actions with positive, loving thinking and choices, every part of my being is supported, and my quality of life improves dramatically! This is *also* in line with my destiny! I know that part of my pre-birth plan was to learn about loving and respecting my body as much as my mind and spirit. I know that in many past lives I had focused more toward the spirit, and in this life it is part of my destiny to accept and love myself in every moment, no matter what, and that acceptance and love is how I came to remember *my* Divine Self.

In *Difficult Lives*, by Robert Schwartz, clients presented with a desire to know *if* they had chosen such difficult destinies, and if they had in fact chosen them, then *why* they would make such a difficult life for themselves. When they discovered that they did choose these destinies (including drug addiction, suicide, abuse, and even abortion), their entire outlook on life changed and they were able to come to a greater acceptance of their situation. Schwartz' approach (and I highly recommend his book) was to have a highly qualified medium retrieve information from the client's Akashic records relating to their past and current lives. This or similar helpful information may also be gathered through regression therapy, Life Between Lives spiritual regression, meditation, shamanic journeys and other methods. Having an idea of what our destiny is, and why we chose it, is some of the most life-altering knowledge there is. I would say one more thing in this regard however—that if we are not ready for this information, or if the full knowledge and understanding of our destiny would in any way hinder our life or the lives of others, it will not be revealed, no matter what we may try! Usually, we "know" when it is time to know more. At this time, the inspired thought, the appropriate teacher, or designated facilitator comes to us, and the rest is our beautiful, magnificent, continuing story!

Chapter 5
Choosing Freedom From • Moving into the Unconventional • Change IS

Addictions, distractions, fears and blocks, are neutral things. We make them good, bad, painful, hard, challenging, enjoyable, fun, or whatever, by putting our energy into them.

"Francis" was addicted to work. He simply could not function without working, and not just for the normal forty or even fifty hour work week. He "worked" at everything. He worked at his place of employment, he worked at eating, at his relationships, at the chores he did at home, and even at the social events to which he was invited. To him, *everything* was work—grueling, never-ending, and most certainly not to be enjoyed—work. Like many of us, he defined his value according to how much he "did" during the course of each day. When he accomplished a lot, he felt successful. If he was unable to finish a project, or missed a gathering, he felt he had somehow failed and let down himself and others. His relationship with his wife was suffering, and he didn't know what to "do" about it. At the age of 38, he felt his life was falling apart and he *could not figure out why*. While at first he thought he was "doing" everything right, he was beginning to see that he did not find joy in anything, and this baffled him.

Although many of us are not this extreme, we often accept the conventional belief that our work defines us. While some of us actually *enjoy* life, at least most of the time, Francis did not because he toiled 24/7. After just one regression session, his Spirit Helpers revealed to him the unconventional idea that work was what *he* made it, that it could be fun, it could be peaceful, and it could be joyful! During his session his guides came in and, without reprimanding or judging him, showed him the truth of who he was and how his life experience could change simply by *changing his attitude* and making choices that were in line with what he truly wanted. Once he changed his attitude, everything else changed too.

Francis still works a long, 40-plus hour week, but enjoys his job and life much more. All this changed when he shifted his outlook, his attitude toward something that *was neutral to begin with*. He enjoys the drive to work. He started to set healthy boundaries with his boss, family, and friends, and *he* is setting limits on how much time he will spend on worrying. He even developed a program of walking and fitness that brought new energy, vitality, and value into his life. The job is still neutral but Francis became a different person. He chose freedom from the way he used to think and do, worry, and fret. He chose to move into a more peaceful way of *interacting* instead of *reacting* to his life experiences. Most everything was still the same, but his life changed because of *his attitude* toward the job, the drive, his body, his relationships, his co-workers and life in general.

When one of my sons was young, he did not embrace change. He often bemoaned the fact that he was growing up. Unlike most children his age, he did not want to grow up. He was never "7 ½"—he was 7 until he turned 8. He definitely did not embrace change. I'm not sure how many hundreds of times he heard it from me, but he got used to hearing me say, "The one constant is change."

Change IS. Embrace it, flow with it, be as present as possible in every moment. Gandhi said it very simply, "Be the change you wish to see in the world." Be willing to let go of any ties that bind you to patterns that no longer work. Make choices that allow you to feel good about yourself. Get up, or get out and move… walk, run. Try something different. Laugh, cry, pray, pound a pillow, meditate, but *do* something or *be* someone that allows you to grow (and glow!) from within. Do you know that simply by your being, others' lives are enlightened? Hug someone. Smile when you may not feel like it. Anything done with intention makes a difference. You make a difference *simply by being*. Shine. Be. Smile. Grow. Play. Love. *Enjoy!*

The Spirit-Directives for this chapter are:

Freedom From

There is an aspect of your life that is asking you to choose "freedom from" *something*. This could be an addiction, a block, a distraction, a partner, someone who is no longer a friend, a relationship that is no longer working, an area where you live that is no longer right for you, or anything that could be holding you back from living fully. When meditating on the card, notice the cocoon—how the butterfly is slowly emerging into a different version of itself. It shows freedom from the case it was originally in; freedom from the one thing that held it back; free to be. This card indicates it's time to choose freedom from at least one thing in your life that is holding you back.

Birth, Death and the Afterlife

Surrender

With this card you are being asked to let go, once again. However, this letting go is about surrendering to a higher source on a much higher vibration level, a deeper level that will bring you to another level of being. This surrender will be easier than ever before yet extremely important to your life path. You are being summoned to a greater purpose than before, and by surrendering to the greater good of all, you truly will be able to move into this new life path. Sometime today, imagine you are walking in the woods, like Hansel and Gretel who left pieces of bread behind them, as you walk you are leaving little pieces of yourself behind, to be healed by the Earth. These are aspects of your life or self you no longer need. This process will change your life.

Live Fully

To live fully is to be aware and accepting of your Whole Self—your body, mind, and spirit. It means to be balanced mentally, emotionally, spiritually, and physically. To live fully is to be grateful for every thing, every moment. It's very important to you to have purpose today. What does living fully mean to you? What makes your eyes smile from the center of your heart? This Directive is a calling for you to be wise in the ways of what abundance means to you. What are you truly passionate about? What are you truly grateful for? Focus on these thoughts today or during the course of your reading – it will change your life.

Case Study

When "Cary" presented for his PLR, he was having difficulty in his relationship. His girlfriend at the time wanted their relationship to move forward and that implied marriage at some point in the future. Cary felt a great resistance to this idea but couldn't put his finger on exactly why! For whatever reason, that knowledge was hidden or somehow inaccessible to him before the session. His girlfriend had essentially issued an ultimatum: figure out why he's resisting commitment and heal it or move on.

For Cary's first ever PLR I guided him down a hallway with several doorways, suggesting that he float or move down this hallway as I counted from one to three. When I said three, he would go through one of the doors and be in a past life or an experience that would help him in his current life and that would potentially answer some of the questions he presented with.

> MK: What are you aware of?
>
> C: I'm aware of some tall stacks of some very old books. It's a dark corridor, and it's kind of musty.
>
> MK: Are you alone?
>
> C: No, not exactly. I feel someone else with me.
>
> MK: Are they spirits or are they someone you know? Just like an old movie, just kind of move around in the scene and share whatever you're getting. Heighten up all your senses and just share what's happening.
>
> C: There is an indirect light and wood floor as well, and the shelves are made from wood that's not highly polished. There's a being with me that is guiding me or assisting me.
>
> MK: Okay. Are you a male or female, or is this you in this experience?
>
> C: I'm... that's me. I'm male. There is a cot, and that's just pretty much a wooden platform with some books, blankets, other things, and it is for the times when I am growing tired and I've wished to rest, but most times when I'm here, I am just studying the books that I am here to study. I am to study most of these books. If I can study all of these books, that would be best. But I am studying whatever it is that interests me at the moment. These are texts, ancient knowledge, knowing. They are literature that was written some time ago. They are the books that have been gathered by this group that runs this institution. They are teachings that are supported by a group that runs this institution.
>
> MK: Do you know the name of the institution?
>
> C: It is like Benedictine or something like that. It's like a monastery.

And it is a place of contemplation and study, and work supporting the institution.

MK: How old are you?

C: I am 31.

MK: What's your name?

C: Armond, or something like that.

MK: Okay. Keep moving, maybe have that guide that's with you, the being that's with you, take you wherever you need to go in this experience to help you understand why you are being shown this.

C: There is some resistance that I'm being met with because it is my interest to spend most of my time in this library, reading texts that interest me, not necessarily those that I have been instructed to read. So it is always a struggle to go back and forth between the two, because my teacher would wish me to read certain texts, and these I am not interested in so much, but I feel drawn to read other texts, so the difficulty is I must read the texts that I am interested in, in a way in which I won't be discovered, so that I do not raise the ire of my teacher. It is a delicate balance between reading and knowing what it is that I wish to know and keeping my teacher happy. There is so much here that I wish to know, and that is not necessarily in line with the teachings of the group that I am a part of in this life and my teacher. So I'm always fearing being caught for reading that which I am not sanctioned to read.

MK: Is there anything else from this experience that is for you to know at this time?

C: I feel guided, at an unseen level, to read the works that I am reading, and to read as much as I can because I don't know how long I'll have to be here. There is also pressure for me to be engaged with other activities of the house, so to speak, that I don't wish to engage in these, though it is required of me. So there is constantly this struggle in terms of doing what it is that I feel pulled to do from my heart, and that what the outside world requires of me – requires of my time and my actions. I have such a burning desire to learn, there is so much to know and so little time to learn it in. I also feel that, once I learn these things, that it will grant me freedom in this life that I so greatly desire. If only I can find that. If only I can find that.

MK: I'm going to count from one to three and when I say three, you will be in another time, another important experience from that life to understand it and your current life more clearly. 1-2-3... What are you aware of?

C: I am aware that I am in a kitchen.

MK: Are you older or younger?

C: I am around the same age.

MK: Okay. What's happening?

C: There is the preparation of the meal, and there is much hustle and bustle and activity in preparing the meal. There is much work involved in preparing the meal, and I am doing what it is that I have been asked to do and yet, my mind is on other activities, other pursuits. I am not concerned about whether or not I complete my tasks in a timely fashion, and I am met with great disdain from the other brothers who are working with me. They can see that my mind is not on the task, and that I am not doing my share of the work.

MK: I'm going to count again, and when I say three you will be in another experience from that life that will help you understand it more clearly. 1-2-3...

C: I am on the path, on a road, that is barren, that is rocky, that is dusty. It is quiet here and I am walking.

MK: Is it the same life?

C: Yes, it is.

MK: How old are you now?

C: 34 years old.

MK: Okay. And what has transpired in that life?

C: I have been evicted from the monastery. So I am told that I must live using my own resources and my own skills and my own capabilities, in whatever way that I can find for myself. I have a fear of how it is that I will provide for myself. At the same time I am curiously unconcerned about not being in the monastery, because I feel that there was only so far that I could go personally there. I miss the opportunity to read and to learn in the library like I had once been able to, and I am unsure of how I will ever be able to do such a thing again, but because I have read much, I know that I have whatever skills are necessary to continue to live in this world. So I am without fear, I am angry that I can no longer study in the ways that I have been able to before.

MK: What else transpires in that life now that is of significance for you to know relating to your current life?

C: I see that I come upon a farm and there is a simple farm family that lives in this vicinity—a simple, peasant farmer and his family, and he has a daughter, and he has a simple life that he offers to me, and he has other children as well. And when I see that this is a life in which I can easily move into and live comfortably, and I can work and pull my weight, so to speak, contribute in a way that brings value, so that I will have a place to live and I will have a contented life. But I also understand that if I do this, I am giving up my opportunity or the possibility of advanced planning for the sake of a simple way to sustain, this comfortable way to sustain my life. So I let go of what it is that I had set myself to before—the vows and the commitment that I made, and I now choose to release all of that and live a life where I can contribute what I know in a limited fashion for the good of all those that I am living with.

MK: Very good. I'm going to count from one to three and you are either going to go to another important experience in that life, or you may go to the time in that life when you died. Now you won't feel any of the pain if you choose to go to the time when you crossed over in that life, and you could always be just the observer at any point in this experience, but you will know where it is most important to go. 1-2-3… What are you aware of?

C: I am lying and I am on my back.

MK: Are you alone or with other people?

C: I am with others. There is much love in this room. Much appreciation.

MK: How old are you?

C: I am 78 years old.

MK: Okay, and who's in the room—do you recognize any of them, or...?

C: Yes, I recognize all of them, and they are the descendants of those that I had befriended so many years ago. They are the children of the children. They are the land owners. They are the farmers, they are the people that work this land and this house.

MK: Do you recognize any of them from your current life? Look into their eyes...

C: My son is there. Carrie is there. There are other people that are familiar to me but I do not know them in this life.

MK: Okay. What is it that you are dying from?

C: It is just old age. My body is tired. I am tired. I have lived an industrious life, and I have reached the end of my desire to be in this life.

MK: Okay. As your spirit leaves your body in that life now, and as your spirit looks back into that life, what was that life all about?

C: It was about having a balance between that which is desired from within and that which is required from about. And there was a choice that was made that did not have to be made. And nonetheless, it was not a waste, it was not a mistake. (sigh) There was a choice to either play a political game of moving up the ranks of power within the organization, meaning that I would have full access to anything that I wish, but it would also mean that I would dilute my desires, my clear and pure desires, to learn, because I would be filtering that desire, then, through the work and the activities that I would need to climb through up into this organization, and the tradeoffs that I would have to make for my own personal values in order to attain these levels within the organization. So what that would mean is that as I would pursue those goals, that the desire for the pure learning and the pure knowing would become less and less. And it is not different than the choice that was made to leave that institution and to work the land, and to work in ways that I could work because of the knowledge that I possessed. Because in the same way that choice took me away from the learning I would wish to accomplish from that which was learned in the library. It was a different set of learning and it was valid nonetheless. So there was always a heartache or disappointment that I could not follow my original intent for this life, which was just pure learning, pure becoming. However, the becoming that I did choose was one that would take me along a different line that was valid in and of itself, and that was to selflessly give of myself for the benefit of others. Which meant that I had to abandon my original line of including it more… which desire… I had the tools in front of me, but there was too high a price to pay for being able to pursue that plan of inquiry. And I see then, that in this life, I will wish to strike a balance, because I am not interested again, in this life, in polluting or diluting my pure goal, which is learning… by being enmeshed or entangled in the political movement that would take me away from my pure desire. But at the same time I am unwilling to throw myself wholeheartedly into relationship with others that would distract me from my purposes in this life. Because I see both directions from that life, and where those directions could lead me in this life, for the example of where they lead me in that life.

MK: Do you see… if you could state it, what is your primary purpose in this (current) life?

C: My primary purpose in this life is to recover the lost knowledge that I had learned or gained from previous lives, so that I can integrate it into a whole, and an understanding that is applicable to this time, so that I might bring this understanding forward for the benefit of the world, and not just myself, and not just those who are immediately around me.

MK: Okay. And now, where do you need to go? I'm going to count again from one to three and you are going to go wherever you need to go, because you are in charge here. I'm just a guide, a facilitator. I'm going to count to three and you may go into another past life or experience that will help you understand more clearly how to do this and how to clear yourself of any traumas that may hold you back, in order for you to fulfill your life purpose and live your full potential, you will go there at the count of three. 1-2-3… What are you aware of?

Birth, Death and the Afterlife

C: (Sigh) I understand that I am a high priest in the Atlantean times, and I'm wearing… it's like a cloak or a cape, that is a white, shimmery, silvery material, very light, thin, but very strong. And I am wearing clothes that are of a similar nature, that is like a smock and a loose fitting hat. And I am in a place that is elevated within the building and it is a very simple construct that is a pyramid form above me and about me. I am in the pyramid form. There is what seems like an altar there that is made from a white stone, and the place is empty. There is a crystal that is like the pyramid, is made from a clear crystal, but I cannot see outside, but it is clear, and the floor is… is like a white marble. Everything around me is made from crystal of different sorts and types, it is all from the Earth—it is not man-made. It is all cut by man, but it is all minerals that come from the Earth herself.

MK: You said you are a high priest. Do you have a name? Do you live here, and what do you do as a high priest?

C: Aidon, a-i-d-o-n. And as a high priest I have a concern of the citizens of this local area are my highest concern. And all the work that I do is for the benefit of the community. And I work with energies of the Earth and of the cosmos to maintain a balance so that the people can live their life in the most beneficial way possible, meaning that adjustments are made to the energy so that people can live with ease and not face difficulties or have to contend with managing these energies themselves. I have a role in working with these energies so that these citizens do not have to be concerned with it. I provide the most optimum conditions that I am capable of, so that they can live their lives… so that they can accomplish their goals and their needs with minimal distraction and with greatest support. I know how to manipulate the energies. And I have been taught how to do this, and I come from a long lineage of people that have been taught this and that exercise this in a most selfless way. It is done for the benefit of others. I have no concern for myself.

MK: How old are you?

C: I am 50-51. I am not married. But I know vast quantities of information, as you would term it in this time. I am very skilled in what I do, and I understand the workings of these energy systems that I am working with now.

MK: Knowing that we are a compilation of all those lives, how can you, if you so wish, access that information in your current life?

C: It is a challenge, because there are supporting systems that do not exist in this timeframe. I do not have a crystal pyramid from which to do my work. I do not have the tools that I had in that life. I have the understandings, that is true, but to bring them into this life it is difficult because I do not have the tools that I had at that time. It has all been destroyed. And we lack the understanding in this time, of knowledge that we had in that time, to utilize these crystalline structures to manipulate for beneficial reasons, the energies that come from the Earth, the energies that come from the cosmos in a way that they come together for the benefit of all living beings – all humans, all animals, all plants—and all the other nonphysical beings that come together in the orchestration of life on this planet.

MK: And as you are in this experience, what is the most important reason you have been shown this lifetime, this experience?

C: It shows me that I have been in a life where there has been much knowledge of workings of the Earth and the workings of the cosmos given to me, and that I possess a high level of understanding—so high that I could work with it in a way where I became one with it, and could move it and change it at my will, at my discretion, always knowing that I had the impeccability and that my purpose was beyond reproach—I had the perfect impeccability to be in a position like this, that that potential exists within me in this life.

MK: Very good. Is there anything else for you to know from this life, or from that particular life, or experience?

C: I can see both past and the future, and I understand the cycles of the Earth, and the cycles of the solar system and the cycles of this quadrant of the universe, so to speak, of all the galaxy, and I understand the shorter cycles and the longer cycles, and I see that, because of where we are and the time sequence of Atlantis, that there are many negative influences that are coming into play, and that my job of balancing these frequencies has become more and more difficult. I also know that there will come a day when the negativity, the influence, becomes greater than I can balance out, and when that day comes, then I will no longer... I will no longer need to be here. And then as I look forward, I see a time in the future when these energies are coming together in a like fashion, and... (sobbing)... it is my desire to assist all, so that we can overcome the negative cycle, so that we can move beyond this negativity into the higher plane that we are destined to reach. So it is my desire to bring forth all of who I am and contribute to that process, so that we can accomplish our goals this time! And I do not want to be distracted in that life, in this life, even though I know that I must work in the currents and the forces and the distractions and the needs and the desires that will be in effect at that time. And I need to find a balance so that I can get what it is that I need to satisfy my physical comforts and needs, but at the same time not lose focus with the purpose that I came to accomplish in this life.

MK: If I may ask a question, and because you can see future in that life, in your current life then, we have the possibility, the full potentiality of going into that next level of consciousness, so to speak?

C: Yes. Now, in this time, is when we move, when we have the opportunity to move into the higher level of being. The energies are upon us now, and there are just a few years left before the point is reached, where we either move up or we fall back, and repeat the cycle once again.

MK: Is there any more information from this experience you wish to share, or is that another time?

C: It is another time, because in this life we did not have the distraction of family, we did not have the distractions of living and working within a society in a way that you understand it. The priesthood and the priestesshood, so to speak, was always kept separate from the general population and did not have an experience of what it was to be those that they guided the energies for. And so there is limited input from that life, for this life.

MK: I'd like you to simply move now, without me even counting, you can simply move into another life or experience that will help you to release any block or traumas that hold you back in our current life, so you truly can do this work. Just move into it now… and share whatever you're getting…

C: Well, I'm being shown the life that I was shown the last time that I did this. So I am a merchant in the late 19th Century London, man.

MK: How old?

C: Hmmm… I am in my late 30's… no, no, that is hard to determine my age.

MK: Okay, then it's not important. There is obviously something you didn't get from the last time that is important for you to know at this time, so I'd like you to go to that experience when I count to three, you will go to an experience from that life that is to be revealed to you now. 1-2-3…

C: (Sighing)… I am a strong man, I have a large body, but it is from muscle and hard work, and I am a very driven individual and I am most interested in being successful in my life and providing for my family, and I can do that—I know how to work those people in my life—the politicians, and the other traders and vendors that I work with. And I am a fair man, and always negotiate a fair price and a fair deal, and I always am concerned that everyone gets their due, but no more than what they are due, and it is a great percentage of my life. But also I have my family which I do love—I have my wife and I have my daughter. (Sighing)… and they are ill. And I am not ill, I am strong. But they are the reason that I do what it is that I do, because I wish to provide for my family, and I wish to give them those luxuries and those conveniences that I did not have when I was a child, that seem to be out of reach from the common man, but because I am skilled and I know how to do these things, it is my desire to bring this to my family. But there is no point now, because they are ill, and they are dying, and I do not know what is the purpose of all this? Why be so strong? Why be successful? There is no one to give it to if they don't remain healthy and strong, they don't remain here with me. So life seems pointless to me, and now I see that they have died, and that there is no reason for living, but I am so strong and I know so much about being successful, for being healthy, for being strong, for accumulating wealth, for negotiation, for being favored in this city, but there is no purpose to it. What can I use these skills for? My whole reason for being is I love them. (Sobbing)… they are no longer here, so I just give up. But I am so strong that I cannot get away from it, so I spend most of my time at the tavern, because when I drink I cannot feel my pain, and I don't care whether I have a purpose or not.

MK: Let's move now, to the time in that life when you died. Again, you will feel none of the pain if you have it, you can detach from it. Go to the time in that life when you died. 1-2-3… What are you aware of?

C: I feel a relief now.

MK: As your spirit is leaving your body now, are you alone? How did you die in that life, if it's important?

C: I died alone.

MK: What age?

C: I was in my mid-30's, or mid-to-late 30's.

MK: As your spirit leaves your body, what's happening?

C: All the pain is gone. I am leaving the body that was hopeless, that was very sad.

MK: Okay, and who are you with now, as you leave? What was that life about, and what's happening?

C: I am with those that left me earlier in that life—my wife and my daughter. And that life was about… (sighing)… it was about how I had placed all of my focus into my family. All that I did was for the one that I loved most dearly, which was my wife. I would have done anything for her, and then to have a beautiful child… and so, I was, in some ways, out of balance as well. But I could also see the potential of what it would mean to fully give my heart over to another. And so I see now, that, because of the great pain that I experienced, that I am unwilling to do the same thing now, because it's just too painful. There must be a way to find balance between the two.

MK: Yeah. I'm going to suggest that you go to a place now, to of all knowing, or there may be a place like in nature, I don't know, everybody's experience is different, in the interlife. Connect with your guides, or... I don't want to make any suggestions on what your experience is, so that you can have some very specific questions answered about all of this you are learning today... which is a lot. And just share wherever you are, just be in that place now...

C: My desire in this life is to be alone, and I have done that, sometimes, but many times I have done it where I am in a family situation, too. So even though I have been in a family situation, I have been trying to find time to be alone, and I have not given my heart fully because I know that I do not want to experience any pain that might come with that. So what I want to know in this life is how I can strike a balance between being alone and being in a family situation and learning what it is that I need to learn. Because my first thought is always to be just alone and to be on my own, but there is always a part of me that would wish to have someone to love, and to be loved by someone, to not feel alone at those times when I feel alone. So I need to know how to reconcile those two... (sighing)... so, I'm told that I have choice. I can either choose to live a life that attempts to balance all of these things, but at the same time it would dilute the focus in either of these directions. So I can either balance these and know that my learning and my pursuit of remembering will slow, or I can have (humph) focus beyond family relationships, and have that piece that I feel is missing from my life. Or I can choose to let go of all of that, and focus solely on what it is that I'm learning and that I am remembering, from the past lives, knowing that there are just a few short years left before the shift takes place, and that if I am willing, that I could have this aspect, this family, this love aspect, come later in my life. So it is a point of choosing that I must make now. And it is a difficult one.

MK: Can you ask, I'd like to ask, this isn't a suggestion, that you be shown some potentialities based on some choices that you might make. Let's say you make one choice, what are some possibilities? You kind of know that I'm certain this would just be kind of a review, but I'd like to test or be aware of how you're feeling in each of these,

Birth, Death and the Afterlife

in your own spirit, in your own mind, in your own physical body, so that you can... because you are in a heightened state of awareness, you can be more aware of what truly is best for you and everyone concerned. Does that make sense?

C: Yes, I think so.

MK: Okay. So, I'd like to ask the energies that you are with or your own self—whatever experience you are in right now, to present to you, some of the potentialities if you were to make the choice to...

C: (Voice changes) Well, it is all very simple from this perspective, because there is no choice to be made. The choice has already been made. The choice was made before you came into this life. And so you see, it is just a matter of... ahm... remembering what your choice is, and continuing to hold that.

MK: Okay, and what is that?

C: The choice that you made when you came into this life was to remember the knowledge that you had in previous lives, and to have the experiences that would cause you to remember those pieces that are missing from your conscious recollection, so that at some point in the future, as the shift is occurring, all these pieces will come together and you will be able to... perform that which it was your choice to come here to perform. And so any distraction along those lines is to be... removed, or put off until that which time you have accomplished the goal in this life. It is very simple from our perspective, but we understand that from the human perspective, it is a very difficult... it is not unlike others that have come before you, where the temptations and the urgings and the desires of the human ego, of being human, are great, and difficult to overcome, although overcome is not the word because it is not that you overcome these, what you do is you learn to live with them, even though they are present, and be ever mindful of the goal that you have, and that you act in accordance with accomplishing the goal. Because once the goal is accomplished then, there will be time for all those other human pursuits that you desire.

MK: And are your counterparts then, and I'm going to actually say our counterparts, because this will probably involve a lot of people—are our counterparts then aware of that and will work with us in that? Will they wait, in other words?

C: Those others in our lives who are our loved ones, is this what you refer to?

MK: Yes.

C: They understand that at a deep level, that they, too, are dealing with their human ego issues—the human factor, so to speak, and even though they may understand at a deep level, a personality issue, there will be difficulties that must be managed, that must be experienced. It is the way of life, you see. So they will understand at a deeper level. And for those that are awake and aware, will have the opportunity to learn from the Greater Self, what is at play, and they will come to understand over time, and then this will ease their difficulty, and ease the strife or discord that comes as a result of this.

MK: And they have free will choice along the way, too, so that's all part of this?

C: Yes, they do. You see, each person has that choice. For those who have come forward and who are more aware, they have the choice between… that which pulls you as a human, the human desire, so to speak, or the purpose that you came into this life. And if you choose to fulfill the human desires, then that is a valid choice. And it can be as simple as recognizing and acknowledging within yourself, that that is what you wish to do, is to appease and to fulfill the desires of the human ego—the human desires, the human condition. And if that is so, then fulfill that and let it go and move on, you see. But if it is that you wish to fulfill the goal and purpose of your life, then you will always have those distractions pulling at you—you always have the temptations pulling at you—but you must always remain fixed on that which is the goal. And know that it may be painful to let go of that which is a pleasure or a fulfillment of the human desire, but these are just temporary. You have lived many, many, many lives, where you have had the opportunity to experience the human condition and to fulfill the desires of the human ego. And

so it is but a small period of time that you have left to do that which you came here to do.
MK: May I ask who is speaking?
C: We are Cary.
MK: Okay. Very good. Is there anything else for Cary to know at this time?
C: (Sighing)… it is a painful time that he lives in now. And knowing that as he fixes his primary goal that he wishes to accomplish in this life, that it will be easier to say what must be said, to do what must be done, because the purpose that he has is not a selfish purpose, but is a purpose that is for the benefit of many, not just the one. And so in this way he can be comforted knowing that it is not a selfish desire that he pursues, that it is for the greater good, the greater benefit.
MK: One of the questions is how to cleanse his karma?
C: Well, the greatest way to cleanse karma is just to participate in those areas that are there to be participated in. So if there is any resistance, this is an indication of an area of karma that needs to be cleansed. It must be understood that life is lived to cleanse karma—that is the purpose of life—but most times individuals in our lives will avoid cleansing their karma because of the pain and difficulty, or how it distracts them from fulfilling their desire to… ahm… their human desire, that is—the human condition—just in fulfilling that which pulls them in that human condition. So you see, most people turn away from cleansing their karma. In each life they have the opportunity to do so. So each time there is or a fear, that is a clear signal to move forward in the direction where that fear or that resistance is coming from, and when that forward motion is made and the interaction is made, then the karma is met and released.
MK: Okay.
C: It is funny… a dilemma, because it is those areas of resistance and fear that all their karma can be cleansed, but it is of course the areas that you would wish to turn away from because they are uncomfortable or cause difficulty or seemingly are difficult. But it is where the solution lies.

MK: Thank you very much. One of the other questions is, what should Cary be eating? What is proper diet?

C: (Sighing)… he has learned much in terms of diet over the years, and essentially, what it comes down to, is that foods that are simple in nature must be consumed. Foods that are not processed, foods that are generated in an environment of great positivity for the most part. So this would include fruits that are grown by people that love to grow food for people, and typically these are foods that are organic foods, but not all organic foods are grown in these conditions. Understand that when the human cooperates with the nature spirits and with the Earth in growing food, that is the highest form of food to be consumed. Also, it is true with animals as well, because it is important for the human to consume animal flesh as well, although as we reach higher and higher vibrations, this will become less and less of a need. But again, it must be that the food that is consumed, it was… had its life in surroundings of love and surroundings of concern for all factors. So this is something that must be sought out and typically is something that can be found in those retailers that would sell food that is made by people who are concerned and aware, and is not typically available through restaurants and in situations where the food is prepared by others. Typically unless you purchase this food from these retailers that have obtained it from people who know and care and have love for what they do, and then you must prepare this food yourself to be consumed for yourself or for others—this is the highest and most pure energy. And so we would instruct you to continue with what it is that you have learned and are learning, and then just to see by gauging the reaction in your own body, what works and what does not work for yourself. And then there is a way of testing the food with your hands so that you can ascertain the level of love and cooperation in which that food was created, and the higher the level of love and cooperation, the better it is for your consumption.

MK: Is that just placing your hands over it, or how do you do that?

C: Yes. You can put your hands over it, with the intention of feeling the intensity that that food radiates, the intensity of the amount of cooperation and love that was present at the time of its nurturing and growth. And so there can be a relative comparison of foods done with this feeling of the intensity of the energies that are given forth.

MK: Okay. Okay, is there anything else that you'd like to share, that will help Cary at this time?

C: Well, we would caution Cary to have more fun in his life. You see, he takes his task very seriously, and he is always looking at how what he does contributes or detracts from his purpose in this life. But it need not always be so—it can be that he has fun at the same time.

MK: So another way of balancing? That seems to be a theme here.

C: Uh huh.

MK: I can really understand that. Is there a way that Cary can more consciously connect with you? I know that he could by coming here again, but is there a way that he can do this in the dreamtime or on his own, or does he do that without knowing consciously?

C: Well, it is interesting, because he has been holding onto two competing goals most of his life—one of fulfilling his purpose and the other of fulfilling the needs of the human condition, you see. And once he has been able to fulfill… once he has been able direct his energies along the path of fulfilling his purpose in this life, then he will easily connect with us. But you see, this is an area of fear and this hasn't been touched upon in what he has written in his question. And so as he continues to hold both paths as equally valid, then he is also holding the fear of moving forward away from him, and not moving into it because he sees that fear represents a choice.

MK: And he moves through that, how—by just making the choice?

C: Yes. And the choice must be made and it must be definitive. There can be no holding onto these mutually exclusive paths, you see. One clear choice must be made. Because neither goal will be accomplished if both are held onto.

MK: Neither will be accomplished if both are held onto?

C: One or the other must be chosen.

MK: And he could do both in this life, though?

C: One after another, not at the same time.

MK: Okay. I just want to have it very clear, because sometimes it feels so clear when you get it, and then you have questions after, so to make it as clear as possible… Is there anything else you need to know at this time?

C: Just remember that anywhere there is fear, that is a marker or a beacon for opportunity. And so you should always go into the fear. Always go into the resistance. Always. This is the path—the most and direct and straight path available.

MK: And… how do you do that? Sometimes… when fear seems to really block you, or you have some karma related to it—how—what do you do? What would be a step or two that could be done?

C: In those opportunities where you are confronted with a fear, and you have the opportunity of choosing one way or the other—choose then and there, without any thought—take no thought, and just go with it. Choose to move, to take the next step, to say the words that need to be said. Do not resist it, just take the next step. It is like the example that has been made before in another setting—when someone asks you a question they ask you a yes or no question, and they say, "Is it yes or is it no?" And you answer right then, yes, or no. You know in your conscious mind that it is not really, as far as you are concerned, a clear yes or no answer, or that you would wish to qualify your yes, but then that is an example of how you can move forward into your fear or resistance, by making an unqualified yes or no in that instant. And then owning that choice that you make, and moving in the direction that that choice moves you in that moment. When you resist or put off or wait until later or qualify your yes or no response, you are delaying, you are turning away from the fear, you are trying to dull the sharp edge of it, and you are trying to skirt around the edges of it as opposed to moving directly through the center. So this is one example of how you can act. Now there are situations where you do not have the opportunity to act in the moment because it is something that you know will have to be done at a certain time the next day, for example, and the best way to do this is in the moment, choose what it is that you were going to do, and then let it go—forget about it—until the time comes, and then just repeat the choice you made in that moment. Do not think about it. Do not agonize about it. Do not add any energy to it. Life can be very quickly decisive. It can be that way. It should be that way, in many cases. Certainly for those who understand where it is, or what it is that their purpose is in life. These decisions can be made quickly and easily, and they may seem unfeeling or heartless, but there is a greater issue to be considered, so in that way, it is not heartless. It is done in a way that is for the greatest good. It is best not to entangle oneself first, if they are going to choose not to be entangled.

(Note: After Cary and I thanked his guides for coming through, the guides once again reminded him that his belief that he can follow a dual path has continually blocked him from the life he planned, that his resistance was not helping. After again thanking them, the client was brought to full awareness, with the suggestion that he will remember everything.)

End of PLR

As a result of this session, Cary realized that marriage (and his girlfriend's two younger children) represented a direction opposite of his heart's desire and was actually contrary to his path. He not only wanted, but needed the freedom to travel to learn new things and follow his passion. Marriage and family was the antithesis of that. Within a few weeks of the session, the couple broke up. He chose freedom from what was holding him back.

Four years after this session, Cary sent in the following update to his session, which is printed in its entirety.

"I had divorced in October of 2003 after 13 years of marriage. For years I had had a strong urging to pursue my heart's desire. I knew climbing the corporate ladder, living in the suburbs and appearing to have all the trappings of success did not sustain me. I left that marriage vowing I would do whatever was necessary to find joy in living every day. As the reality of my situation settled in, I realized my most essential concern was providing for and spending quality time with my 9 year-old daughter. In time, I moved closer to my daughter and took a well-paying job in the field I thought I had left behind. I began to date, meeting women with children. A feeling of regret and hopelessness began to set in but I didn't understand why, at the time.

My girlfriend noticed a certain reluctance to move forward in our relationship, "moving forward" implying marriage at some point in the future. I felt a great resistance to this idea but couldn't put my finger on exactly why. We talked about this issue in great depth but the reasons for my reluctance were hidden or somehow inaccessible to me. Soon after, my girlfriend issued an ultimatum: "Figure out why you're resisting commitment to me and heal it or I'll be forced to move on."

Being familiar with the power of hypnosis to reveal hidden or buried emotional issues, I contacted Madonna Kettler in June of 2007 for a private hypnotherapy session.

After the session, I began to realize I had been settling back into the very place I had left just a few short years before. I remember having the thought "You're right back where you were, all you've done is replace one family for another!" Even worse, I couldn't be a father to my precious daughter in the same way ever again. I wouldn't be there for all the little things, the discoveries, the joys, the tribulations. I would always live in "summary," listening to her stories after-the-fact, never being there to share in her life first-hand like before.

But as the memory of the session resurfaced it became clear to me that marriage to my girlfriend (and her two younger children) represented a direction opposite of my heart's desire and was actually contrary to my path. I also began to see that even though my relationship with my daughter had changed, it had changed for the better because now I was a positive influence in her life, the opposite of the way I had become while married to her mother. And as these realizations set-in, I suddenly had a sense of well-being and the path before me became clear. Within a few weeks of the session, my girlfriend and I broke up.

Since that time, I have given free expression to my desire to travel and explore and have been very happy. With the understanding I gained from my session, I have a better appreciation for what drives me and I know that as long as I honor that drive, my life unfolds with ease and joy. Carey"

Chapter 6
Filters and the Unseen • Dreams • Acceptance of What Is

My mother was raised in a strict Austrian-Catholic home. Our family was brought up in this same genre, yet each sibling chose to accept different degrees of the doctrine the church imposed. Need I say, when we get together and discusses beliefs, it can get pretty interesting!

Mom was never sure if she approved of or trusted my spirituality. She loved it when I channeled healing to her, because during the session she would see a vast field of flowers of every color and would feel wonderful afterwards. Yet she remained unsure about "that psychic stuff," and didn't like talking about it much, so out of respect, I usually avoided the topic with her.

Then one day during a routine visit Mom told me about a LOUD, BOOMING voice that came out of nowhere and said, "Pray for 'Arnie.'" I asked her what she did next, and she said she got up right away and started to pray fervently. Then she scrunched her face, tilted her head and asked, "What was that?"

Not wanting to alarm or frighten her, I said that it could have been her angels talking with her, or her intuition could have been telling her very strongly to pray, or that God really wanted her to pray right away. I asked her if the voice felt scary or good, and she said it didn't feel scary, just loud and urgent. We agreed that prayer was the right thing to do.

After a few moments of silence, she sat down beside me, looked me directly in the eyes and timidly asked, "Was that psychic?"

I chuckled and softly replied, "Yes, Mom, that was psychic!"

Mom continued to pray ardently during her entire Earth life. She prayed the rosary daily, recited Novenas whenever requested, and went to mass every day she was able. Over the years that followed this psychic event, she had many more requests for prayer, both psychic and human, and the more she prayed, the more she seemed to connect to the other realms. The more she allowed herself to go into any type of trance state, the deeper her conscious spirit-connection was.

Dad, also raised Catholic, had a near death experience around the age of 35. During this experience he "knew" there was a presence that loved him beyond a shadow of a doubt, and that this love was unconditional. He called this presence God. He felt that as long as you believed in a higher power, that was okay. He only revealed this to me in his late 70s after reading an article about NDEs in the Minneapolis Tribune. I was the first person to whom he spoke of this.

From what I have learned, many people have visions, or psychic or intuitive experiences, but for various reasons do not choose to share them. Dad was afraid to share his for fear of ridicule, and Mom shared her experiences with only a couple of people besides her children. I believe Mom's many experiences with her Spirit Helpers aided her during her final transition at the age of "almost 94."

The psychic incident was definitely a turning point in Mom's and my relationship. Just like Dad's NDE was a contributor to his "looser" version of Catholicism, I believe that because of Mom's psychic episodes she learned to trust some of my abilities a little more, and we were even able to talk about the possibility of past lives from time to time. (She said if she ever came back it would be as a yellow tabby!) I believe we both shared a new respect for each other that grew deeper as we continued let go of some of the expectations we had for each other as mother and daughter.

One time a few months before she transitioned, while I was channeling a healing for her, she told me again of her doubts for my salvation. I quietly responded, "Mom, when you are in Heaven, you will understand." We were both able to leave it at that, and from that point forward (at least from what I remember), she only focused her prayer on the positive, praying that "we will all meet again in Heaven." We may have struggled with our beliefs over the years, but our love and respect for each other allowed us to move past our differences and focus on what we knew: we love each other, no matter what. Mom *still* loves her family, just from another dimension. About a year after her transition she appeared to me while I was meditating. She was radiating pure light and love as we embraced. She understands.

We are much more than our Earth-suit-selves. We are always connected to beings that are *not* in physical form. They are right here with us, just in a different vibration. When our vibration matches theirs, we "hear" them. Sometimes they lower their vibration to match ours, and other times we raise ours. In "Arnie's" case, prayer was desperately needed *in that moment*, and it was prayer that most probably changed the outcome of an auto accident from being potentially deadly to a very frightening close call. It was not "Arnie's" time to have a major accident, therefore Mom's Spirit Helpers instructed her to pray. I'm not sure how all this works, yet I know of far too many similar incidents to not believe that we are *never* alone.

Another realm that many are familiar with is the dream state. I have been journaling my dreams for over 25 years, and some of the information that has come through has changed my life *forever*. I have consistently asked for guidance through this medium, and have always, eventually, received a response. I have asked to meet with loved ones, which is always a wonderful event. I have also allowed my spirit to be "of service where needed, for the highest intentions," which could include healing or comforting people in times of need. Sometimes during traumatic world events, it seems my day hours are less busy than my night time hours! We are spiritual beings first, so this travel/work is not new to our spirits: it's only new to the current body and mind in the present incarnation.

We all dream. *Recalling* our dreams isn't quite as common. I was just getting started with other-worldly contact when I wanted answers to some fears I had in relation to being a healer. My deepest self knew I was a healer, but my conscious, egoic self doubted it could be a career that would support me and that I was "good enough." At the time I had only one or two dreams I remembered during my *entire life*, so after stating my conundrum to my chiropractor, she told me just to say, over and over again, while drifting to sleep, "I dream, I remember the dream." I knew I also wanted to record the dream, so I changed it to, "I dream, I remember the dream, I record the dream." I had also heard it was helpful to put a glass of water by the bed, drinking half before retiring, which causes you to get up during the night and in turn can help in the recall process. I diligently repeated the mantra, over and over and over again, for quite a few nights. I was determined to remember!

My question to God was, "Am I *really* supposed to do this healing work, and if so, please give me the message through someone I trust." I had no idea whom that person would be. On the third night after the request my uncle Eugene, who had crossed over about two years earlier, came to me in a waking dream (a dream you have just before awakening in the morning). In the dream I was sitting and talking with some of my cousins (Eugene's children) when he "floated" toward us. I "floated" toward him and we hugged as he kissed me with so much love, it was breathtaking. He looked directly into my eyes and said, "This is just a piece of the love I experience every day. God told me to tell you He loves you very much and that you are doing exactly the right thing. Even more healing power will be sent through you, and know it is good." Then he "floated" away.

I woke up from the dream, sat up, and hugged my knees. What a blessed validation *that* was! When I told my aunt, who was living at the time, about this experience, she quietly said, with loving tenderness in her voice, "Oh, I always thought Gene was going to be some type of messenger."

Whether this was an actual visit from my uncle or my unconscious self relating the message, it doesn't really matter. I can still, after all these years, feel his kiss and hug. It was divinely real! This event got me hooked on remembering my dreams, and was only the beginning of many subsequent adventures in the dreamtime.

We can have spirit contact in many other ways as well. Guidance can come while meditating, praying, walking in nature, or just being. Quite a few years after the above dream, I was in a particularly down period of my life, my energy level was exhaustingly low, my emotions were off the charts, and I felt as if I had nowhere to turn. I was being guided to sell my home (which I absolutely loved), and had no idea where I would move or what I would do if this were to happen, yet all the signs pointed to selling my home. As often happens, I fought it for quite awhile. Then during this down time, when I was questioning everything in my life (again!), I got home from getting groceries for my Mom and checked the emails on the computer. One was kind of strange in that it was from one of my family members. It just said, *"Life is either an adventure... or it is nothing... by Helen Keller."*

When I discovered no one in my family had actually sent that email, I knew it was a direct message from the Universe for me to trust the messages I was receiving. And isn't it interesting that I always describe my *journey* as an *adventure?* When we don't listen in one way, they will find other ways to affirm us!

If you find that you are having difficulty accepting things, either messages, challenges, the state of the world, your relationships, the job you have, the losses you may be experiencing, the "mistakes" you have made, or anything at all in your life that could dull your spirit, here is a story someone told me recently. A man was walking down the street, bemoaning his life. Everything was going wrong with it—his job was horrible, the weather was bad, and his outlook was not the best. He came upon a Buddhist Monk, reiterated his failings and disgust to him, and the Monk said gently, "And this, too, shall pass." The next week, the same man was strolling down the same street. He was on a natural high because life was so very, very good. The weather had changed, his job was improved and he was feeling enamored. He came upon the same Buddhist Monk, and as he expressed wonderment and exuberance with his life, the Monk repeated softly, "And this, too, shall pass."

I'm sure you've heard the expression, "When life hands you lemons, make lemonade." If you have practiced and practiced meditation, requested information in the dreamtime, walked in nature with intention, or tried any of the plethora of ways there are to have otherworldly contact, hopefully you have discovered that you can find acceptance with every failure, just as you find acceptance with every accomplishment. They are both good. It's *all* good. Acceptance of what *is* allows us to "flow with the go;" it allows us the opportunity to relish every moment. There are always helpers out there, whether we are aware of them or not. There is always another opportunity for growth. Seize every moment. If you are unable to see the possibilities from time to time, embrace the moment you are in and *do the best you can do.*

Mom often said that phrase to us when we were frustrated or impatient with some part of life. She herself had a lot of acceptance to work through in the years prior to her transition. Her eye sight was nearly gone, she was confined mostly to a wheelchair or walker, her appetite had left her years before, and she needed to wear hearing aids. She had trouble breathing and didn't sleep well due to severe arthritis and osteoporosis, which caused a great deal of pain. She did know, however, that she could pray. And pray she did, nearly constantly. She *did the best she could do*. She loved us unconditionally, and she focused her attention on the positive and *by her being, she made a difference*.

We all can pray in our own way. We all can tap into our intuition, our deep inner self, our outer guidance, our Spirit Helpers. These gifts come from the highest source, our Creator, and they are available to us 24/7. Having access to these gifts can make life not only unique, but ecstatic! The only thing necessary to access them is to practice listening, practice being, practice living in the now. When these practices become more a natural part of your everyday living, gratitude will also become a natural part of every day. If you get frustrated for any reason while listening, practicing being, or living in the now, ASK FOR HELP! One of my favorite teachers, Echo Bodine, a gifted psychic, intuitive, healer and ghostbuster, said "There are a lot of unemployed angels out there. All we have to do is ask."

Coming from one who was a Type A personality (doing, doing, doing, and not just one thing at a time…), I know spirit connection can be achieved. I have gone from totally left brain, to (nearly) totally right brain, to a balance of both, and sometimes using one or the other on demand! When I am doing the bookkeeping for the business, the left brain kicks in, and when I am focusing on meditation or any type of trance state, the right brain is there for me. When I am writing, it can be either a left or right brain function, depending upon where I'm asking for assistance during the input process (right brain) or typing the information into the computer (left brain). Practice, practice, practice, and it will enhance your life beyond your wildest dreams!

The Spirit-Directives for this chapter are:

Guidance

It's time for you to become more aware of your Spirit Helpers, Guides, Angels, or Ancestors. They may speak to you through nature and signs, or they may come to you in thoughts you may have that feel a little different from your "intuition" or your "daily thoughts." This guidance is very important for you. It will help you with the rest of your life journey, and it is important to take time daily to listen to this guidance that is coming in. This daily practice could start with just five or more minutes daily. You could just allot yourself some time and play some quiet music or have no music and sit quietly, take some deep breaths or listen to a meditation CD—whatever works for you. This card is a clear message for you to listen to your guidance—they have important messages for you.

Filters (and the unseen)

With this Directive, you are being asked to see beyond what your normal vision sees. You are being asked to use your inner eye, your third eye, to answer a question or resolve an issue you currently may have. It's time for you to see things differently. Your perception of things could be far different from others'. Be aware of this and allow everyone's perception to be his or her own, including yours.

Dream

    This Spirit-Directive asks you to notice your dreams. Have a journal or a recorder by your bedside so you are ready to record any dreams. This card indicates that your dreams could be prophetic or any other type of dream, but they will be dreams that will help you in your future planning. There are many dream books to help you translate them. To remember your dream, simply say, over and over before you retire, "I dream, I remember the dream, I record the dream." This card is telling you very clearly that dreams are coming from a higher level, and that they are important to your life path.

Connection

It's time for you to connect with the Earth and all the higher consciousness levels. It's time for you to be aware of your connection to All That Is. This can either be through meditation, yoga, walking in nature, or your special way to connect. It's time for you to reconnect with the higher realms around and within you, and one of the best ways of doing this is to sit and BE IN LOVE, or walk in nature. As you walk, repeat over and over again… "I AM loved, I AM love, I love." Every part of our being is connected to every thing else. Begin today to be aware of this deep, profound connection to All That Is.

Case Study

"Kasia" presented for an LBL session because she was curious about the events that had occurred over the prior year. Her fiancé had committed suicide six months earlier. She was wondering what to do next, and wanted to know how to communicate with her fiancé. She hoped to find out if his death had to do with fulfilling a contract and also felt her fiancé might be a bridge to the other realms for her, a notion that she wanted to validate.

Also, the client wanted to inquire about her destiny, and what her draw to Hawaii was all about. She did not, however, have any attachment to the outcome of the session. She was confident that the information that was most important for her to know would come through.

I did my standard regression with deepening techniques and had her go toward whatever she was guided to move toward. I also suggested that she could easily "change her vibration" to make a conscious connection with whatever beings were there for her to connect with.

> MK: What are you aware of?
> KB: Feels like a tunnel… it wasn't darkness, it was full of little lights, like stars. Moving toward this light at the end, but it was always kind of light and dark at the same time.
> MK: Okay. Does it feel like you're male or female?
> KB: I don't know; it's more like I'm an observer.
> MK: Okay. That's very well how you can do it. I didn't talk to you about that – you can always be an observer in these experiences. So just kind of move it ahead and share whatever you're getting.
> KB: Waterfall is coming very strong, because it's outside, this whole scene is outside.
> MK: Okay. Can you get an idea where this is at?
> KB: Hmmm
> MK: Sometimes, especially if you are an observer, you can sort of shoot yourself out into the Universe and see where you are, if it is on the globe… you'll see a dot or a star…
> KB: South America is coming to me.
> MK: Okay. Sometimes it's not important to the session, too, and that's okay. So if you don't get the information, it may not be important or it will come to you later.
> KB: Because it's almost like a jungle but the whole scene is very strange because these people don't look like they are from there.
> MK: Okay. What are they dressed in?
> KB: They are dressed like a traditional wedding – white dress and dark suit. Very strange. The whole scene is like a jungle. There looks like no one else…

MK: Do you recognize the couple—are you one of the couple or are you just observing this scene completely?

KB: I have a feeling that I am but I cannot see which one.

MK: Okay. Okay, very good. I'm going to count from one to three and when I say three you will be in another scene from that life, or whatever it is, that will help you understand it more clearly. 1-2-3...

KB: Now I'm in a kitchen. Also it's in some kind of a jungle, but… it's quite a modern kitchen. I feel like it's like a family life, and there are children, too. Now I feel that I'm a woman.

MK: Okay. What are you…

KB: I just feel like crying… I don't know…

MK: Well, maybe that's good, just get into it… Why do you feel like crying? What's going on?

KB: I don't know, I just feel this deep sadness in me…and it feels like I'm alone there with the kids and there is no man. And this strange environment… we don't come from there, really.

MK: Okay. How old are you?

KB: 35, maybe 40?

MK: What's your name?

KB: Clarissa came real strong, whoof!

MK: Okay. Very good. So what do you do in this life? Are you the mother to these children?

KB: Looks that way. I have a feeling that we came on some mission in that jungle, and that this man is either working all day or he's not alive—I don't know.

MK: Just kind of go through a day and see what happens… What are you aware of?

KB: Yes, I feel that I'm alone with the children. I'm kind of lost in a foreign world.

MK: Yeah. How many children?

KB: Two.

MK: How old?

KB: Mmmm… around four and six.

MK: Do you recognize them from your current life? Look into their eyes…

KB: No. But I have a feeling that that man in that wedding, that it was Robert. But the children, no.

MK: (Counting, 1-2-3...)

KB: The first image that came to me was a man who looked more like a Hindu from India, meditating.

MK: I didn't mention that sometimes you go from one life to another. You may jump from one to another, or you can go backward or forward in time, so just stay with whatever you're getting and you'll understand it later.

KB: It's almost like he's my teacher, but he's not saying anything, he's just sitting there.

MK: Can he say anything to you telepathically?

KB: Just that you know we have all the answers. This one is more peaceful, there's... it's more peaceful, and just fulfilled.

MK: Where are you in that life?

KB: You mean geographically?

MK: No, you said you saw the Hindu man...

KB: I'm just like a young woman, traveling... I am alone and just exploring.

MK: Okay, what is your name and where do you go, and what do you look like? Tell me all you can...

KB: I have curly, blonde hair, quite long. I'm wearing a dress, very colorful, and I'm really young, probably in my 20s, early 30s. Just really excited about life—I'm curious... but this man... hmmm, it's somebody that seems really important.

MK: Do you recognize him from...

KB: But it might be like Keya?

MK: Yeah, okay. What was he in that life—just someone you went to visit or something, or...?

KB: Uh huh, somebody when I went... to India. And I feel we have some kind of psychic connection.

MK: Okay. Just kind of move forward in that life and share whatever else there is that's really important for you to know...

KB: I have a feeling that I am in some kind of temple or ashram. I feel really good, I don't have any expectations, and just...

MK: By what name are you called in that life?

KB: I don't know.

MK: Okay. Now I'm going to count from one to three again and when I say three you will be in the most important life that will help you understand…which might still be that one, but it will help you to understand your current life more clearly. 1-2-3…

KB: I am still in the same ashram, and it seems like that man is a Guru or… now I see a tree… now I am in a different place. It looks like Scandinavia… but again, I am alone, and just walking, like a wanderer, or…

MK: Male or female?

KB: This time it looks like male. Kind of lonely, too. I'm lost, like there is no purpose, and no… I am feeling that there is a mother who is very sick—that I had a mother somewhere and I don't really want to take care of her, and at the same time I feel guilty… I know I should, but I don't really want to. Oh, it's a terrible life! Really meaningless, and… cold and terrified and nothing is really happening in this life. The feelings of guilt, and being lost.

MK: Okay. Let's see if you can move now to your most recent past life and see if there is anything there for you to know or experience. 1-2-3…

KB: I'm flying in a helicopter and it's flying over a jungle.

MK: Male or female?

KB: Female. I have a feeling it's the same life as the first one…

MK: Okay, good, that's good validation, too. Just share whatever else you're getting. What was that life all about?

KB: It seems like me and this man were scientists and we came to explore something in the jungle, so we build a house there and we had children, and then… I don't know what happened to him, but he's not there.

MK: Okay. I'd like to go to the time in that life when you died. Now just like you did before, you can be the observer—you don't have to feel the pain or anything like that, but I'm going to count to three and when I say three you will be at the time when you died in that life. 1-2-3… What are you aware of?

KB: I have a feeling that I died really young and it was some kind of a sickness from then.

MK: Are you alone or are there others around you? Just share whatever you're getting now, as your spirit leaves your body from that life...

KB: I feel peace. Also I'm concerned about the children who are still small. What's going to happen to them. Maybe that's the sadness... maybe this is the sadness I felt before, about this sickness... Yes, this is really powerful, the sadness of what's going to happen to them, and that I'm abandoning them.

MK: Can you tell what you died from?

KB: Mmmm... malaria, or...?

MK: Okay. Now your spirit has left your body. Is there anybody you would like to go to, to comfort them?

KB: Mmmm... I just don't know what's going to happen to them.

MK: Would you like to go and check out what happens to them?

KB: No.

MK: Okay. Very good. Is there anything else for you to know from this past life?

KB: No.

MK: Okay. My sense is that you will get more information about this, either in the dreamtime or just in flashes or whenever it's safe and if it's important for you to know, you will get more information. Now... I want you to just go a little deeper and as you regress, I want you to just trust in your ability to just look at the pictures and feel the feelings... (deepening techniques with suggestions that the personal guide may come to help and comfort... suggesting she will go deeper than she has ever been...) Do you feel it's important to review your current life right now? (I always give the client the suggestion that they will recall more—either in the waking state, in the dreamtime, or anytime when it is safe. This helps them recall the vast amount of information they are receiving that is not able to be understood at the time of the session.)

KB: It's like they don't feel like talking...

MK: Okay...where are you?

KB: I'm floating...

MK: (Deepening, with suggestion to float to Mother's womb.) What are you aware of?

KB: It's dark.

MK: What else?

KB: I didn't want to go outside, into the world... I want to go back, actually...

MK: Do you hear your mother's thoughts at all? Can you connect with them?

KB: My mother is kind of sad, because she was the daughter before... just before she was pregnant. And I just want to go back—I don't know what I'm doing here. (crying)... I got side tracked.

MK: Well, we'll find that out soon...

KB: It's kind of nice in this womb but it was much nicer before.

MK: Yeah... So let's just... go back into that floating place where you were before... just move... you can see how easy it is to just move to wherever you want or need to be... in order to get whatever information you need to get. And I'd like you to just move into space, where you left that body from your most recent past life. You are in spirit, you left the young children behind, and just share what you're getting... what are you aware of as you are in space, in this area...

KB: Looks a little bit like a night sky with dots of light.

MK: Does it feel like you're moving away from Earth or are you already far from Earth?

KB: I'm far away from it already...

MK: Okay. Can you see or sense it at all anymore?

KB: Uh huh.

MK: Okay. Are you moving slowly or are you moving faster now?

KB: I'm moving very slowly, floating, almost like I'm one of those lights... in the vast space of lights. Looks like a night sky, that's how I could compare it.

MK: Okay. So you are now fully in a soul state... (LBL script for final deepening that guides the client into the super conscious.)

KB: I see someone who looks like an angel. It's very big, with beautiful wings. And I also feel pressure in my third eye—is this... a normal sensation?

MK: Okay. Often times that can happen, it's very common. I can't explain it but just be aware of it. It feels okay, right?

KB: Uh huh.

MK: Okay. So just describe what's happening.

KB: I'm standing in front of a, like a line of beings who look... they're male and they look like they are OLD and they have long beards and gray hair, but they are all like light. It's strange. I know that they have gray hair, but... at the same time they are just light. I don't know, they are kind of looking at me in a strange way. They don't say anything, it's just... like acknowledging that I'm there.

MK: Okay. How many?

KB: How many? Oh... seven.

MK: Does one stand out from the other or are they pretty much the same?

KB: They are similar... acknowledging and also welcoming, or...

MK: Okay. Does any one of them come out to greet you particularly, or are they all kind of pretty much the same?

KB: They're all kind of... the same.

MK: Are any of them talking to you telepathically, because your third eye opened up? (long pause)

KB: I have a feeling that it is something that is beyond words... I ... that they are sharing with me, but it's not words. It just feels good.

MK: Okay. Are you to stay there for awhile and just receive that? (long pause)

KB: It's a very new space for me. There's no words... saying, it seems like some kind of a transmission, but with no words.

MK: Okay. So you should just stay there for a little bit, right?

KB: It feels like I could just stay there forever, actually!

MK: Well, you won't, but that's okay, just enjoy it. (long pause)

KB: Hmmmm, now I feel like... again, there is a female... they are standing... on the right side of me... and she is like this very kind...

MK: Okay. What's her name?

KB: I don't know… Marie… Mary?

MK: Is she your personal guide or is she one of your guides?

KB: I don't know. I just feel a powerful connection. It's feeling, she's like a protector… I don't know… And she tells me that she's with me now. She is quite bigger then, too… in posture, in size.

MK: Is she to take you somewhere or is she… see what she is for you…

KB: She took me somewhere, to a place that looks like… this is weird… looks like a cinema? But it's also… I believe it's kind of like, it's not really tangible and physical, just more like… I can see it clearly but it's more like energy or lights… wide world of energy and light.

MK: Okay. Is there something that is going to go on at the cinema? Is that what this is all about?

KB: Hmmmm… it could be, I could see something on the screen but I don't need that.

MK: Okay. Where is it you are to be going next, then?

KB: She is telling me that I don't need more information because it will create confusion? And that I know everything that I need to know at this time. She also said I can go to that place anytime I want to.

MK: Okay. How?

KB: By meditating, by just asking her to help.

MK: You mean—does she mean going to the cinema or going to this place, this state that you are in?

KB: Going to this state, going to this cinema, going to this world.

MK: Okay. Good. May I then still just ask her some of those questions that you had, is that okay?

KB: Uh huh.

MK: Okay, because sometimes, even though you get those answers and you know everything, sometimes to confirm things, when you are in this state, because you can feel it at a higher level. So some of the questions we have—What is your destiny? How can you contribute? What did you come here to do?

KB: To connect and to connect people and places, and to see beauty in everything and everyone, and to help them see that in themselves. To draw this beauty out from people and places, so that they can shine.

MK: Is part of that then, through the work you are already doing, I would assume, like the event planning and the... and just what you're doing already—so you are doing that already, aren't you?

KB: Yes.

MK: Is there a specific healing method that is for you to learn or to do?

KB: I have a feeling that it's talking, just talking with others, letting them talk from their heart, in a circle.

MK: Is there anything else? Really get into the feeling of it.

KB: I'm really touched by this place and the feeling... I'm getting the message that just being and trusting... and that by being and trusting and loving, that evokes a trust and love in the world around.

MK: Yeah. Did Robert have to die in order to fulfill a contract? Was there a contract there?

KB: I feel that I had both, or had two routes, but his death helped me to move me to what I'm supposed to do here... otherwise I wouldn't fulfill my destiny, if he stayed.

MK: Or at least if he were here. Yeah, okay. Wow. Wow. Do you get a sense of him around you right now?

KB: Yes, he is standing next to me.

MK: Okay. Does he have any message for you? I'll ask more questions, but does he have any message for you?

KB: Just says that all is well, and that he is in the right place. And he is thanking me for visiting that place!

MK: Okay. Well, I think you'll be visiting it more as the days go by. What about your connection to Hawaii—what is that? Is that some past life or part of your destiny or what?

KB: (Long pause) I get a feeling that it is part of my destiny and I just need to go there, but it's not from past lives, I don't feel.

MK: Okay, very good—that's what the draw is then. What about Keya? Is he a teacher, or who is he in your life?

KB: He is a teacher, but I am ready to do it now, by myself. And

I'm getting a feeling I should do some ceremony, or… I don't know if cutting cords is it, or just stepping into my own space. And it can be very simple and short, this ceremony.

MK: Okay. Kind of a cutting cords but not really—a little different from that? Just cutting the teacher cords and becoming the teacher?

KB: Uh huh.

MK: Yeah. And then what about Kuba? Who is Kuba in your current life?

KB: They don't… they won't tell me. (laughs)

MK: Okay. Is there anything for you to know about Katie or Patricia—your girlfriends—or do you kind of know that already?

KB: I'm getting with Patricia, re-examine her messages after you receive them, like think them over, and select what's hers and what's really from me and this is like Robert speaking, and from the Spirit. That she is putting some of her fears, and… or thoughts and beliefs around that.

MK: As many of us do… very good. With your permission, before I bring you back, I'd like to ask… I think I talked briefly with you about this, I have a friend and he's writing a book on grief… and when people die, and how to move through grief, and I'm wondering if there is anything that Robert or your guide or you, in this realm, could tell me that could help that person, or anyone that is going through grief. Maybe Robert can share from the perspective of how you moved through yours, or anything relating to grief and how that can help.

KB: We can talk about that because I wrote an article about it. Robert says to be open to the messages, because nobody really dies, and if you call them, they will be there. There is nothing wrong with death, nothing bad, it's just part of creation. It's just transition, and accepting someone else's path, it is very important, acknowledging that this is someone's path, and to allow them to walk that path. While they allow us to walk ours. And they don't take us with themselves to the other side… and we're still together, all together, right here and right now. Nothing disappears. Nothing really dies.

MK: Wow. Is it always part of a contract or do sometimes people go off contract when they die, either accidentally or in any manner?
KB: There are no accidents. But there can be, sometimes, several contracts, several different ways.
MK: Wow, okay. Several possibilities, you mean?
KB: Yes, and all of them are… are fine.
MK: Okay. For instance, you and Robert could have contracted to be together, but another alternative, another path, was that he leave and you stay?
KB: Yes.
MK: And then your destiny changes a little bit, too?
KB: Yes, it's like accelerating a little bit, because of that. And all those parts are perfect, they are all for the highest good. There are no wrong choices, trust me! And it's not about external events, it's all about our reactions. It's all about our heart, what we do with it. So basically, it doesn't really matter.
MK: Yeah. Is there anything else for Kasia to either know or experience before she comes back? Otherwise, I will allow you to have a little silent time, just a little time before I bring you back, but is there anything else?
KB: Yes, to get into that state of meditation… and do that on a regular basis, to reconnect with my guides and angels… and also he said that I don't need to hear anything or see anything or understand, but it's all happening anyway, when I ask, they answer and this answer is with me, even if I don't know on a conscious, mental level.
MK: Okay. So you know, but you don't know?
KB: Yes, but it will be manifested. And I don't have to comprehend it really, with my mind.
MK: Okay. It will be manifested if it's for your highest good or will it be manifested if you desire it?
KB: If it's for my highest good and the good of everyone, if I request that. And that they will not do anything without that request. And that they are there and ready to help, and it's true for everyone, they are there ready to help, you just need to ask. And just let it happen, without expectations and controlling the effect.

MK: I'm going to be silent for awhile. You can still share anything if you wish it to be on tape, but I'm going to be silent for a few minutes, and just allow yourself to experience, okay? You can share if you wish, but you can also share it after this experience... and I'll bring you back in a little bit... just enjoy... (long, 4-minute pause)... Would you like a little more time?

KB: No...

MK: Okay, before I bring you back... as I suggest, very strongly, that anytime you meditate, or anytime it's safe, you will be able to get into this trance state so you can receive all the guidance, all the affirmations, all the love you need, easily and effortlessly... (closing script from LBL).

End of LBL

Summary

There is much wisdom in Kasia's experience, which is why I chose to include it in this book. Many of the things she was told, she and most of us already know. But it was validated once again through Robert's words and her LBL experience, which assisted her in moving forward with the rest of her life. She is a prime example of Acceptance of What Is.

Some of the primary messages were:

1. We already know everything, we just don't always know it consciously, until we are ready.
2. Suicide has many purposes, and this was another example of where it was a contract between the two souls.
3. Nobody dies, and if we need someone, just call on them.
4. There are no accidents.
5. We do not make mistakes. (In my first book, *Becoming Multisensory*, I stated "We don't make mistakes: we have different outcomes based on the choices we make.")
6. Not everything is revealed to us, and this is either per our contract or based on our need to know.

Birth, Death and the Afterlife

Finally, I am including a letter Kasia sent to me in response to my request that she summarize her after-experience. Here is her email, in its entirety:

"Madonna:

Amazing things are happening, miracles are happening. Everything has accelerated, the pieces of the puzzle are falling into place, and the prophecies of all the indigenous tribes from around the world are connecting into SOMETHING that is difficult to comprehend with a human mind...

After beautiful events with the Grandmothers of the Turtle Island and Grandfather Keya in Europe, events that touched around 1,000 people, where so many hearts have opened and we felt divine energy on the Earth, we learned that one of our brothers and friends Kuba Dzienkiewicz, who danced hula at the Gathering has crossed to the other side in a car accident. So many people remember Kuba with a great smile, burn candles for him and help him to cross over. Our prayers create a bridge that allows him to walk with a great smile on his face...

Many people wrote that they feel that Kuba's funeral is going to be a shift, something important and that Kuba's crossing has a deeper meaning that we will comprehend with time. It is so true!!!

I met Kuba when I wrote an article about Hawaii and he told me that he wants to come to the Grandmothers' Gathering. After he crossed over I felt that he wants me to fulfill some of his dreams... Kuba loved Hawaii so at first I dedicated him a prayer and a song, *Somewhere over the Rainbow*, by Iza Kamakawiwo'ole, (http://www.youtube.com/watch?v=w DKWlrA24k&ob=av3n). I did not watch this video, the song was important to me but yesterday Keya showed me the video and I was shocked to see that it is about Iz's funeral in Hawaii, beautiful, colorful and light...

Grandmother Susan wrote that in Hawaiian language

there is no word for good bye, only *aloha* (*alo*—to share, *ha* – breath), so during funerals people are thankful that they could share their breath with that person and are grateful that now they can be with her or him in a new way...

I felt that Kuba's funeral is supposed to be in Hawaiian style, light and colorful and then Kuba's brother wrote that he wants to include some of Hawaiian elements in it and he asks me for help. I imagine his funeral full of flowers, music, and hula dance. Then Grandmother Susan sent me an email asking if I could come with a Polish group to Hawaii in September as a translator. Kuba wanted to go to Hawaii this year so I felt that he wants some of his ashes to be spread there. I wrote to Kuba's brother about all of this and it turned out that his family wants the same: FLOWERS, MUSIC, DANCE and that they want to take some of his ashes to Hawaii.

Two days ago we had a talking circle with Grandfather Keya and a Pipe Ceremony done by Maria Lewanska. It was a ceremony for Kuba. There were 12 men and 12 women there. Kuba was born on 04.08, and crossed over on 08.04. More 12s...

Keya rarely shared his experiences and visions from the Spirit. This time he shared them. When a ceremony started he saw a candle's flame dividing into two. Each of the flames turned into a rainbow ray (somewhere over the rainbow...) that shoot up. One of them was Robert Sieklucki (my beloved man who crossed over in November and is with me all the time. I feel that thanks to him, Grandmothers could come to Europe), the other one was Kuba. Suddenly there were many rainbow rays; each of them was one of our ancestors. The room was filled with ancestors as though Kuba and Robert opened the gates. The veil between the worlds has lifted. We became one... The rays were touching us during a prayer. Each person holding Cannupa was filled with light. We were all filled with the light of the ancestors... The boundaries between us and the ancestors are thinning, everything is becoming one, the past and the future, the world of spirit and the world of matter, the Heaven and the Earth...

I feel that Kuba's crossing has a global meaning. His greatest dream was to become a healer. It is happening already. Kuba is acting. He is changing the way the funerals are performed in Poland and the way we perceived death. For such a long time death in Poland was a burden, full of grief and sadness. Everything was so final. Our attachment to matter did not allow us to see beyond, our restricted perception did not allow spirits to contact us. So many spirits got stuck between the dimensions. We did not let them go. It is time to change that. Death can be a joyful experience. We met that person and now his soul is free. It is time to free the spirits so that they can ascend higher and higher and be on the Earth at the same time, helping us and supporting. They want to help us, we just need to ask. We are all one. There are no boundaries.

During the Cannupa ceremony many people saw Kuba and Robert, even those who have never met them in the body. More and more people see the spirit world. It is TIME to enter the space of the heart. Nobody is alone here. We all carry a divine spark, powerful and of unlimited possibilities. Let's experience the divinity through our unique being. Each of us is important and only together we create wholeness, the tapestry of existence. Let's remember HOW BEAUTIFUL WE ARE!!!

Kuba's funeral with flowers, music and dance will take place on Military Cemetery on Thursday (16 of August) in Warsaw.

It is interesting as Grandmothers Gathering in Hawaii took place in a military camp. The energies of the places are channeling as well.

Let us gather to show Kuba's way to light and change the way we perceive funerals, come in colorful dresses, with respect, lightness and love in our hearts to dance a Dance for Kuba, for Life which does not cease to exist, only changes form... We can change the world thanks to the filled with love and light ceremony for Kuba...

We are the ones we have been waiting for. Let's not wait any more. -- With love, Kasia"

Chapter 7
The Power of Words • Seeking Deeper Truths — Inner Reflection • Deception and Perception

The Power of Words

When we are on what I call a "conscious spiritual path," our choices change, at least somewhat. For me, that means there are some things that simply are no longer an option, like intentionally deceiving myself or others, or feeding my addictions. Most every choice I make, or thing I do, is intended to move me toward a deeper conscious connection with my Creator. Most every word I say brings me to a deeper remembrance of who I really am, and every movement is intended to be positive, peaceful, and in balance with my actions, choices, and spoken words. I strive to be a reflection of my Creator, and a role model in every way, without ego, without attachment, and without judgment of myself or others.

Over the years this journey has been one of extreme highs and lows as I slowly but surely move into a more balanced, less egoic, and nonjudgmental part of the mass consciousness. I love the quote where the initiate asks the sage, "Master, am I done with my life purpose yet?" and the sage answers, "If you are still breathing, you are not done." If we are still on this Earth and breathing, there is a reason!

How do we live our best life? How do we see the adventure or opportunity in every moment? One way for me is to intentionally choose positive language and to have an awareness of how my and other people's words affect me. What words, thoughts or beliefs did you accept when you were young that encouraged or even embedded these beliefs into your psyche?

Are they still as true for you today as they used to be? Do they still work for you? And why do we so often feel less than, *or* more than? Why do we accept thoughts and beliefs that are not beneficial to who we are?

Having been raised Catholic, there was one mantra I said over 250 times a year, from my First Communion until after grade school: "I am not worthy." Even at an early age, I didn't really like saying it, nor did I realize at the time what an impact those words would have on the rest of my life. Now my entire being is now focused on knowing from my deepest core that I *AM* in fact worthy. Pshaw to that unworthy crap! I *AM* worthy, simply because I *AM*! Of course, this doesn't mean I am *more* worthy than anyone else, and it doesn't mean anyone else is more or less worthy than I am. It simply means that I am loved by my creator, no matter what. It means *we* are loved by our creator, no matter what! We are all in this together, and we are all loved equally, no matter what.

Thoughts are things. Our thoughts, words, and beliefs, are something we *can* be accountable for. By observing our thoughts, we are better able to respond to any situation that presents itself. For example, if I catch myself in a negative thought such as, "That person really gets me angry, and I wish he'd just get out and leave me alone," by observing the negative thoughts, I am able to respond appropriately to it and change it to a positive thought. My negative inner dialogue could immediately be switched to a more positive thought such as, "Isn't it interesting… I'm allowing that person to really bother me… so, in order to respect his emotions and my feelings, I'm going to just walk away and let him be."

By observing our words we can control our speech as well as the words that come into our ears. We can choose our words wisely, and if others' words affect us negatively, we can choose not to allow them to affect adversely. One way to do this is to say "cancel/clear" to ourselves, or walk away from the situation (if possible), or turn off the offensive TV or radio program. It's not as hard as you may think!

And just how do we "accept what is?" How do we begin accepting ourselves as we are, in every moment? How do we get from "there" to "here"? Training, practice, and baby steps to the elevator. We move toward our intention in as positive a way as possible, and eventually we enjoy every experience that presents itself. Experiences *are* opportunities, and opportunities are how we evolve! There are a lot of suggestions on how to accept what is in this book and I'm certain you can figure out what will work for *you*.

What is the difference between a painful experience and an opportunity? Any experience is neutral, so the difference is how you respond to it. I've mentioned this before, but it bears repeating. The pain or challenge in any experience is what we give to it. Likewise, the opportunity in any experience is what we can glean from it. A senior prom is neutral, what we bring to it is how we will experience it. The prom can be exhilarating, exasperating, emotionally stressful, utterly relaxing and enjoyable, or a plethora of other experiences. Whether we experience an event as a challenge or an opportunity is up to us. The event, in and of itself, is neutral. All experiences are neutral. Which way do you wish to experience life—as a painful experience or an opportunity?

For example, you have three possible career opportunities in front of you. You could see them as 1) overwhelming, (How in the world do I choose one?), or 2) exciting, (What a gift that I have three to choose from!) or 3) not enough, (Why don't I have any more choices? I really wanted…)

The three possible career opportunities are all neutral, until you put your emotions into them. It's up to you to decide where you choose to put your energy, your thoughts. Do you focus your energy toward the positive or the negative of any experience? Energy flows where attention goes. Use your energy wisely and you will be rewarded in so many ways!

And what happens if we feel we have failed or we feel like giving up?

When we attend a workshop, lecture, class, party, or other gathering of any type, or when we read a book (like this one!), or watch a TV show or movie, each of us brings in our own way of experiencing it. If six people view the same movie, odds are each one liked it for a different reason, and one may not have enjoyed it very much at all. Our perceptions, ideas, beliefs and baggage are ours and ours alone. We bring this not only from our current Earth life, but from all our past and future incarnations. Each of us perceives and sees, unique to our own experiences, and each of us makes choices based upon these experiences and perceptions. In remembering the prom situation, which one were you? Perhaps you didn't even go to one, so you have only others' perceptions on what a prom might or might not be like. When I ask a group to imagine the color blue, there will be as many shades of blue imagined as there are people in the group. One may imagine the morning sky blue, another the night sky blue, and still another could envision the aqua blue of the ocean! When I say "imagine peace," or ask questions relating to an event that was experienced by many, the same thing happens. When I am writing these words and you are reading them, each of you perceives what I am saying and digests it differently. I remember the first time I read *Seat of the Soul* by Gary Zukov, or *A New Earth* by Eckhart Tolle—and then read them again at a later date. I doubt the words changed, but how I perceived them certainly was different. Words we use all the time, like Love, Gratitude, Surrender, Trust, Allow, Peace, Fear, Anger, Judgment, God, Spirit, Soul, Energy—what do they mean to YOU?

This is why, when giving instructions to someone (especially your children!), it's beneficial to have them repeat back to you whatever they heard you say. Or when having a serious conversation with your spouse, ask them what they are hearing you say. This can save hours of frustration and non-peace!

May I suggest you try the following the next time you are with some friends, family, or in a group setting: Write down three words, like God, Peace, and Pink, and put three lines below each word. Then have your group write down their first thoughts relating to each word. Take about ten minutes to do this, and then compare notes to see how different the outcomes are!

What happens if we feel we have failed, or if we feel like giving up? We see now that failure is just a word, a neutral word at that. What you attach to it, what it means to you will be very different from another's perceptions. And how you perceive it can change as well. Walking a mile may feel like failure to you, but to someone with severe arthritis it is a supreme success!

No wonder relationships can be confusing! No wonder we can feel misunderstood, not heard. No wonder it is important to be impeccable with our word as talked about in *The Four Agreements* by Don Miguel Ruiz. No wonder? No—WONDER at this, for it is absolutely amazing. We are absolutely amazing in all our uniqueness!

Birth, Death and the Afterlife

Seeking Deeper Truths – Inner Reflection

How do we find our truths? How do we know or create our belief system?

It is within us. All we need to "do" is listen. Be. Listen more. Be. And listen again, with our inner ears. Go deep within to find yourself. You already know. Our process, or the adventure we have taken during our Earth life, is solely to remember! It is all there, within us. The truth of who we really are is often times very well hidden, but it *is* there, nonetheless.

Zip the lip. Quiet your mind. Close your mouth and open up to your inner guidance, your High Self. It is egoless, it is light and free, and it is YOU. Somewhere in there is the YOU of your dreams, the YOU of your remembering! Find a way, YOUR way, to move through this life-adventure. When something is said to you during a discussion and you are uncertain about it, go within to see if it is true for YOU. As you read a book, check with your intuition on what feels suitable to YOU and your life-adventure. This book and others that will come to you relate valuable wisdom. Read. Remember your light, then dwell upon and be the love you are. The more we are able to remember our True, Divine Selves and live within that deeper, inner wisdom, the more peaceful we are, and the more we remember the one Universal truth:

We are love.

And that's the truth!

Some of my greatest inspirations have come during or after what seemed an intolerable, disastrous, or extremely painful event or experience. This pain forced me to go inside to listen and look at it from a broader perspective. Our ego is continually focused on challenging us. It is a large part of our humanity, and it can block us from seeing the big picture in order to get its way. An intolerable, disastrous, or extremely painful experience can trigger a variety of emotions that lead to a fast road to discovery, or if we so choose, it can lead us further down a rabbit hole. I've gone both directions, and to many levels in between. The only way "out," from my experience, is to embrace wherever process I choose, as much as I am able.

While writing I am reminded that the more I write, the more I share, the less I am certain about anything—because nothing is static. Everything changes. Our perceptions, our truths, our beliefs, all change.

Oftentimes when I am preparing for a talk in front of an audience or workshop, I suddenly realize I have *nothing* to say, *nothing* to teach, only things to share. All I can "do" is stay in the immediate moment and *be present* in it, speaking from my heart. There is nothing else. I have nothing to prepare for, nothing to practice; only the "moment of truth" that is automatically in every moment.

Does this mean I have not "prepared" for the talk or workshop? Not at all. I LIVE the talk. I LIVE the workshop. It comes from within my experiences; my entire life has prepared me for the present moment, the present talk, and the present workshop.

There have been times when my original plan went down the tubes during the workshop, because the needs of those attending would not have been met had I stayed in line with it. When I shift gears and decide to start clean, with an open agenda, listening to that little voice within or the usually louder ones all around, at the end of the day each person's intentions have been met and there is an overwhelming sense of peace and connectedness within each participant as well as the group.

In the same manner, when we plan our day, we often make lists, or at least have a mental image of what we want to do. Detailed planning can work for or against us. Why not try, one hour at a time, listening to the wise one within? If you insist on having a list, then listen as you perform your duties, for anything you may have missed. It can make life the adventure it is intended to be!

And what if our day is planned for us? What if we have jobs to do, duties to perform, children to raise, places to go? We can still choose to go within throughout our day. We always have choices and options. We may not always be *aware* of them, but they are there. Sometimes a friend or co-worker, child or spouse, will point us to that choice. Sometimes nature will give us signs that guide our choices or direct us toward a decision, and sometimes we just do *not* feel we get what we need, but we *do*. Every moment is perfect, when we are in the present moment. Inner reflection is an amazing way for us to be present in each moment.

Deception and Perception

There is no "one way" Home. There is no one way to live or believe that works for everyone. I repeat, as Dad used to repeat to me, "If everybody were the same it would be a pretty boring world."

How do we face our demons? What are our demons? They are whatever keeps us from love. If looking in a mirror causes me to judge and berate myself, or even to feel sadness, in that moment it is my demon. In another moment when I am looking in the mirror and feeling gratitude or having positive thoughts, I am in a place of acceptance. For someone else, the car may be his demon because it is the place where all his aggression is released and is screamed at other drivers. To yet another person, cooking a meal is a demon because it is being done while feeling used or manipulated: ("Why do I always have to cook for them and they don't even appreciate it?") In another person's experience they love to cook and share their food with loved ones. One person's demon can be another person's passion! I certainly don't always love to cook, and driving can be a chore sometimes, but the more I focus on being in a positive, loving place while doing these things, the better I feel.

When we are in our Dharma, in the place of perfect balance, living in the present moment, everything is perfect. When we are in that place, everything flows, everything is in order. We know in our deepest core that everything is right in our world.

Yes, sometimes a demon may continue to present itself. Old patterns of questioning and doubt enter, and the negative, unworthy, stinking thinking sneaks in. What do we do?

We keep on keeping on. Every time this process unfolds, it gets easier to accept that we have all the answers within—we can choose to move back into the feelings of peace, and follow that deep, inner guidance. The guidance that is always there and never lets us down.

The Spirit-Directives for this chapter are:

Believe

You are being called to trust and believe in someone or something in your life. This may be something you have not allowed yourself to believe previously, or something or someone you have not understood. Believing sometimes calls for releasing judgment, shame, blame, or guilt in order to allow a new perception into your life. Belief sets a firm foundation, yet in this current energy, beliefs are changing, being repeatedly challenged, and new beliefs are replacing the old ones. This is a time of change and transformation for the Earth and all her beings—believe this is so, and allow the process that waits to unfold. Allow your beliefs to change and transform you into a life that is free from anything you no longer need. Write down three beliefs you currently are questioning, meditate and/or discuss them with others until you once again have a firm understanding of what they mean to you.

Adventure

How do you see adventure? What does the word adventure mean to you? Is there fear involved in it or does the thought of it excite you? Meditate on what you have done in your life—the adventures you have experienced, and how you felt before, during, and after them. Meditate on the figure that is climbing. Life is a climb, a journey, a road, an adventure, that each of us experiences. The attitude we have relating to life in general is how much of an adventure we will experience.

Flow with the Go

Realize that everything is going appropriately and as it should be. This card indicates that you are on a roll, and that everything is happening as planned. Notice the little leaf gently moving down the river. You are truly flowing with the go instead of padding up river (without a paddle)! Look at nature and see how it just IS—it doesn't have to DO anything, it simply goes with the flow. See the peacefulness of nature and how everything simply lines up.

Story

Years ago I worked with a client who was on her way back to Israel. She requested an LBL session to have many questions answered. She wanted to meet her guides, and find out what her next step was. She was in her early 30s and told me in the intake interview she felt she was on the right track but she wanted more validation for some of the decisions she recently had made.

Since she meditated regularly, it was easy for her to get into a deep trance state, where she heard and saw her guides. She gathered what I felt was a vast amount of information and had all the questions she brought to the session answered. From my perspective, it was a very successful session, yet when she returned to the Beta state, she was somewhat disappointed. She said, "I know all of this already." Her guides had also told her during the session that she already knew all of this, yet she wanted me to continue asking the questions she had prepared. As the guides answered her questions one by one, either she or they would state, "You know this already, but…" and a response to her query would follow.

Our inner self *does* have all the answers. It is up to us to quiet our mind in order to tap into that deeper knowing. During the course of an average day, our ego can interfere with this inner reflection and cause us to stress, worry, over-process or second guess that wisdom.

After processing her experience awhile longer, she came to realize she truly did have all the answers within her and was grateful for the validation received. She realized how intuitive she was, and said she would now trust her choices and her intuition more. What she did during that session was raise her vibration (see Chapter 11), listen, and ignore the ego (or at least move it to the side during the session), in order to remember her true, Divine Self, the self that is connected to everything, the self that knows all. She walked out of my office a changed person.

Everything we need is within us. It is only the veil of our ego that can cause us to forget. When we choose to stay on a conscious spiritual path, that veil thins, and the ego is fed less as our spirit maintains the remembering for longer and longer periods.

Over the years I have seen hundreds and hundreds of clients who have had this awakening. Once we tap into the unlimited power that is our Divine Self, everything changes. Sometimes these are baby steps, sometimes great leaps, but always there is change. Always there is movement towards *remembering*.

Chapter 8
Forgiveness and Happiness • Worthiness • Manifesting and Empowerment

Have you ever been *forced* to forgive someone? How do you feel right now, as you are thinking about that incident? When you said, "I'm sorry," how did you feel inside? Do you think that incident was true forgiveness, or was it coercion?

If you have had an incident where you were forced to forgive—and most of us have—it may have worked, but that's not the level of forgiveness I'm talking about in this chapter. According to the American Heritage Dictionary, to forgive is "To cease to feel offense against; to pardon. To excuse for a fault or offense. To stop feeling anger toward or resentment against." To me, forgiveness means "the act of forward-giving," similar to the act of paying it forward. It allows us the freedom to move forward because we are no longer focused on sending negative thoughts or anger to an incident or person, *including ourselves.* Forgiveness is giving up the hope that the past could have been different.

In most cases, the hardest person to forgive is ourself. If I find that I'm angry at myself for *any* reason, I use the phrase "in this moment," which tells my conscious and subconscious that my intention is to forgive fully, yet recognizing I may not be ready to forgive *fully* "in this moment." It gives me some leeway, takes away some of the pressure, and allows me to process the emotion at my own pace, without creating even more unforgiveness.

Often I practice the art of observation by saying or thinking the words, "Isn't it interesting that"... (fill in the blank.) These simple words allow every part of my being to *observe* the situation, and release me from the shackles of judgment, which moves me toward the freedom to surrender any situation.

For example, I just made a mistake in balancing my checkbook and the negative thought comes in, "How stupid is that? I'm a full charge bookkeeper who cannot balance her checkbook? What's happening to me, anyway? Why does this always happen to me?"

The sooner we recognize the negative effect this has on us (and therefore on everyone and everything), the sooner we can neutralize its energy. Once we recognize the unbecoming thought, we can immediately change it to, "In this moment I am being really hard on myself... and this too, shall pass." The next thought is more conscious and goes something like, "Isn't it interesting how I allowed a little mistake like this to cause me such angst." With these new thoughts, we can easily let go of any lingering unforgiveness or surrender any situation—and Heaven forbid—we may even be able to *laugh* at the incident! How freeing is that?

Forgiveness doesn't condone a negative behavior or act, but it *does* allow us to *let go* of whatever negative emotion the act or behavior created within us. And this allows us to move forward as we neutralize the negative energy from the behavior or act. It still happened, but it ceases to affect us (or others) negatively, and we can see it for whatever lesson it was there to teach. We can then move into a place of self-empowerment that is amazingly freeing!

Forgiveness, Observation, & Non-judgment = Freedom, Happiness, Worthiness & Inner Peace

By practicing the act of forgiveness of self and others, then observing the situation from a higher perspective, we move from a negative, non-productive place to a state of non-judgment, then to a feeling of freedom. From there we are free to express happiness, which allows us to feel worthy, and we move into a place of inner peace. When we are in this state, many gifts will come our way; we only need to be open to receiving them. Marianne Williamson's book, *A Return to Love: Reflections on the Principals of a Course in Miracles*, contains one of my very favorite quotes that begins: "Our deepest fear is that we are powerful beyond measure. It is our light, not our darkness that most frightens us." Once we realize *our* magnificence and the magnificence of *every thing*, we easily come into our personal empowerment and are able to manifest whatever it is we desire, because our desire is aligned with the greater good of all. It is a sweet, delicious place to be. It is a place of empowerment vs. power, a place of happiness vs. sadness, a place of worthiness vs. worthlessness, and love vs. fear. It is a place of true inner peace!

The Spirit-Directives for this chapter are:

Happiness

Giving your attention to the picture on this card for a moment, notice the soaring birds. They are reaching beyond the rainbow, over the rainbow. The rainbow is higher than the mountains, and the border on the original card radiates abundant green. The numerology for this card, "9", signifies endings, with the birds representing soaring to new heights, into the great unknown. With endings come new beginnings, freshness in your life, more happiness than you can imagine. So get ready because there is even more of that happy energy, that enlightened or light energy, coming into your life. Perhaps the birds are bluebirds of happiness! My goodness, reach for the *sky* with your happiness! Let it be new and fresh and let it bring you into

Birth, Death and the Afterlife

this next phase of wherever you are going. You are worth it! This card says that happiness is you!

Worthiness

By reading this card, you are being asked to see yourself as worthy, no matter what, at all times, in every experience. Focus on the pot of gold in the picture—this is YOU. You are worthy! You are golden! You are the golden child of the Universe—act as if this is so, because it IS so! Accept this into every cell of your being. This card is filled with abundance and beauty, showing you your worth. The love and compassion, the golden magnificence of who you are, is being revealed to you, beginning today, and it will continue to be revealed for the next 30 days until you GET IT. And by getting it, you are inspired to be all you are.

Laughter

For goodness sakes, LAUGH MORE! Lighten up! Take a break during this day to do something you have wanted to do—even if it's for 10 minutes. DO this. Laugh out loud! Focus on the picture—look at the laughing Buddha. Notice the musical notes, the strong, flowing energy. Bring music and dance and laughter and giggles into your life more – especially today. Focus on being more in tune with the laughing fairies, the wind, and the colors in nature. This will bring you to another level of consciousness you may never have considered. Laughter brings more laughter. It inspires you and others. It makes you feel good, so DO IT. Laugh more and often.

Birth, Death and the Afterlife

Cooperation

You are being called to help someone or yourself in some way. While focusing on the picture, ask yourself a few questions: Where have I been helpful to someone lately? Have I been of service in some way? How can I help my fellow man, my son, my daughter, my partner, myself? Then listen to what your intuition is saying on how you can be of service in some way. It may be only for one day for now, helping a young child, someone you know or don't know, or it may be a commitment to work at a food bank. You can decide what is best and most appropriate for you in order to fulfill the message this card gives you.

Story

Many years ago, I worked with a client who was probably the most self-deprecating person I have ever met. She felt she was ugly, rude to people and did not deserve anything in this life. She was quite the enigma to me because, despite this, she had amazing abundance in that she had a family, friends, and a spouse who loved her dearly, and a career that kept their family in a very comfortable setting. Yet, during the intake interview, she constantly put herself down. She explained that she did not know where this came from. Her spouse had asked her to come see me and try to get some help with this because nobody could understand the reason behind her self-loathing. They could not figure out why she had these disrespectful, negative thoughts about herself because there was no family history of abuse, there was no current life incident she could remember that may have caused her to feel so unlovable; no neglect, either verbal, physical, or mental. She felt she never did well at any job she performed, even though she had a successful job in the career of her choice. This client was *way* beyond not feeling worthy, she was completely *off the chart* in her lack of self-acceptance. She felt she was about as worthless as anyone I have ever met.

During the session she went into several lives. What was almost amusing to me was the fact that *even while she was in the past life experiences*, she held onto that ego part of herself that didn't feel worthy of knowing why she was so self-deprecating! That's how deep these feelings and thoughts were embedded.

First she revisited several past lives where she had the same pattern of self-loathing and lack of positive self-image. She discovered she had been with the same group of people/souls throughout these lives—a group that had no positive self image whatsoever. They were everything from a band of thieves to a group of self-made outcasts. As she moved through these lives, it appeared she was making *some* progress but not as much as the rest of her soul group. Then, after revisiting her most recent past life, she visited the interlife and processed all of these lives. She began with expressing her dissatisfaction with her evolutionary process, and her Guides suggested that in her current life she may want to finally move toward feeling worthy. She was astounded that none of her Guides reprimanded or judged her in any way! The discussion with her Guides and other Spirit Helpers assisted her in finding different ways in her current life to move past this unforgiveness and move into true happiness and worthiness for herself and for others. Next she was shown several different lifetimes where she had made a positive difference in other peoples' lives, and all of this helped her realize she *was* worthy! Her guides also helped her formulate a plan on how to begin this process, and gave her some steps she could take toward the fulfillment of her purpose. It amazed me that these steps were very similar to the I

AM WOWED™ Program outlined in Chapter 15 of this book! (The client knew nothing about this program at the time.) They told her they were very pleased that she had had this session, because it was helping her remember her Divine Self, which helped facilitate her process of being at peace with herself and her life.

She came back from her regression experience with a dazed, glassy look in her eyes. Even though she was perplexed with all the information she had received, the understanding that she was first and foremost a spiritual being was already setting in. She knew now that she had purpose, and that purpose was to love herself! She also knew the first step in this process, for her, was forgiveness of herself. It was an amazing session!

The client immediately committed herself to the I AM WOWED™ Program, and together with the wisdom gained from the regression session, was able to move into a state of happiness and inner peace with remarkable ease. Many of the suggestions given to her she already knew, yet after her session everything finally made *sense* to her; *she finally got it*. She began manifesting *with wild abandon*, with peace in her heart, and she has created an amazing rest of her life. She continues to this day with working her program, and she is amazed with herself and with life.

When we have a conscious awareness of who we are and why we are here, we can achieve most anything. This person's soul had struggled, lifetime after lifetime, but she slowly yet methodically managed to move into a place of happiness and peace. Once she *remembered her Divine Self*, she could finally let go of the self-deprecation, the negative self thoughts and all that was attached to her old way of living. She found herself on the elevator of life, moving upwards toward the fulfillment of her destiny.

Chapter 9
Universal Love • Releasing Fear • Living Consciously and Loving Unconditionally

When I wake in the morning and begin a new day, I deliberately take time to reflect and plan. First I review if I had any dreams I remember. Usually I have a light breakfast, then walk or do Yoga, draw a guidance card for the day, meditate, and write, followed by seeing clients. If facilitating a training or seminar or while traveling, I try to wake a bit earlier so I am able to do a shorter version of this routine, because it gives me the focus and balance needed to maintain a state of peacefulness throughout each day. I am very blessed to be able to take this time, because there is nothing more important to my personal well-being than the ability to have peace within. However, this was not *always* how I chose to experience life. There were times when it took every ounce of my energy just to get up in the morning, have that first cup of java, and get to work. I knew life was a little stressful but I was generally okay with that at the time. Upon reflection, it was exactly where I needed to be *at that time*, and is exactly where I could *never* be now.

Isn't life interesting: how it evolves, how *we* evolve as we gather wisdom through our experiences and education, and how we shift our perception of nearly everything during the adventure? The life I chose in my 20s and 30s was exciting, stimulating, fast-paced, and filled with drama and stress. As I moved into my 40s, priorities changed and now, after more than twenty years of spiritual seeking (remembering), my days are filled with a totally different type of stimulation: that of living consciously and loving unconditionally. I still work and play just as much, but this is because my intentions and goals have changed. The choices I make throughout each day are based on whatever it takes to maintain a healthy place of inner peace in body, mind, and spirit.

So what is your intention as an Earth being? What is your motivation as a spiritual being, as a Child of the Universe? How do you perceive yourself in this moment? Is your heart filled with love and compassion for all things, or is it allowing fear, anger, or judgment to run your life? Do you often feel out of balance or have you taken steps towards staying focused and peaceful within? Have you made choices today that will help you in experiencing a sense of peace and balance, or are you focusing instead on what you have *not* accomplished? What is truly important to you in this moment? What *one thing* can you do in this moment that will allow you to feel peaceful? Here is one way…

- Stop now and breathe deeply
- Hold it a moment
- Exhale
- Feel it—be present in this moment
- Return to reading *after* you feel at least a little more peaceful inside
- Practice this regularly…

There is no separation between you and me and All That Is. We only perceive this separation due to the "Earth suits" we chose at birth. We are all connected. What we feel is experienced by others and what others feel is experienced by us, although our perceptions of these feelings and experiences can be vastly different. When I walk in nature and look at the trees, feel the sun or wind on my face, and hear the birds, it will be a different experience from your walk. The trees will allow a slightly different experience for every thing, the wind will have a distinct effect on each of us. Birds may or may not be present, perhaps noticed by some of us and not by others. Our perceptions are unique to our own experience.

There is one thing that connects us all, and that is Universal Love. Unconditional, all-encompassing love. This is a vibration, an energy, that we all share, that is US. It is from where we came, and is where we all are headed.

The Spirit-Directives for this chapter are:

Release

The next step for you to take is to release anything that is holding you back. This could be a fear, a block or distraction. It could be anger, shame, an addition—anything that no longer serves you is to be released. Then you are being called to forgive yourself for having held onto anything that held you back in the past. This is calling you to forgive others and yourself. This card indicates it's time for you to let go of the past and live in *the eternal now*. The drawing indicates the Phoenix being released from the very core of your being. We all have a Phoenix within us. Allow it to be released and expanded into every part of your life, so you are truly FREE to BE.

Balance

There is a need for you to consider ways to become more balanced today, either physically, emotionally, mentally, spiritually, or all of the above. Whichever one came to you first is most likely the area that needs balance. If it is physical, choose to do something that makes your physical body feel better. If it's mental, adjust your thoughts to become more balanced—get rid of the fast-paced, chattering "Monkey Mind" and find peace somewhere within your mental mind. If it is spiritual, do something that enlightens you and allows your soul, your spirit, to feel good. If it's emotional, let go of any emotions that are causing you to feel out of balance and bring in only the emotions, the thoughts, the feelings, that are positive and enlightening.

Dare to be You

    You are being called to help someone or yourself in some way. While focusing on the picture, ask yourself a few questions: Where have I been helpful to someone lately? Have I been of service in some way? How can I help my fellow man, my son, my daughter, my partner, myself? Then listen to what your intuition is saying on how you can be of service in some way. It may be only for one day for now, helping a young child, someone you know or don't know, or it may be a commitment to work at a food bank. You can decide what is best and most appropriate for you in order to fulfill the message this card gives you.

Birth, Death and the Afterlife

Imagine

    This card is calling you to become more creative. Imagination is creation, and this card is calling you to create your highest visions. Write down 10 things that you wish to create in your life. Be very specific. Pay attention to the emotions you feel while writing the list, then keep the list with you, post it on a mirror or make little sticky tabs to put your imaginations everywhere around you. When you read them, FEEL them. Read your list daily as well. This card is calling forth your imagination. Enjoy this creative process.

Madonna J. Kettler, PhD

Unconditional Love

With this card you are being reminded to love yourself unconditionally in some way. You may be asked to love someone else unconditionally. In the card, the beings are embracing beautifully, lovingly, the border on the original card is the pink rose of compassion and love. Meditate on the peacefulness and strength that unconditional love bring out in this picture and in you. This card signifies everything that is, which is love. The Course in Miracles states that everything is either a call to or a move toward love. This is where you are moving by drawing this card. You are being reminded that the wisdom and peace that unconditional love brings is part of who you are NOW. Write down three times when you felt unconditional love and what it did for you. Write a story about each time. If you feel you have never experienced unconditional love, then write a story about how you imagine it would be to experience it.

Stories

In my first book, *Becoming Multisensory: A Guide to Discovering and Trusting your Inner Spirit*, I wrote that fear is the absence of love, just as darkness is the absence of light. We are either in love or moving toward it. All we need when in the dark is to turn on the light.

The first 40 years of my life were loaded with fears, and after many years of personal inner work, I have been able to release a plethora of them as I accept more and more love into every moment.

Over the years there have been many sessions where clients presented with some very challenging fears, some of them are:

- Flying
- Public Speaking
- Failure or Success
- Being alone
- Rejection/not being good enough
- Heights
- Water
- Authority Figures

Fear can serve a useful purpose. It can keep us safe in certain conditions, such as refusing to speed because of a fear of authority, or not flying because our gut is telling us it's not safe. It's when the fear keeps us from driving a safe speed (driving too slow also causes accidents!), or keeps us from *ever* flying, that the fear is running our life. It is in these instances that hypnosis and regression therapy can help.

Yes, there is "healthy fear," but *usually* our fears keep us from living fully and consciously. If we are a team leader at our job, yet we hesitate to present an idea we may have for fear we may be rejected and take that rejection personally, the project may not get finished on time and it could jeopardize several jobs. If we run a business where flying is mandatory to the company's success, and we have anxiety attacks before boarding an airplane, it would be beneficial to everyone who works with/for us to overcoming that fear. Likewise, if we have a fear of public speaking and were just asked to do a speaking tour, eliminating that fear would be paramount to our success.

We all have *some* fears: I believe some are from our current life (fear of driving after being involved in a major car accident), and even more are from past lives: <u>All</u> can be released!

The following stories are taken from several client experiences. Sometimes a person revisits more than one or two past lives in order to heal, but oftentimes only one is necessary. Whatever the guides and the person's Higher Self deem necessary, is what will be revealed. For this story, I combined three clients into one story of a woman I'll call Maggie. The name is fabricated and situations altered; however, the facts of what transpired remain real and relevant to how fears were released.

Maggie was a beautiful person, full of life and ready to experience everything life had to offer. When she wrote a book, she knew she would need to be out in the public to promote it. She was terrified, even though she was passionate about getting the word out relating to the discoveries she had made in the field of health.

During her session, she revisited several past lives. In one, she was an object of ridicule in a gypsy show. In another, she had been killed in a plane crash, and in yet another, she was stoned by a group of her peers for practicing what was deemed to be witchcraft (she was an herbalist).

When Maggie first saw herself as the object of laughter and ridicule in a freak show, she was mortified! This feeling softened when she realized her parents from that life had to sell her to a band of gypsies because they, the parents, were desperately poor. This was their only way to give her any life at all. She was then shown that her parents in that life were also her parents in her current life, and that in this life they were able to support her in a much better fashion than before. Maggie also revisited another life where she had sold out these same parents as Jews in the Holocaust. She did some "logical recall" where she reminded herself that she was not a freak in this life and, in fact, had a lot she could offer the world. She was also told that the karma from these lives was now balanced.

In her second recalled life, where she was killed in a plane crash, she moved out of the memory to see the bigger picture and was astounded to discover that she had been a spy, that her spy plane had been sabotaged, and that it was a good thing because it changed the course of a major battle in that time period. Some of the characters from that life were also present in her current life, and it helped Maggie to understand why they were having trouble trusting her. She then asked for and received spirit guidance on how to heal those karmic relationships in the present.

Birth, Death and the Afterlife

Although it didn't appear that any of the people responsible for stoning her were in her current life, she wondered if she had not met them yet, which brought up much fear in her! We decided, after she witnessed the past life, to have her move forward in her *current* life, where she witnessed herself speaking in front of several groups to see if her fears were founded. *From what she was shown*, she felt there was no more karma to work through; that the stoning had in fact balanced karma from a different past life. She was given the guidance that she did not need to revisit that past life. Sometimes our guides or Higher Selves do not reveal every past life, especially if the memories are not relevant to the current life. This was the case for Maggie.

After these revelations, other information was gathered in the form of Spirit Guidance, and each participant was amazed at how easy it was to release fears that had caused them to put off moving forward in their current lives.

I have no updates to these stories, since I have lost contact with the subjects, yet when each session was concluded, the clients were ready to face their present circumstances and meet their public! I have no doubt they are out there somewhere, fearlessly fulfilling their destinies!

The final story for this chapter is from a client who then became a long time student and dear friend. Her story is printed here verbatim, and it strikes true to so many things we all share—doubting, questioning, and finally, believing… at least *most* of the time!

<u>Bev</u>

My story belongs in the "You Just Never Know" category. It begins about 1998 when my sister-in-law mentioned a transcriptionist she was using who knew of a psychic. I had never even considered visiting a psychic until then, but I thought it would be a hoot so I booked a visit. During my reading I mentioned a chronic foot pain that had been cramping my style for many months and she suggested I try a hands-on healer, something else totally out of my realm of experience. The healer was none other than Madonna Kettler, my relative's transcriptionist, who was experiencing a major awakening into the world of metaphysics. I scheduled a session with Madonna. I don't remember if she healed my foot pain, but I know for sure that she changed my life!

Madonna invited me to one of her spiritual development meetings held weekly in her home. I went one time and was hooked. The people I met there, and the ideas I was exposed to made me feel enlightened, empowered and loved. Life in general simply began to make more sense. However, even though I attended faithfully for years, I never felt that I "fit" with these wonderful people. I believed each group member had "powers" such as healing, receiving messages from spirit guides, and communicating with rocks and trees. No such powers for me. For example, one evening Madonna guided the group in a past life regression. Everyone else had cool experiences, but I fell asleep, snored, and received nothing. While I never doubted these experiences for the others, I never believed it was possible for me.

Month after month with the group I searched for my special niche, but my only talent seemed to be taking fast and accurate notes. The group began to call me their "Scribe" and I kept records of events at our sessions. This was certainly not the "Power" I was searching for. As the group watched me take notes so effortlessly they encouraged me to use this ability to contact spirits. They suggested I try meditating and then writing my thoughts.

It seemed silly to me but I trusted their judgment and was willing to give it a try. I even had the perfect spot. I had been teaching elementary school for 33 years and was preparing to retire. The room in which I prepared lessons was undergoing a bit of a redecorating change. During that year I had been receiving gifts of angel figurines and pictures. I never told anyone I was collecting angels because I didn't know I was. They just kept showing up until instead of a school room, I had an "Angel Room."

The perfect time was early in the morning. I put a "Do Not Disturb" sign outside my Angel Room, lit an angel candle, meditated, and began to write. I thought the results were totally weird and it felt like I was making it up. However as I read through the pages it was undeniable that these words were totally unlike me. I am a typical stoic, down-to-Earth Scandinavian and never even call anyone "honey" and never, ever use any flowery language, but here's a sample:

"Good morning, precious one. We wrap our wings around you in love.

It is a jewel of a day. Enjoy the minutes. Be in each minute. Own the day.

Use it with love. Trust. Love. Peace. Joy. Inspiration. Slow, feel, enjoy. Be.

We send you our love at each minute. Sparkles are healing."

The thoughts were so unlike me I had to wonder if maybe this was really real.

I trusted the process and I must admit the words were comforting and made me feel wrapped in love, so I continued this on and off for years. Then, like all good intentions, doing this simply faded away. Over the years I remembered this notebook filled with love and supportive thoughts but as time passed it was easier to doubt and harder to believe. Plus, I lost the notebook.

Then a dozen years later, in a cleaning mood, I dug into the mess of my basement and happened upon the dusty old notebook. Glancing at the writing I thought it looked pretty stupid so I began to tear out the writing and planned to keep the rest of the notebook. Then, for no logical reason, I put the pages back and kept the notebook. I just couldn't destroy it. It was back in my heart.

Almost immediately after finding the notebook again I began to notice 11:11 on clocks with increasing frequency. I wondered, "Was this a coincidence, or was there meaning here?" Sometimes when I saw 11:11 I felt goose bumps which Madonna often said means, "This is real. This is the truth."

A short time later I had an opportunity to visit another psychic. I mentioned the notebook I had almost thrown away. Her response was that I was a "Scribe"—the very word my friends had used so long ago. She gave me strong advice to continue meditating and recording my thoughts. She insisted the messages I was receiving were real and, in fact, important. She encouraged me to begin a blog and told me that these messages which seemed a bit goofy to me, would be enlightening and even healing to others.

I was excited and wanted to hope she was right, but my doubtful nature overtook me and I was afraid to try. I just thought that I would be making things up in order to make myself believe they were real. However that is when my 11:11 sightings became eerily insistent. I would walk into a room and see those numbers on every clock and phone twice a day, almost every day. In fact one day I was shopping at Best Buy when my daughter-in-law called me to tell me it was 11:11 on 1-11-11! Now this was getting just plain creepy. My brother and I were chatting and he looked at a clock out of my vision and told me it was 11:11. He was unaware of the meaning for me, he just thought it was cool. So now just seeing it wasn't enough; I had people bringing the numbers to me. I even saw 11:11 on television. It was on the alarm clock behind two characters on "Everyone Loves Raymond." I was watching an old, old show from the 60's ("Have Gun Will Travel") and a character took out his pocket watch and declared something like, "It's eleven eleven and it's not too late."

It was time to get the message: continue to meditate and write. I haven't yet begun a blog because I don't exactly know what that is. But I am confident that it will happen. I think of my messengers as angels but I don't actually know who or what they are and I don't think it really matters. I am beginning to believe, however, that the messages are real. The story is an ongoing process. I have learned so much since a "chance" meeting with a psychic so long ago. I view my life now from a more positive and broader perspective. I have become better at trusting subtle messages the universe sends me. My story teaches me that you just never know when a seemingly insignificant chance meeting or comment might change your life. Pay attention because, as my angels tell me: "Believe. Trust. Love."

Chapter 10
We are Eternal, Divine Beings • Self-Empowerment • Respect

We forget.

When we are on the Other Side we forget how challenging Earth can be. Because of this, some of us plan excruciatingly painful experiences, difficult lives with challenges that may not seem to be so extreme *during the planning stage*. When everyone's free will comes into the picture, it can further exacerbate the life lessons we choose.

When I was a guest on a local TV show, one of the interviewers asked me, "Do we really *choose* our parents and our families?"

"Yes," I replied. "Based on my work, we do." Not only do we pick our family and friends, but we choose what body we will be in, our brain, and the place and time of our birth as well as our life challenges, although this may not be the case one hundred percent of the time. Then after we incarnate, we promptly forget we made these choices.

Everyone forgets their plan to *some* extent. It is wise to be respectful regarding these plans, because they are *sacred* contracts. We may have an agreement with others and we usually have a very personal plan to fulfill, as well. What every person does (or doesn't do) affects the outcome of the group plan as well as their personal contract. When we respect not only ourselves in our agreement but everyone involved, we allow these agreements to be fulfilled more easily. What matters most is our eternal soul and its sacred contract.

Our contracts are created specifically for our soul's evolution. This is why we incarnate. What we do in our career, what we look like, how much or how little we eat, how we present ourselves—none of this really matters unless it has to do with our contract. When we transition from this Earth, only our eternal soul continues on, and all that we identified within our physical body is gone, dead, dust. Books written, homes passed on, and all we identified with while in a physical body may continue to be available to others, but our physical body is no longer, until we decide to return from the spirit world once again to fulfill another contract that is, once again, at least partially hidden from our conscious awareness.

Would you like to know one way to remember what your contract is?

Right now, bring your attention to this moment, to these words, NOW.

Beautiful.

Now, bring your attention to your inner self: the beating of your heart, how your blood is moving throughout your body and the peaceful energy that is moving that blood. Bring that energy, with your intention, throughout your body, all the way to the tips of your toes, fingers, and then to the top of your head. Feel this peaceful presence everywhere within you.

Next, whatever you need to do in order to relax in this one moment, do it. Feel the energy moving throughout your body, and in your mind's eye, ask the question, "Why am I here?"... Then:

1. Breathe deeply
2. Release excess thoughts
3. Feel and be aware of your Divine Light
4. Make a conscious choice to BE here, NOW
5. Be thankful
6. Be loving
7. Be respectful to all that is, including yourself
8. Release judgment (of self and others), and finally,
9. Listen... and *Remember*...

Birth, Death and the Afterlife

The Spirit-Directives for this chapter are:

Respect

Beginning today, you are coming into a time of profound change in how you look at yourself and others, because it's time to look at how you treat yourself and others. This card is reminding you to respect every being and every thing. Focus on the card and hold the image in your mind. Notice how the older adult is embracing the younger one. Tap into the feeling of the card—how these beings can emote such respect without even having eyes. This is a call for you to respect yourself and others on a deeper level. Discover what respect is to you, and then treat others as you wish to be treated.

Self-Acceptance

 It's time to accept yourself unconditionally, on a deeper level—deeper than ever before. This card is a higher consciousness card that represents self-acceptance on a much higher level than ever before. It is calling you to the highest level of integrity, belief in yourself, and acceptance of who you are in this moment. You are also being asked to look in the mirror (as in the picture) daily for 30 days, and simply look deeply at who you are. Let your eyes glaze over, and see your higher self, until you come into complete acceptance of who you are in every realm. This is self-empowerment in its greatest expression.

Abundance

Observe the picture, the tree of life. Become one with the deep, wide trunk with far-reaching branches, and the hole in the base of the trunk, possibly representing openness to receiving. Imagine the roots of the tree—how large, how deep they are—and how they allow the tree to grow even larger with every moment, with every drop of water, with every ray of sun. Abundance isn't just about money, it is about feeling and knowing that everything is perfect. It's about trusting that the supply and demand continue, that the circle of life continues, and everything is provided for. If you drew this card it may be important for you to look at the abundance in your life—re-evaluate what you have—what you THINK you have and what you REALLY have. Focus on being grateful for everything. The abundance of nature is all around, no matter what season it is. Just as the tree observes everything around it, under it, and above it in order for it to flourish, if you drew this card, be observant of everything around you. What are the signs from nature telling you? What are the signs gifting you with, and how are they honoring you? And in that same sign/message, how are you gifting them? How are you honoring them? This card calls you to be aware of and grateful for all the abundance in your life.

Partnering

This card expresses the importance of working together in some way. This could be working with yourself more compassionately, cooperating with another person (life partner, child, friend, business partner). It reveals the need to be with others or more at peace with yourself.

Sandy's Story:

When Sandy presented for a session, she was confused as to why she had not been able to trust her husband, and was concerned because it was getting worse as time went by. She said she had known from the moment she first met him that he was the man for her, and there was absolutely no reason for this distrust. It bothered her that no matter what her conscious self told her, her suspicions kept gnawing at her. She wondered if learning to trust was part of their contract. When she called for an appointment, she was ready to find out what this was all about in order to be done with it forever.

Sandy was easy to get into a trance state and was able to resolve her conundrum in a very short amount of time. I suggested that she regress to the time when her issue of mistrusting her current husband occurred. Here is her version of the session, unedited:

> "I'm a normal person living a normal life, perhaps not as exciting a life as some, but better than most. I have four wonderful daughters, a beautiful home in the best country in the world, and a great husband.
>
> I should have been the happiest person around, but I had one serious problem. I just didn't trust my husband. I had no reason to distrust him. I had never even caught him telling a little lie, but I couldn't get past this distrust. If he was a little late home from work, I thought he was in a bar somewhere. If some woman we met on the street smiled at him, I asked, 'Who is she?'
>
> When I started menopause I got really weird in many ways, but I became even more suspicious of my husband. He had been very patient, but this was bothering him a great deal and it was putting a great strain on our marriage. One can only defend oneself against false accusations for so long before you give up.
>
> Luckily, if you believe in luck, I talked to Madonna about this and she suggested we do a past life regression to see if we could figure out where this distrust came from. In this regression, she suggested that I go to the reason for this distrust.
>
> I immediately went to a life in Europe where I was an older man pacing around my wood shop in a city. I was very frightened because there were men in uniforms outside who were coming to take me away and execute me because I was Jewish. My husband in this life was my oldest son in that life, and he had sold me out to the authorities in the hope of saving his own life. I said, 'It isn't going to help. They are going to kill him anyway.'
>
> We went on to other lives that he and I had lived together in various relationships as I seemed to need to get all our stories out of my system, and when she brought me out of the hypnotic state I felt as though a great weight had been lifted from me. I am completely over the suspicion and I feel sooooooo much better.
>
> The most interesting part is the fact that when I was telling my

husband about the life where I was the old Jewish man, he said, 'I sold you out,' before I told him that he sold me out.

How about that? -- Sandy"

Summary

When Sandy incarnated into her current life, the memory of being betrayed had been *consciously forgotten*, yet it was still in her *cellular memory*. When this unconscious memory was brought to her consciousness, she understood why she had been suspicious of her husband and, consequently, was able to move past those feelings since she now knew where they had come from. These cellular memories can be revealed in many other ways, for instance during meditation (with the intention to remember), spontaneously during a massage, in the dreamtime, during a regression session, doing the simple exercise mentioned earlier in this chapter, or by other people recalling them. It doesn't matter how we get them, but I believe if it is important to our life work, they *will* be revealed to us at the appropriate time—one way or another.

Chapter 11

Thankfulness and Gratitude • Do Be-ing

For more years than I'd like to admit, I chose to be a victim. I felt persecuted, denied, "less than," never good enough, forgotten, alone and different from everyone. I had fun times and good friends, yet the way I remember it, my vibration was pretty much in the mud, especially during the times when I was drinking heavily or in the midst of a drama—which was often.

Then something happened. I had an awakening unlike anything I had ever experienced (at least in this life, so far) after which I *knew* I was *not* alone. I was catapulted into unknown (unremembered) territory. In bed and emotionally crushed after an argument with my then-husband, I had withdrawn into a fetal position. In the depths of despair, I heard a voice. "Relax," it said. I straightened my body. Immediately I was propelled into the most splendid, fantastic, uplifting journey through the clouds. I had no body. I was bright, and sparkly, and light as a feather. As I passed the clouds, going at breakneck speed, thousands of stars whipped by. Clouds parted as I flew ever upward, climbing to an unfamiliar realm of peace, calm, and serenity. I was aware only of whiteness and warmth. I was enveloped in unconditional love. Then I heard the words, "You don't need that any more."

The words shocked me and brought me back to my Earth reality. I then drifted into a deep and profound sleep." (Read more about this in my book *Becoming Multisensory: A Guide to Discovering and Trusting your Inner Spirit*.)

This experience opened me up to a new life that was adventurous yet peaceful, scary yet comforting, new yet familiar—and *loving* beyond all measure or description.

As I began the process of releasing the old challenges, pain, sadness and fears that had plagued me, my "Higher Memory" was activated, and with a more conscious awareness of that "Higher Memory" came a freedom I had never known.

That was only the beginning! Since that time I have made many other phenomenal excursions to unremembered realms. Because of them, I have also had questions, doubts, and fears arise within me, until I finally moved into a place of trust again, at a new level of be-ing. Little did I know what adventure was beginning to unfold after that first conscious reconnection to Source. And *had I known what was in store*, I probably would have stayed right where I was, out of fear. Because my guides know me pretty well (smile), I was told *only enough* to titillate me to the next step in my awakening!

I have moved from fear and sadness to understanding and balance, from victimization to acceptance of what is, then into thankfulness and gratitude, and finally to peace within. With each challenge, the positive became clearer and the gratitude deeper, until living peacefully became the norm.

One of the first healthy practices I attempted was a fitness regimen, with a goal to "move" at least 20 minutes a day. It took me years of forcing the issue (I call this "fake it until you make it") before I finally *got* that the movement helped me in other ways and that I was *worthy* of having a healthy body! Twenty years ago, when I decided to meditate at least 5 to 10 minutes daily, I did not know the positive affect it would have on my life. But I stayed with it all these years. Over time, as I started valuing myself more—taking "baby steps to the elevator,"—meditation, journaling and fitness became a permanent and integral part of my daily routine. I treasure the preciousness of every moment and every thing, *including* me, and I have reduced the negative self-talk and the "monkey mind" to a bare minimum.

By choosing freedom from whatever I feel is holding me back, I more easily remain in a place of thankfulness and gratitude, and nearly always can, as Gandhi said, "be the peace I wish to see in the world." With every peaceful thought, my vibration is higher and lighter. The other dimensions I regularly travel to are enlightening, fun, and educational. My otherworldly experiences are part of *who I AM*, and I am naturally more thankful. Self-acceptance, peacefulness, and gratitude are more consistently a part of who I AM.

When we are in a lower vibrational field, life can be extremely challenging. We struggle to feel any type of gratitude because we "can't see the forest for the trees." We are more apt to complain, there doesn't seem to be much happiness anywhere we look, and frustration and anger can run rampant.

As we awaken and begin living a more conscious life, our vibration can increase, or get "higher." The holistic methodologies outlined in the Supplemental Information section at the end of this book can help this process, yet the number one way I raise my vibration is through the mind; my thoughts.

What am I talking about when I say vibration? The American Heritage Dictionary says to vibrate is: 1. To move or cause to move back and forth rapidly. 2. To produce a sound; resonate. 3. To be moved emotionally; thrill. 4. To fluctuate; waver. The slang version of vibration is more apropos to what I'm talking about: A distinct emotional aura or atmosphere capable of being instinctively sensed or experienced.

If we rate our vibration on a scale of 1 to 10, with 10 being our highest vibration, where would you choose to be?

The Law of Vibration, which is a Universal Law, states that everything vibrates at a certain frequency. For example, you are driving to work after a spat with your spouse. Traffic is slow and you're already late. Let's rate your vibration at about a 3. There's another person driving the same road who is in a more peaceful state, let's put her at a 5 on the vibration scale. Still another person is driving to work who is resonating at a 7 (he had a very peaceful morning)! There are others on this road as well, some vibrating the same as you, some lower, and some higher.

In the lower vibrations, we are more likely to experience negative events. So let's say the level 3 vibrations have a car accident. Those that are at a higher vibration will NOT be involved in the same accident because they are in a different energy field. They may assist with those involved in the accident, or they may be somewhere else entirely during the accident, maybe because they slowed down or decided to take a different road that morning. The vibration they are holding will keep them with others on that same level.

Thought is the most potent form of energy, so it follows that negative thoughts carry a lower vibration, and positive thoughts, higher. Therefore, it's not that everyone in a lower vibration will be involved in an accident, but those that are holding the same vibration *will* tend to have or be involved in the same experiences. Besides thoughts, things can lower or raise our vibration. Watching TV (especially the news), sugar, and alcohol are only a few. It is said that the tone of Ohm is the vibration of Mother Earth. Dr. Masaru Emoto took pictures of water crystals and proved that our thoughts, both positive and negative, are captured in water, which affects the properties of that water. (See http://www.masaru-emoto.netl for more information.) In his studies he captured the vibration of the water after different thoughts are infused into it. Since our bodies are primarily water, these thoughts also affect us.

It's this simple: What we think *matters*. Energy flows where thoughts go, not only to us and our energy field, but for everyone. The more aware we can be of our energy field, our thoughts and our actions, the higher our vibration.

Here are the Spirit-Directives for this chapter:

Vibration

You are moving into a profound new vibration—the vibration of love. This is a higher vibration than you have ever experienced, and you are being asked to trust that you are ready for this love, this peace that is coming in through the higher vibration. In order to achieve this higher vibration, you may be guided or asked to tone or sing or pray, meditate, or dance. Whatever tool can help you raise your vibration, this is what you are being asked to do today.

Change and Movement

There will be dramatic change in your near future. You will either move through something that has been blocked or you will change the way you are doing something. This card instructs you to call and accept the change and movement happening in your life, for it is all moving you toward your highest intentions. Ask for help from the nature spirits during this period. The one thing we can be sure of in life is change. At this time in your life, there may be more than the average amount, and it will be easier for you to move through it, into that next phase of your life, if you use the energies of nature—the sun, the Earth and water. Allow those parts of creation to be your helpers through this time of change and movement.

Do Be-ing

Are you doing, doing, doing? This card indicates it's time to *do be-ing*. This card means it's important for you to be active in your inner work. Be active with meditation, or more accurately, do *meditation*. Do be-ing indicates it's time to meditate, take time for yourself, even if it's only five minutes daily to start with. There are many types of meditation—you will find the one that fits you. This card also indicates that nature is a very good surround for your beginning meditation practice—simple walking meditation or sitting quietly in nature, clearing your mind, and be-ing in the moment. In the picture, the Nature Goddess is on the tip of a beautiful plant that opens in a lotus-type blossom. This represents the outcome when you commit to be-ing.

Case Study

"Rachel" came for her LBL session because she felt it was time for her to know more, she wanted to be reminded of what she needed to do, she wanted to regain her self-confidence and embrace the positive aspects of herself. She said she felt lost and didn't know why. She, too, had played the role of victim and was tired of it.

I always ask clients to prepare not only a Cast of Characters for their LBL experience, but to bring in any and all questions they may currently have, in case the guides are ready to answer some (or all) of them. This has proven to help the clients feel more supported, helps them get to know their guides a little more, and reminds them not only that they are never alone, but that they have all the answers within them. Rachel had quite an extensive list of questions, and all of them were answered. It was an amazing session for both of us!

For this case study I chose to take excerpts from her session instead of revealing everything that was told, since many of the questions overlapped and responses often were similar. Some of her questions, also, were more personal than I feel is appropriate for this book, so they have been excluded. As with any client requesting the interlife experience, my intention was to have her walk away with gratitude and thankfulness for the experience of *remembering*.

<u>LBL of Rachel</u>

> Rachel: (Most recent PL) Daytime, warm, I'm outside, female, age 19, wearing a skirt and white top with buttons. We live in the city. I'm really thin, like a stick figure. Name is Anna. I'm walking down the street, observing people, streets kind of busy. I'm in England, 1876. I just got done helping with the children. I have three siblings. I don't recognize them from this life, at least not now.
> (Next scene) We're very sick, the whole family. Some sort of flu-type thing. I'm taking care of them but I don't appear to be as sick as they are. They're all in bed, I'm sweating, trying to fight it. I'm 20 now. Just my Mom and siblings here. Dad died.
> (Next scene—Rachel automatically goes to the death scene from that life.) I didn't want to be alone, so I married someone older. All my family died from that flu thing and I didn't want to be alone. He was abusive and choked me to death. He is Michael in my current life.

MK: What was that life about?

R: Being true to myself, not sacrificing my happiness out of fear. It was about not putting myself into situations where people could hurt or control me because I was afraid. About having faith that I can be okay by myself. But I sacrificed happiness because I was worried, so I just chose this route.

MK: Where are you now in relation to your body?

R: Floating away. Only my husband in the room when I died. He's trying to get rid of the body. Wrapping it up. I'm feeling sad. I'm going further away. Two guides here, one on both sides. Earth is gone now.

MK: Where are you now? (Client enters the Gateway):

R: I just came back to my home. I have my guides and two angels. The angels are very tall. One has long hair but it's male. The other feels more female. Angels are Josephine and Zacheil. Their purpose is to bring me back home. Other guide is female, dark hair, tall, name Arizellie. Also Nham, not my guide normally but here for now, feels male. They have been with me all the while. They will also be my guides in the interlife. Now I'm going to the Hall of Records. Big pillars, white and gold in color. Everything bright and shiny. I'm brought here to show me my options. I don't go inside yet. I don't need to go right now. First I'll go meet everybody. Here's even one more guide. My Mom from that life is here, and the siblings, and Dad, and other people. My friends, too. I know my Grandmother is there. I speak with them telepathically and I see them, too. Everybody is just happy I'm here, not saying anything to me. I have a conversation with the person who molested me for 10 years in this life. He says he's sorry for what he did but it was necessary because of the path I chose, and what I chose to learn. It was an agreement we had. My soul just wanted to experience that. It would help in the next life (her current life). Because of my fears, I didn't trust in myself, so being aware of that would cause me to be more conscious of my choices. Now I'm just spending time with Angelo (son in her current life). He's awfully tall. Spirit color is blue-purple. Mine is orange, maybe?

MK: What happens next?

R: I'm just enjoying being here. I feel like my mind is fighting me. (Deepening again) Now I'm being rejuvenated, I feel the energy and the colors. Don't know how to word this... energy moving through me. Now guides with me again. They take me to where there's grasshoppers and grass. A little house with a porch, lots of flowers. I created this place. I've actually dreamed about it. My primary guides (2) are with me here. The first two that I mentioned. I feel like I'm getting recharged now, yes, and they're laughing because they see I'm struggling with this. They will be taking me to the Elders.

At this time I suggest that Rachel will be able to return to this place any time she wishes, simply by taking the time and asking, then listening.

MK: Where are your guides taking you next?

R: They're taking me to the Elders. There are ten of the Elders, eight plus my two guides. They look all knowledgeable, wise. Very compassionate. Some of them change from incarnation to incarnation, but not all of them.

MK: What messages do they have for you?

R: Not to be so hard on myself. We love you. Don't worry, you'll know what to do, just trust. Listen to yourself.

MK: How can you know when it's your mind and when it's your soul talking, and when it's really important?

R: Because I will feel it. Yes, I know when it's my mind and when it's something higher. It's a knowing, and my mind likes to get me into trouble, my mind is always loud, and there are always forks in the road, and when it's knowledge or knowing, there is no question. Like I knew I was supposed to come here.

MK: What are some ways to not have the mind get in the way?

R: I chose to have this kind of a mind, so then I could help others on how to use it. To help them overcome like I do. If I already know how to do it, then I can't help others on how to overcome it. It's something I would like to focus on, to help others.

MK: How do you do that?

R: I quiet my mind by allowing it, then resisting, and discipline, become undisciplined with it, not in a negative way, but it's important to stay focused on reaching that goal. They say I know everything I need to know, but I do need to allow myself to heal myself first.

MK: What is the best way to heal?

R: To know who I am. I do that by remembering that we're all love. And remembering is a choice, it's all about how I want to look at it. I know when I'm going through it, I think there might be better ways to think, but I have enjoyed not… I'm to keep on searching and not give up, knowing it's there for a reason (the challenges). They are there for my growth and learning compassion and to help ourselves and others to realize our true being. Forgiveness is important, too, really important. And remember that we are never alone, even if we think we're alone. Always just ask for help. Just ask verbally, but it would be more effective if you meditate or pray with that intention. They also tell me not to give up, as hard as it seems, don't give up like I've done before. Do not sacrifice my own happiness like I've done in the past. They're reminding me that this is all I need, this information, to remember.

MK: Are you on track with soul purpose?

R: They're telling me not to sacrifice my happiness, to speak my truth. The way I do this is to just continue to meditate, use the energy healings, to continue with the search, the self-exploration, my spiritual journey.

MK: Okay, just let go, change your vibration… feel your vibration raising as you go deeper… then ask your guides to take you wherever you need to go next.

R: I'm sitting in a chair… like a desk. The guides are with me. It's a room, a classroom. I'm here to get questions answered.

MK: Okay then, what is your purpose for being here?

R: I'm going to work on healing myself so I can help others find ways to do this, and remain loving to myself and increase my love towards others, unconditionally. I am to do things that lead to me loving myself unconditionally. Loving, like it is here in this classroom. So by remembering this experience, that will also help.

MK: So really absorb how you are feeling in this experience, and maybe a guide will give you a key word that will be special to you, that will help you immediately remember this feeling, this experience, of unconditional love.

R: Namasté is the word that will remind me of this.

MK: Where did your soul come from?

R: They don't want to tell me, because then I will obsess over it. It's just not important.

MK: How many times have you been on Earth?

R: 300?

MK: What was your most important life on Earth?

R: Many important, for different reasons. In some I was more awake than in others, but it doesn't defeat the purpose.

MK: What patterns are there yet to be resolved that may have gone on over many lifetimes?

R: Feeling that I can't take care of myself, that I need others, like a parent or a spouse or family. And then when they're gone I give up. This is also one of my lessons in my current life, yes. That's why I don't have much attachment to my son. I still have a pattern that when I'm with people I end up having an attachment to them, so this is something to work on.

MK: So how do you break that pattern?

R: To practice non-attachment. Just remembering that I'm able to make it without others, not that I'll be alone, but that I don't need to depend on them completely. I can still share a life with them though, just not to give up my strength or power because of them.

MK: What is the depression about? Is this something you chose?

R: It's necessary to give me the need to search for other things. If I didn't go through that it wouldn't have been a necessity to search spiritually.

MK: Now that you know this, can you let go of the depression and still do your searching?

R: I'm always kind of prone to sadness, but it just doesn't have to get so debilitating now. It won't have to be as severe as long as I can remember.

MK: How can you regain your self-confidence?

R: Unconditional love. By remember that everything is the way it needs to be and that I'm really… whether or not I make a mistake, it will lead me in the direction that can help me grow. To remind myself that everything is in Divine Order. Even the things that appear wrong, even the choice in the last lifetime to be murdered, I needed to be beaten up because… there wasn't any other option, but I shouldn't judge that, either. Because it's not real anyway.

MK: So that murder was planned, a contract?

R: Yes. There are no accidents; there are just different probabilities that happen with different choices. So some of them have more benefit, or rather not "more" but you accelerate faster with other choices.

MK: What about your low energy? What percentage of your spirit did you incarnate with?

R: 40%. That's why I have such low energy. It's what was decided I do. Because the more work that is needed, the more profound the results.

MK: So you were just given only what you would need and no more?

R: That way, if it was more, then maybe it would be a little easier, but there are benefits to making it harder to accomplish the plans. Then you are able to try more ways, you appreciate there are other ways, other things that maybe you wouldn't otherwise know. To remember something, remember who you are, with less energy, will take more work but then you are able to transfer that to other people you are then able to help.

MK: What is the feeling of being lost, then?

R: Pleiades… that's where I'm from. The feeling of being lost helps me strive for something. There is the feeling of being lost, and that can be disruptive, but it will also help me focus on regaining direction. That's all about the self-confidence, too. And not being afraid to face whatever is going to happen.

MK: Where does some of your paranoia come from? Is it from a past life or what is it?

R: I've learned that certain people will use certain things against you.

Birth, Death and the Afterlife

So I'm ultra-sensitive on what people know. That's from the past, being persecuted for what I know, and what I've said or believed, so there's a need to protect that. Also in this life, I'm to be aware of other people's feelings, to be sensitive to them. It's more just for protection.

MK: How do you embrace the positive aspects of yourself?

R: First thought is the part of the St. Francis Prayer – be an instrument of peace... then I had the thought... if we're perfect, not from an ego sense, but knowing where we're from, we shouldn't be too hard on ourselves when we make mistakes. Maybe use the word Namasté for myself, too.

MK: How can you get over the feeling of never being safe? How do you move through that feeling?

R: Well, in the past it has been beneficial to not trust, but if I can just cut the cord attached to that feeling... and choose not to be a victim. Right here, I am cutting the cord. I do it with intention. I'm ready, and I'm doing it now.

MK: Remember, any time you cut a cord you fill it with light, empowerment, self-confidence, a feeling of ultimate safety yet knowing you will be warned if there is a need. You can balance all those lifetimes now and bring into this lifetime a feeling of self-confidence and security, caution whenever needed, knowing you are always protected and safe. Now, the next question is why do you talk in codes?

R: Because I don't want people to know what I'm talking about. It comes from being persecuted for what I've said. It's from this lifetime, too, having parents that weren't open to certain things.

MK: What is your soul color?

R: Yellow... yellowish gold color.

MK: Who is your most predominant soul mate in this life, or maybe they can describe what a soul mate is?

R: Someone you choose to... you're in the same soul group and you choose to experience your lives together. You're there to help each other grow.

MK: Who are your primary ones in this life?

R: My grandma, my son, and my friends, Monica…

MK: What about your dog, Cookie?

R: She is here with me. She's good, she's in the house with the flowers.

MK: What about what you talked about, the ADD-type feelings you may have?

R: It's just if I'm not interested in something or want to explore something else, my mind just wants to go somewhere else. It's not that serious, just a bit annoying. I just need to remind myself not to do things I typically don't like to do unless it's a thing that's necessary.

MK: What about your fear about getting into trouble and not wanting others to know what you said? What's that all about?

R: Because they have been physically and emotionally hurt. The best way to overcome that is to have the understanding that's their reaction but I don't have to be affected by their own issues. To not put myself in situations or with people who are going to mistreat me if I do or say something they don't like.

MK: Did you choose to mother your mother—is that part of your contract?

R: Yes, to guide her. Yes, part of a contract. She is not part of my soul group, though.

MK: What about Angelo, your son, how he always wants to protect you?

R: He knew that he had a purpose, too, of helping me coming into this life. That's part of contract too, because I was so self-destructive and wanting to hurt myself. He knew that he would give me a purpose and he just had the need or feeling to protect me. Even he has had that role before, of protecting me, and he didn't feel like he did it right before.

MK: Is there another place for you to go, where your guides would like to take you to experience?

R: I'm talking to my guides now. I'm asking them to help me out a little bit, find a little more purpose. They're saying there's not one clear path, there are many options. You can have the same intention of helping and working with others, trying to improve myself and others' lives, and no matter where I go. Even if I don't think it's going to make a difference, it's going to make an impact. There is not just one option.

MK: Can you get your spiritual, immortal name?

R: I'm getting it's the same one I was given. Gamprasad. They said they can't give me exactly what I'm here to do because it's part of the journey. They say now there's not much to be searching for, I just need to continue to increase listening to my inner guidance. Also it's not to say "this is what I'm going to do with my life" because it changes. It changes. There is still the major theme that stays the same though.

MK: And what is your major theme then?

R: Service.

MK: So there are different ways to serve, that's your choice?

R: Yes. That's the path and I can choose what I want to do on the path, and change it in a year but I don't have to define myself by what I'm doing, and I don't have to get frustrated with myself because every day, is just to find a way to serve. And most importantly, to serve myself, if I want to be most effective. It begins with myself. It's part of the walk, yes. It would mean every day, one way to serve yourself and serve others, yes.

MK: Is there another place for you to go?

R: Not important for me at this time.

MK: Is there any way you can heal your body with the stomach or thyroid? How can you best heal that, or is that serving some other purpose?

R: It's to show I can heal myself. Do the affirmations, the positive thinking, use the Reiki, the meditation, use the crystals, herbs. I can do this and get help from others, too, uh-huh.

MK: What is the most important individual characteristic as a soul that defines the real you, that is carried from life to life?

R: Compassion. That's why I had to learn compassion for myself. If I don't have it for myself, I can't have it for others. Feeling and self-acceptance and letting go of what isn't for me, are all ways to have that for myself. Because if I don't do this, I will keep attracting people that will judge me, and not let me be comfortable with myself where I have to speak in code and be paranoid and not be me.

MK: Why were we brought together for this session?

R: This is a way to facilitate the healing, to remind me, it's a wake up call, and just an opportunity to remind myself that I'm not a horrible person and that I'm not alone, and I am loved, and that I can deal with whatever is going to come, and be whoever I need to be, and sometimes you just have to allow instead of trying to figure it out with your mind. There's all this stuff I already know but it's just carried over.

MK: Really feel now, all the energy that's around you. Go to a place of relaxation and allow yourself to remember your Divine self, absorb all that has come to you, kind of review it like a movie, allow the mind to process this in every cell of your being… as I tap, really get into this experience. Integrate everything from this session, and all you were and all you will ever be, into this present moment, and feel your Divine Essence. Feel how perfect this process is, and how loving everything is… now (long pause).

R: I just have to remember the present moment. I'm always concerned about what I'm to do, what I'm going to be, and I'm just supposed to enjoy the moment. Be loving. That's really important. If I don't give myself that unconditional love there will be reminders. The people in my life may not be so loving or so kind, that they won't accept me. So it's important not to judge them, they are there to help me remember. Don't let what they may have said or done towards me take away from who I really am.

MK: So is it like all these things are just distractions to you not remembering who you really are? Did they just keep you from remembering, and the more you can allow that remembering, the easier it gets?

R: They help facilitate the remembering in order to get through the challenge. To know what you are and who you are, you have to know the opposite. On the Earth, anyway. Be more open to things that others may think are not real or true, and just trust in my own guidance.

MK: Any other gift or word other than Namaste for you to know? Anything else they'd like to present to you or say to you?

R: They're showing me the necklace I'm wearing—to remember that. It's gold. They love us and everything will be fine! (Tapping one more time while giving the suggestion that anytime you state your intention and take the time to meditate or listen, you will be able to go deeper into the remembering of who you really are... love.) They're saying that's it. That's all we need! It's perfect. That's what I needed to know.

End of LBL

Update from Rachel, received three months after her LBL:

"The past few years I have found myself to feel somewhat lost in life. I had moments where through meditation and expanding my spiritual awareness such as through reading and classes that I seemed to gain some insight however, none of it seemed to sustain the peace that I was looking for. I truly believe that I was guided to do the Life Between Life to remind me of who I am and what I came here to do. I think that sometimes throughout my life I have allowed self-destructive thoughts to take control of me and cause me to see the world and the experiences that I have encountered in a negative light. I have allowed victim consciousness to guide me and attract situations and people in my life. The session reminded me to be aware of that, as well as be thankful for those experiences. Perhaps it was necessary so that I could break the karmic pattern in my life as well as in my family. The session reminded me that even though some things happen that seem bad or negative, something positive can always be gained from it. More compassion, understanding, love and acceptance for ourselves and others is what is necessary in order to evolve as souls. I am sure that there have been some choices in my life that were made out of fear instead of love, but now I know that there is always an opportunity to find our way back to the path that leads us is (the direction of) our highest good. Perhaps through forgiveness of ourselves and others we can find the way back. I know I have a lot of work to do, but I was reassured during the session that we are never alone and that there is perfection in everything, even if we don't understand it. With Love, Rachel."

Summary

Some people choose extremely difficult lives... others relax after muddling through several challenging *previous* lives. After reading these chapters, are you recognizing a theme? Do you have a greater understanding of why you are here and who you really are?

Most every client who comes for a session has questions relating to why they are here and why certain "horrible things" (illness, early death, suicide, abuse) happened to them, their family, or their friends.

Usually they leave the session with the answers they sought; other times, their guides or Higher Self blocks them from these answers for various reasons, the primary one being that knowing more than they already know would interfere with their lives. It is not up to us to judge our own or anyone else's illness, challenges, or "lot in life." Often times we choose difficult lives in order to further our evolution and the balancing of karma has nothing to do with it!

After either experiencing some type of transpersonal hypnotherapy such as a past life, connecting with their Spirit Helpers, or experiencing the vastness of our life between lives, a client will walk away with a deeper sense of who they are. Most always, the client will hear the words you have heard throughout this book—*we are never alone; there are no accidents; be thankful in every situation;* and *we are all loved unconditionally.*

How many times do we need to hear this before we finally *get it?* Fact is, it's different for each one of us.

Chapter 12
Celebrating our True Selves

In December, Christians celebrate Christmas, Jews celebrate Hanukah, and Buddhists continue to celebrate every day, which is what I prefer to do. All these holidays (holy days) are symbolic of the awe and miracles that abound everywhere, every day. The biggest miracle of all is that we are DIVINE, ETERNAL BEINGS. *We are living miracles!* Holidays are the material manifestations of the awe that is everywhere, in every thing. As Earth beings we tend to forget this as we move through each day, which is a major cause of the *illusion* of separation.

So why do we struggle some days (even holidays), while other days flow beautifully?

I've talked about this before but it bears repeating. The primary reason we have "good" or "bad" days is because of our perception and our thoughts. When the sun rises, one person sees it as a joyous event, allowing it to take their breath away, thanking the sun as they move into another day filled with that joy and thankfulness. The neighbor may grudgingly awaken, grumpily take her shower and routinely face the day as best she can. Another neighbor may simply stay in bed and vegetate, mourning the very day he was born. One more neighbor is unable to get out of bed due to some disability, yet he notices the sun rising and is thankful for the breath he is breathing and the bed to which he is confined.

Only our thoughts and perceptions make the difference. It is the same neutral sun, the same neutral day, the same neutral morning, but it's perceived differently by each person. If we are having negative thoughts we can shift them to positive ones, sometimes even *forcing* ourselves to think positively until, amazingly, our attitude shifts and the day gets better. Really—it's amazing! Sometimes we need help in this endeavor, especially if there has been long-term depression, abuse, crises, dysfunction or addiction. At these times we may choose to get help in the form of a healing of some type—Reiki, massage, hypnosis, psychotherapy, acupuncture, volunteerism, counseling, meditation, yoga, walking or any of the methods described in the Supplemental Information section. Any of these techniques (and others not mentioned) may help to switch your perceptions. *What creates the outcome of each moment is our thoughts and how we perceive that moment.*

Eckhart Tolle says the *primary cause of unhappiness is never the situation but our thoughts about it.* So when the sun comes up in *your* morning, be aware of the thoughts you are having and create a day of thankfulness and gratitude.

When Jamie came to me for severe depression, feelings of worthlessness, not believing in any type of higher power, and a sense she was always alone, I was still a fledgling hypnotherapist. As she lay on the table, I started the induction and she immediately went into a light trance state. Part of my induction has always been for the client to "find a light within them," which is the spark of the Divine, or our soul. However, on this day when I mentioned a light, Jamie contorted her face, saying adamantly, "There's nothing there."

I kept encouraging her, saying, "Oh, it's there somewhere, look deeper. Maybe it's hiding behind your liver or pancreas…" She quietly grumbled, but continued to look within for her light. After a few *long* minutes, her mouth shot open in amazement as she pointed to her solar plexus and said, "It's there! I see it!" We then proceeded with the regression as she reviewed her current life. As she looked at several events from a different, higher perspective, she noticed what she was creating. Even many years later, she sometimes slips back into the depressive thoughts, yet says she is able to move through them more quickly each time. She realizes that it is her thoughts that create her situations, she remembers her light, and knows that she is much more than her depression.

Our True Selves only have loving, peaceful thoughts and experiences. There is no judgment, anger, fear, or hatred—that is our ego. The more we become aware of our True Selves, the more we experience the awe, the miracles, the joy in every moment. Sometimes it can be tough—I remember my first "funk" (what I call my depressed state) lasted nearly three months. Three months of anger, sadness, depression, negative thoughts, lots of physical and emotional pain in the body. It was horrible. I would experience short reprieves during meditation or while seeing a client or friends, then slip back into the black pit of despair. What finally shifted? I *forced* myself to think differently. It is during this time that the phrase "fake it until you make it" came to me. So I began faking it, and lo and behold within a short period of time, "I" (my True Self) was BAAAACK!

Do whatever you need to do in order to remember who you really are. This book outlines many ways to get the help we need in order to switch our thoughts to ones that enhance our lives. Find what works for YOU, because what worked for me may not work for you, and what works for me tomorrow may be something different. Educate yourself on the many ways you can shift your thinking to the way YOU want it to be—then forge into that constant, perfect "now" moment and celebrate your True Self.

The Spirit-Directives for this chapter are:

Feeling

Feeling

This card indicates it's time to get more in touch with your feelings, your deepest, inner feelings. This card is asking you to feel the love and energy around and within you and become more aware of all this beautiful, loving, feeling energy. The higher consciousness that is coming to you will bring you to yet another level of consciousness. These deep feelings may come during meditation, during the dreamtime, or anytime. Be aware of the power of feeling.

You are What You Think

Isn't it interesting that Card #44 is an 8 and the last card in this deck, and the numerological value of the words is also an 8, so you have the energy of the empowerment of the 8 as well as the 44, double anchoring in all that you think into every part of your being. It's no accident that this card is the final card of this deck, for this is the final step toward your becoming self-empowered, in love with all things, especially yourself. This is truly a self-empowerment card, expecting you to now love yourself unconditionally in whatever you are thinking, doing and saying. Look at all the pictures on this one card—and see how this card brings you into a place of awareness, in every moment, of what you think—because that IS what you ARE in that

Birth, Death and the Afterlife

moment. This card is asking you to BE all you can be in every moment, and letting go of anything that is not serving that pure intention. It is a calling for you to BE IN LOVE! If you are not feeling positive thoughts, *FAKE IT UNTIL YOU MAKE IT—IT WORKS!* Focus on the pictures within the picture and place these in your conscious and unconscious mind. This is truly the most empowering card in this deck—BE IT! IT IS SO!

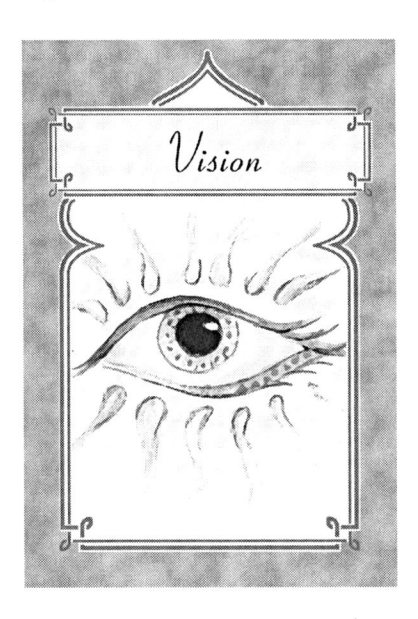

Vision

Your vision, or the way you see things, is changing. Let go of the old, and allow the new vision to be an integral part of who you are. Because this card came to you, you are being asked to shift your awareness, to change your vision. Focus on the eye and the expression—how the eye looks deeply into you. You are being asked to look deep within yourself and find ways to live fully today and every day. It's time to remove the veils, the things you have not seen before, and see beyond what is there.

Partnering

This card expresses the importance of working together in some way. This could be working with yourself more compassionately, cooperating with another person (life partner, child, friend, business partner). It reveals the need to be with others or more at peace with yourself.

Birth, Death and the Afterlife

Community

It may be time to form a community or become part of an existing community. This could be a spiritual community, a family community, or any other type that came to your mind. It is time for you to get out and become more involved with your community. This involvement will allow you to enhance who you are and help you be of service to this community. The outreaching hands and loving embrace in this picture signifies the benefits that come from being of service to others.

My Personal Experience

With my second Life Between Lives (LBL) session I had some of the usual questions, but my primary question was "Who Am I?" The intention was to have an experience of who I Am to share with you. The intention was *not* to show you *how* to have an experience like mine, or that my experience is any better or worse than someone else's—all our experiences are valid. Even when I explain my experience to you, each of you will perceive it differently and learn something different from it. My intention was to have something *to share with you*, and I was not disappointed!

There are a lot of books that talk about discovering who we really are—that we are not what we think we are. I facilitate seminars that help people discover that they are more than their skin, their flesh, their ego—we are *much more* than this. This life is temporary, and is only one part of our being-ness. Our spirit, the fluidity that we are, the energy, the life force, the consciousness that we are that is shared with everyone and every thing, is far more complex *and* far simpler than we think.

When I had my second LBL session I didn't go into a past life. I didn't have any need or desire at this time to go into a past life; however, I was open to remembering one if it was pertinent to my current life experience.

The following includes verbatim excerpts from my LBL. I chose to take out sections that were either personal or not appropriate to this chapter.

Madonna's 2nd LBL Experience
October 2010
Facilitator: Eric Christopher, MSMFT, CHT, Life Between Lives Spiritual Regressionist Dave Ellman Induction and other inductions including intermittent crystal bowl tones to assist in deepening my experience...

> EC: Indoor or outdoor scene? (supposedly going to a Past Life)
> MK: Whole bunch of colors. Swirling like a spiral. A ringing around the back of my head like when I meditate... now colors coming from right to left. Like a big purple head, expanding out, and the background is just... vague. A lot like... blue and red sky, purple and red. Almost like the Aurora Borealis. Feels really good. No sense of where I am. Feels like I'm starting to move because the colors are spreading now... not sure what... Colors have kind of stopped now—am really relaxed, but still not aware of any experience or feelings much. It feels like a void of sorts. The thought is that I'm in another chamber but not sure what that means. Different from where I was before. It is a more spiritual realm... I don't think it's Egypt... feels more spiritually oriented. The feeling is I come to this chamber a lot in order to quiet my mind and body. It feels like there

Birth, Death and the Afterlife

are other… not energies here, but other… it's so light, not energy even, more of just an essence or a being-ness that's here. Feels full yet not distinctive, other energies. Give me a sense of connection, or companion, connectedness, closeness, like when we do this there is something that happens, I don't know what… kind of like, I get the thought of drops in the lake create the lake. Trying not to analyze this… They are not images, but there is… different impressions, formed impressions. Not sure what the forms are. Not beings, just, instead of spiraling energy, they are like… then they move away, they're gone now… it was almost like silhouettes but not people or anything… just like sporadic silhouettes. Seeing if my guides can come in or somebody can come in to help here.

I've never really met my guides… The chamber is just a place to experience our oneness. It feels like I'm getting deeper and deeper into this oneness. I'm less able to talk. I'm going deeply into something like an abyss. I'm connecting deeper with the oneness this way, into the abyss.

I know something is happening because I'm very warm. No idea what this is. It's very nice. I have no body awareness at ALL… (I surrender to the experience…) It feels like a pulsing energy in front of me, but not in front of me. It is me, and it is everything… What I feel, what I sense, yes. The thought is, the answer to all the questions is yes! Do what you will. It's all yes. Whatever the desire is, focus on the desire and the feeling, and the oneness of all, and the answer is yes. It's just whatever the desire is… whatever—there are no wrong answers. And in my mind I'm remembering about how it's been getting more challenging to even speak (in front of groups) because they answer is always yes… so futile… just yes. There are no questions, there is just the answer, yes. Whatever it is. Then my conscious mind says, "yeah, but…. Where is my destiny then, what is that? Whatever I want. Ach… I want more direction…

EC: Do you mean you are guided intuitively by what it is you're kind of supposed to do, so if you even get the thought of doing a book or a program, then it's yes, of course, you're supposed to do that? You wouldn't have gotten the thought to do that unless that's what you're supposed to do?

MK: Yes. Yeah, that's even a better way to say it. It's just... we're here to be, and whatever that is, is right, and the thought is the answer, and if the thought changes, then that can be the answer again. There are no wrong or right answers or questions. It's all inspired through our thoughts.

EC: So the answers can change as the thoughts change?

MK: Yes. I'm kind of arguing with whatever is coming in because I want more...

EC: What do you want to say to it?

MK: It is me, too... this thought, this energy... It feels like one of these thoughts where a guru just talks around in circles and you don't understand it but it is clear on a deeper level... frustrating on a conscious level. Hard to articulate, or hard for my conscious self to accept... I want more clarification on the conscious level... for this body. The whole experience is just to be...

EC: And what is it about being that comes to you as about that experience? If the experience is about being, is there anything more you can share about that, If you can articulate it?

MK: The closest would be just experiencing... make even... doing, being. No pressure, no... just letting go and just allowing. Flow. (big sigh)

EC: Like being fully present and immerse yourself totally in whatever it is you're doing? It doesn't matter what you're doing as long as you're being while you're doing whatever you are doing?

MK: Yes. Later it will feel frustrating to hear this, but yes. It's frustrating because I don't feel like they're clear answers. I don't know that I'll get them because I don't feel there are any clear answers. I know that, too. The clearest answer is yes. Now... I'm just among energies that don't hardly... it's just total, TOTAL peace. Peacefulness... Just everything... sometimes when I come here I do get more images but not today, today it's all oneness... well... ask some of my questions.

EC: Who am I, really? (deep crystal bowl tone one more time...)

MK: Seeing and experiencing pulsing, a deep, purple heart about 10 inches away, then it comes closer in again, and now it's surrounded by… maybe more like a gold, I guess. It's beating with a rhythm and the message I got was "I'm experiencing who I am." And to be okay with that… this abyss with a connection to everything. And that more of this, or what it is, will come to me later… again. The heart represents love… just love… very subtle yet clear. Purple represents the Divine.

EC: Is it part of my highest purpose to finish the PhD and book and promote the I AM WOWED™ Program?

MK: Now the heart is coming to me instead of getting smaller. Yes, that is the message. It's what has been told to me, it's what I have experienced and pursued, why would I not continue and finish it? Yes. Of course, I should share it. That's why it came to me! That's why I went through the addictions. If it hadn't come to me I wasn't supposed to do it, but yes, it came to me. Yes, do it. Finish it, write it. Promote it. Yes.

EC: Is speaking and traveling part of my highest purpose?

MK: Always has been, always will be. I've done this in other forms before and there was reason to be fearful before, reasons to be afraid to speak in public and I still did it then, and now there is no reason to be afraid. It will be provided, yes. It feels like I'm getting images but I'm not. It feels… I'm getting the sensation of what the fears were before and why, and of course the things that happened then, I don't need to know that. That won't happen this time. There were other incarnations on Earth when it was more dangerous to speak in public in this manner. That won't happen in this incarnation. It was more dangerous before to go against the predominant thinking.

EC: Is it important to my life purpose to travel to Australia?

MK: I have a sense, relating to Australia, I don't even have a sense if I was incarnated on that continent or not, but there is something about… and someone has actually told me this but it feels so right… where I was more of an energy there, long before it was ever Australia. So it would be like… an integration if I chose to go. And the feeling is, but it's always yes, and you don't have to go along with the "yes" but it is yes. "I won't have to reincarnate again if I don't go" type of thing.

EC: So there's an energy available there if you choose to go?

MK: Yes, like a reconnection of energy available that would happen if I go, and if I don't, it's not... I guess this part I'm not sure if I'm making it up or not but it feels like if I don't go I can connect through energies like this... in other ways, if necessary.

EC: Is channeling or being a channel part of my life purpose?

MK: It feels like I could choose to channel but I will reach more people in other ways, it feels like I channel just when talking anyway, but I don't have to do the "official" type of channeling or to call myself a "channel"... it just happens anyway, when I talk.

EC: It just happens anyway. Is Australia part of your work to raise the consciousness of the planet, or it is more of a personal experience?

MK: Personal. Yes. Awakening at a deeper level personally, which will help all others, too... I may want to go there when I can promote the book but the "urgency" I feel to go there is more a personal urge.

EC: Okay, is there a best time to go?

MK: 2011 and I'm not sure if this is conscious interference but I felt like NOT 2012... to be here in 2012 and go either 2011 or 2013... and it's not THAT important, but it is just that I will be more called to be here in 2012 for other things. Maybe just to stay home. Huh! Whoa, my sinuses are really heavy... *something is happening right now*... my whole head is really, really heavy. Whoof... (Long pause)

EC: Just go into it if possible, and maybe there's a reason...

MK: Okay. I had that sense again that there isn't anybody or any specific guide... that I am... my guides, the entourage. I don't just have one guide, there are a whole group of them and they change from time to time. There are a lot of them to assist me with the work on this planet. They are pretty funny, too. They have a lot of patience. And it feels like they are just SOOO much a part of me that they don't... I don't see the distinction except with little color variations or pulses, and that has been nearly all my life...ever since

I was little. Once in awhile stronger energy would pop out if needed, an individual spirit or an ancestor or a relative or somebody that wanted to specifically give me a message, not a guide.

(A tremendous amount of static here… tape is nearly inaudible)

(Personal questions continued)

MK: I'm on the right track.

EC: Anything regarding career? On track or? (Nearly inaudible)

MK: I'm on the right track… doing the right things. Just continue the way you are. I get a lot of my guidance/information in talking with others, including clients. More people will be coming to me that will guide me on the path…

…I *swear* I have no body, yet *know* it's here with me.

EC: Is channeling something important for me to do?

MK: Not important – not now – although I am already getting information… just not the "typical" channeling way. (Totally inaudible—LOUD STATIC)

(More personal questions)

EC: What's the best way to help others and myself to live fully and remember their Divine essence?

MK: By my own experience of it, then share it. Experience it, live it, then share it… in the book, in the talks, in regular, daily life. Live it, share it.

EC: When I meditate, who are those that I call my Light Companions?

MK: Light Companions are about loving of self, higher consciousness connection, getting to the next level of consciousness, have the function of moving forward and cleaning out the old, letting go of needing approval. There was work that needed to be done on every part of me. So they helped with that during the "experiences." Now that is almost done, there will be another or other beings coming in to assist. They served a specific function and now there are other entities or guides or whatever companions coming in for the next "chapter" or level of being. We all channel most everything. Record and video self during meditation and while channeling. Have fun with it. They're glad I got the new car… I hear them applauding and laughing and feel their glee. Will need these wheels. White is perfect... *no accident... trust!* (Long pause) There is an energy of playfulness and lightness all around and within me... (huge static here... HUGE STATIC... LOUDER AND LOUDER...) I'm in the experience of the abyss more now... amazing... (LOUD STATIC... inaudible for a long time, then static finally diminishing a little here....)

EC: Last question is to clarify... what is my main purpose in this lifetime? Am I on track?

MK: They're showing me a scene and a track running through it, and even if I go on either road, it's all right. I take the right path. I am on the right path. Wherever I choose to go, it's right. I am always guided. (Horrendous static... then it stops abruptly.) One of those little pedaling things, with my face down, noticing the track, and it's getting lighter and lighter and lighter and moving faster, and going towards that light at the end of the tunnel. That's cool. I'm just absolutely, yes. Man.

(Personal question)...Even if I'm lonely, I'm never alone. I have more time with the Light Companions at home. There is more happening, more going to happen in Silver City over the next 5-10 years... more that will involve me and others... more reasons for why I am there. Interestingly, I'm starting to come back... is there another question?

EC: One last question: Is there anything else I should know that I have not asked about?

MK: I got a nice image of two people standing together, I'm healthy, my hands are up and I've got the peace sign on both, so it looks really good... but it's cartoonish, which means it's fun I'm told. Have fun, always. I forget that so often – to just have FUN. They're showing me, because yesterday one of my sisters and I took the day off and just goofed off. Such fun... so nice. I so seldom do that. Just have fun. Make it a priority, and everything else follows. I'm reminded of one more thing—I can't move my hands yet, but my hand is going to my heart and it's something I say at the talks and should continue to say this... *Whatever brings you to a place of peace, that's what you do.* They're kind of saying "peace is better than love or joy… it encompasses it all… it is all that. Peace is the word! I use the word love, and that works for me, but peace works for everyone. Yes.

EC: Why is peace better than love?

MK: Peace encompasses love. A lot of people have issue around the word love and it's abused, where peace is easier to be acceptable by everyone… we each have our own perception of peace. Chills are going all the way up and down my body when I say this… other people's perception… *whoa*, waves and waves of chills up and down my body… everywhere… of love have been skewed and the energy of it… not even sure about the numerology of the words… but everything about peace is universal. Love is not necessarily, even though it is in that. It's more…people can get angry with it. Even the phrase "loving yourself" to some may feel like ego, but "being at peace with yourself" is more acceptable by all beings… it's less threatening. Wow. I still like love, but peace encompasses love. Wow, those waves of chills. They're gone now, but it was very important… I'm to always have that in the talks.

EC: Anything else?

MK: Give me just a few more minutes of uninterrupted silence to see if there are any other messages before I come back.

EC: And have them fill you with that vibration of peace and playfulness. (One more deep tone from the crystal bowl)

MK: (Long pause and major static again, during the process of my "coming back"…. Then static abruptly stops when Eric begins the count-back.) You can bring me back now… (This is where, as he counts from 1 to 10 to bring me back to full consciousness, I have the experience of making myself into cookie dough. I was trying to figure out how to ground myself back with the "normal" energy… almost panicky about this because I wasn't sure how I'd "come back"… so I decide to make myself into dough then form myself into a cookie cutter shape that "popped out" like a cookie rises when it's baking. I had to figure out how to get my "form" back. More notes on this to follow.)

On the count of 10, a major spurt of static. Then nothing—all the static is gone.

End of LBL

⸻

Personal Notes

What is verbally expressed during a session, and what the person is experiencing, can be vastly different—not to mention the large percent of a regression that simply *cannot* be articulated. Because of this, I chose to share here, exactly what I recorded one hour after the above LBL experience.

"I was in a pool; I was the pool. There were no mountains around this pool, this was an abyss. A vast... vast... abyss... and I was a drop in the abyss... and I was the abyss. Yet I was very aware—as deep into the experience as I was, not having any awareness or any feeling in any part of my physical body except my lips that moved when I answered questions, to get something on tape that would explain this experience, if at all possible. I was not aware of any part of my body, or rather, I had a conscious awareness that I had no feeling in any other part of my body except my lips. So my comical mind created my lips as my ego. The lips were there to help me, metaphorically and actually, express what I was experiencing as articulately as possible.

So I am in the recliner, having a co-conscious awareness that I have no feeling in any part of my body except an awareness of my lips that are moving, cartoonishly, when answering any questions. I was a drop in the abyss and I was the abyss. It was peace. Serenity. Then I had my questions answered as the facilitator asked them. And my guidance was *right there with me*, it *was me*, yet sometimes I said... 'they say' but we were all one. I was them, they were me. And 'they' said, in response to any questions, 'the answer is always yes.' The answer is always yes? 'Yes,' is the response. 'If you have an inspiration for the thought, the answer is yes. You can always change your mind—the answer is always yes.'

When I was asked I knew, being a hypnotist myself, that I would be coming out of the experience soon—I knew I was done for now. The facilitator was beginning to count me back from 10 to 1 and I'm almost, though the word isn't really panic, but I was concerned, when he started counting from 10 to 1, my conscious thinking was 'How would I bring myself out of this abyss so I could explain it to others?' How can I do this? How can I do this so I remember and am able to explain to others?' And I noticed, rather sadly, that my eyes were tearing, knowing I was going to leave this experience soon. *I did not wish to come back.* Yet I needed to come back. I wanted to come back. It's my destiny to return and share this. All these thoughts going through my mind and my ego/lips moving cartoonishly as I answered another question. Then the facilitator counts from 10 to 1 while the thought comes to me, that I could be as rolled dough, and there was a cookie cutter shape coming and entering the presence that I was, and it was cutting my shape. It was quite cartoonish, the shape. I have never seen a cookie cutter shape like this!

And when he said '1, wide awake, alert, and feeling wonderful'— the cookie cutter shape jumped out of the rolled dough, took form. It took awhile for that cookie that was my human self, to shake off and put form and substance into the cookie shape. But I did. I shook myself. I was quite disoriented, quite dizzy, light headed. So I took time, he brought me some water to drink to ground me. I knew all that could happen. It felt like I needed to plump myself up, like a cookie when it bakes, so I shook myself and took some deep breaths. I kind of changed the shape because I couldn't hold that silly shape in my mind for very long. Then I was back. I was out of the abyss. I had an awareness (and still do) of the abyss, that it was still there. I continue to have the thought of it, yet I was the cookie shape, the human formed shape, that had ego again, and had a different type of consciousness than I had just enjoyed."

Summary

I have had similar experiences during some of my meditations with an energy I call the "Light Companions," yet during meditation I have not been able to respond to any of my conscious-world questions. With a qualified LBL facilitator asking the questions for me while in the superconscious state, I was able to respond, at least somewhat audibly, to the questions he asked. It was amazing, even after I had been doing this work for nearly 20 years. I now know and understand and *remember who I really am!* I am certain that my understanding of this will change as I evolve, yet at our core, we are all one, united in peace and love. Our True Selves are all connected and one with our Creator. *The path to all healing is peace and love.*

Chapter 13
Courageous New Beginnings • Be In Love

The one constant is change. We've heard this over and over again, and still we can be resistant. As we choose to release the old to make space for the new, many *opportunities* arise. We may be asked to let go of patterns or habits that have been a part of how we identify ourselves, as in the case study below. We may be challenged to wait beyond what we feel is adequate time for something to manifest, yet the Law of Gender states that everything we create has an incubation period. We may get a clear message to move to a new location, start a business, leave a partner, or write a book—anything that challenges us to think differently or move out of our comfort zone. We may feel an urgency to clear out all excess in our home, or to finish up a creative project. All these things take courage and patience, because although we may have received very clear guidance that we are to move, that move may not be for a few months or years—and we may have a very busy schedule. We may clearly know that we are to leave a partner, yet there seem to be roadblocks to that separation, which can be a sign that the timing may not be right.

The primary way to know if something is in accordance with our soul's path is to listen to our deepest, most inner voice, our intuition. If progress is blocked, relook at the situation and ask for more signs, more information, related to your situation. If you feel fear or anger around the choice you made, keep questioning, releasing, and processing that decision. The more we are able to let go and let God, the easier life gets.

"Sharon" and I have shared friendship for many years. Recently, on a trip to her hometown, she and her ex-husband rekindled their love. She moved back to be with him. When she first decided to do this, she absolutely *knew* it was the right decision. She confided that she felt this from deep within her gut, and that she was confident in her decision to return to her hometown.

However, before moving, she found herself questioning her decision. Before her decision to move she had been blocked from any type of income in her current situation, was having health challenges, friends were changing, and this confused her. She felt torn—excited that she and her ex were rekindling their relationship, yet wondering why she would leave a place she loved so much—vacillating back and forth—until we met one evening to chat. I shared that, based on what I knew, when something feels this *certain in your gut (intuition)* yet *confusing in your head (ego)*, often it is a soul contract. I said that perhaps, if this was indeed part of her soul's contract, she may be *blocking herself* from living comfortably in her current situation in order to fulfill her contract and return to her hometown. I suggested that maybe it was only her *perceptions* that were changing in order to make the move easier. Waves of tingling rushed up and down my body as I said this (my indication that truth was being spoken). She affirmed that it felt right as well. Her feelings of excitement and anticipation immediately returned.

Even though *we make these contracts with ourselves* with the assistance of our guides, *we still have free will*, and can change our minds once we incarnate. However, when we are not on target with our contract, life is often more chaotic, disruptive and difficult than when we are "flowing with the go."

When I heard voices that told me to move to Silver City, NM, (yes, it was actually an *entourage* of *very loud* voices!) it was exciting at first. I *knew* it was right, yet questioned the WHY of it. Actually, I still question the WHY from time to time, especially when I miss my family and friends in Minnesota. However, from the time when I first heard the voices to when I actually purchased a home here, there were at least a hundred physical signs that validated this move. The first time I visited Silver City, it felt familiar and I knew, beyond a shadow of a doubt that I was supposed to live here. When something pulls us this strongly and when everything flows with the follow through, it is a soul's contract—something we planned to do in the interlife that is an integral part of our upcoming incarnation.

As you have read in the previous chapters, many of us choose some

Birth, Death and the Afterlife

extremely challenging life experiences. When we are oblivious to these challenges, life can be more difficult. It helps immensely to know consciously at least some of what our Divine Self has designed. It helps immeasurably to *remember* that part of ourselves that is not of the ego, in order to commit to our contracts and be courageous when necessary.

The most succinct Spirit-Directives to end this chapter (and the 24th week of the I AM WOWED™ Program) are:

Patience

Something you have been waiting for—perhaps for a long time—is going to happen, will be manifesting. Patience is still required towards the end result of the project or endeavor, but this card clearly indicates it will happen in Divine Timing, and if it is for your Highest Good. Look at the picture and hold the image of the seedling in your mind. Notice how the sun, the Earth, the sky—everything—is supporting that seed in its growth. And the seedling trusts that the sun, Earth, and sky will continue to support it until it has reached its goal. Hold this picture firmly in your mind.

It's All Good

Your Spirit Helpers are asking you to change your attitude just a little. It may mean there is a need for you, specifically today, to change your attitude to one of gratitude and say over and over again, "It's all good," until you finally get it, because IT IS ALL GOOD! This card is asking you to see every experience, even the challenging ones, as good—they teach you. A mistake is an experience from which we do not learn—every experience is good <u>when we learn from it</u>. This card is asking you to see the world and all beings through different eyes. In your mind, hold the world and all of creation in your hands and see it all as good. Do this over and over again, until you get it. Everything and everyone in our life is a teacher, and has a purpose. It's all good.

Set a Foundation

(Yes, for the first *and* last weeks of the program! Resetting the foundation)

You are being asked to plant roots in some thing or a project you have started, or begin a project you may have been putting off—JUST DO IT. The pyramids of Egypt represent a very firm foundation that has been around for a LONG time—focus on the steadfast energy of those pyramids—how firm they are anchored into Mother Earth, and relate this to your own life, to where you are being called to set a foundation, to begin a book, to create a center, to follow through and be the leader you are. Now is the time to take one step forward into this new beginning.

Freedom From

There is an aspect of your life that is asking you to choose *freedom from*. This could be an addiction, a block, a distraction, a partner, someone who is no longer a friend, a relationship that is no longer working, an area where you live that is no longer right for you, or anything that could be holding you back from living fully. When meditating on the card, notice the cocoon—how the butterfly is slowly emerging into a different version of itself. It shows freedom from the case it was originally in; freedom from the one thing that held it back; free to be. This card indicates it's time to choose freedom from at least one thing in your life that is holding you back.

Commit (to yourself)

It's time for you to come into your power—to accept and commit to your highest calling. The border on this card is purple, which represents the higher self, the higher consciousness. This means for you to commit! Never forget to commit to yourself and anything that will help you to move into the next level of consciousness, your Higher Self, or anything that simply feels right and appropriate for you.

Case Study

As the following Case Study shows, we are much more than anything we see visually. When "William" presented for a regression session, he simply wanted to alleviate some of his worries. He said he was well known for his ability to worry about everything and anything for as long as he could remember, and that he had the hair loss (and sense of humor!) to prove it. He gave me a list of questions he wanted answered. Instead of experiencing a past life, he was asking for Spirit Guidance, without any expectations about the outcome.

I proceeded to assist him in achieving a deep, altered state and very quickly he began gently shaking and twitching. His facial expression went from mildly distorted and questioning, to peaceful and calm—well beyond the normal peace and calm of a relaxed state of being. Tears welled in my eyes and my voice cracked slightly as I felt the energy shift once again, from peace and calm to a feeling of unconditional love and acceptance. I smiled to myself in anticipation of what was most probably unfolding. He chuckled a bit when I dutifully proceeded to ask the questions he brought to the intake, and although I expected he was probably far beyond answering any of these simple, Earth-experience inquiries, after some very, very long pauses, he furthered his Creator/God-connection and embraced the entire experience. (I have learned that when a client returns to the 3-D Earth plane energy, they eventually will still want their questions answered, even though those same questions seemed insignificant or trite during the experience, where everything is perfect.)

After the session, when he was finally able to come to some semblance of "normalcy," William respectfully stated, "I am forever changed. My life will never be the same."
The following is the exact transcript of his session:

Note: Client presented as simply wanting to understand his current life more. He talked of being a perpetual worrier with the hair loss to prove it. He had a few questions he wanted to ask, but was okay with whatever happened.

During the induction I used the suggestion that he could simply "change his vibration" in order to achieve an even deeper state of unconsciousness. With many clients I have found that this suggestion is more likely to guide them into a Creator/God-connection than when only progressive relaxation techniques are used, and that using progressive relaxation with the suggestion of a tunnel with a light at the end of it is *usually* more suggestive of a past life memory. Suggesting that the client "simply needs to change their vibration" has helped facilitate more profound spirit guidance and super conscious (Creator/God-connection) sessions.

> MK: You are now at the light at the end of the tunnel. You are now in a past life or experience that will help you understand your current life more clearly. What are you aware of?

Birth, Death and the Afterlife

W: I don't... I don't... I'm just... I don't think I'm completely in... I'm in a spot here. I'm not aware of anything going on.

MK: Okay. Let's go a little deeper. just raise your vibration. I'm going to gently tap your wrist, and you go deeper... and deeper... and deeper... raising your vibration, deeper relaxed... You are in the experience. All that will happen now is you will just raise your vibration so you can be aware of where you are at, and who you are, and all that this experience is to tell you. Deeper and deeper. Everything is becoming clearer. You can lift the mist... lift any fog... just let go... just let go... What are you aware of? (Dog barks in background).

W: I just... I heard that dog [in the background] and I don't seem to be able to open anything, ah, to sort of see or sense anything. It's almost like a block of some sort. When I got to the end of the tunnel, it just almost felt like I was kind of enclosed by a kind of darkness and I can't sort of get beyond that.

MK: Okay. Maybe that is where you are in the past life. I don't know. That may be part of the experience. See if you can move from that. Do you have an awareness of yourself in Spirit, in the darkness?

W: I don't think so.

MK: Just take some nice, deep breaths then... we don't need to do a tunnel... and really, everything there is at a different consciousness level. Everything is really right here—we need to go nowhere. Just raise your vibration and breath... and go deeper into relaxation... that way... good... relaxing deeper... just feeling yourself getting lighter and lighter... and higher vibration... just feeling free... You've done this before, you can do it again... now... just feel yourself, wonderfully relaxed... (more of the same for about one minute). Where does it feel like where you are at?

W: I'm completely relaxed... I just... I just feel... I'm completely, completely relaxed, but I'm not, I don't... I almost don't sense anything.

MK: Is it... some people actually go into a mist or a black mist, like a void...

W: It is almost like that.

MK: Well, the void is actually a place. It is a place… and it usually is right before people get—either images—they can either move out of it, or images come to them. It's almost like a stage, where you can maybe part the curtains and move into something. It's a staging ground. I'm just going to be silent for a moment, and you take yourself deeper and see what you need to do in order to move from that and get information. It may be that you don't need to go into a past life, and if that's the case there will be spirits or guides that will come to you, and I'll just ask some questions. But you just take your own time now, breathing deeper, because you're really relaxed… It's just a matter of allowing the presence to come to you, or the information to come to you, or the feelings, or pictures… just allow it… enjoy the experience… deep relaxation (Long pause) And now I'm going to count from one to three and when I say three you will be in an experience that will help you answer some of your questions… 1-2-3…. What are you aware of?

W: I… I… I'm kind of alone. I had seen myself in a huge field kind of thing, only it was … it was… there was no field there. It's almost like I was completely by myself with almost no… the beginning of mankind almost. And I had climbed to the top of a green hill or mountain, and I wanted to find other people to be with him, to see what was happening, and if they could help me, and I think I found like a town, but when I got to the edge of it, I never saw it well, and then I couldn't… I couldn't become part of it, or couldn't get to it, so I feel like I'm (sigh), I'm not uncomfortable, but I'm just in a place where I find myself kind of by myself and not knowing which way to go or how to get to other people.

MK: See if there is another road there, or a bright light, or something that can guide you to where to go.

W: Trying to get into… there were like trees and a woods, and… trying to get into the woods and I'm sort of there, but I'm still (sigh) I'm not getting… I haven't seen anybody and I haven't… I almost don't even know. If there are any people around, I'm in a very lush place, with plants and trees, but I don't… I'm not having any luck finding anybody.

MK: Are you male or female?
W: I think a male, but... I don't know that I have a body...
MK: Okay.
W: I'm just kind of... when I went up that hill I realized I didn't even need to walk up that hill, I just, I just was at the top of the hill. And I just kind of came down to the woods and I saw the woods, I don't have a sense of any... I don't have to walk to do that.
MK: Does it feel like you are kind of in spirit with who you are now?
W: Yes.
MK: Okay. Maybe... I don't know, but are you just checking out some places?
W: I don't... I don't see any... I think I'm sort of before—before there were people.
MK: Okay.
W: And I hear some noises that are kind of a little bit like thunder... and lightening, and I see that... I see the... the... the Earth, but there's no... there's no and I'm trying to look and I can move around a little bit, but I'm not seeing anything... there's no actual civilization, and I feel like I am able to just kind of float around... around and see things. I did..there were some animals earlier, but I'm not seeing any animals here yet... but I do see it's all very green, and lush.
MK: Do you hear other energies around you, other beings, like you are?
W: Uhm... no, I don't think so. No, I think I'm (sigh)... I think I'm by myself, and all right with that, I'm not uncomfortable, I'm just not meeting up with anybody.
MK: Okay, why don't you just... let go of any expectations, and just enjoy whatever this experience is. Just kind of flit around, or whatever you're doing, until something or some energies come in, or you find some people, or you discover what this is all about, because right now, neither of us really knows what this is about. So it might just be about having an experience of being in spirit, and being free. I don't know.
W: That's kind of how it... kind of how it... (voice gets more slurred

and slower)… kind of how it feels, and I'm just almost… just almost… (sigh) I'm almost without a care. I'm just there, and it's okay. I don't have any needs. Uhm…

MK: Do you get a sense of who you really are, that this is your spirit? If there's no physical body, it's just…

W: I think… I think… I do… I think it probably is my spirit or something. And there's just no… I'm fine, and I guess I'm totally carefree, but I don't… I don't… (sigh)…it's as if I don't need anything or even need to worry about anything. I just, and when you asked me to go someplace I could, but I just seem to be perfectly happy, just no place!

MK: That certainly doesn't fit with the person who is you in this life!

W: No, it doesn't! (smiling, then chuckling)… No, it…

MK: So, our spirit has a kind of humorous way of showing us different scenarios. So, as much as you can, just enjoy this, and see where it leads you. My guess is, this isn't a suggestion, but my thought is that there may be other beings that will come around or we may ask some questions here soon, but just really enjoy this feeling. I think your higher consciousness really did want to experience this, because you will always remember this. So just have fun with it… yeah… (LONG pause)

W: (Tears rolling down cheeks, smiling, peaceful expression on face, then some body twitching, more tears, then peaceful expression again…)

MK: What's happening?

W: (Sigh)… (nearly unable to speak) I didn't know I was still where I was, but I was just totally, TOTALLY overcome or surrounded with… with just total spirits or power. And I was just made to realize… that even if I seem or think that I'm alone, I'm totally surrounded by things that are… that are just completely, completely… oh, powerful and overwhelming. And it's like… it's like, it's like… I was sort of a spirit and couldn't… didn't need to move around, and then I just (deep sigh)… I realized I'm completely, COMPLETELY surrounded by… like, by every… by complete, by complete power

and spirits and understanding that I didn't visualize at all, but it was almost like just a black wall of things that, that came to me from the sky and ..and even the whole universe just… just filled with… was crowded with just… almost just a wall of spirits that were there, and it was not at all uncomfortable or scary or anything of that sort, it was just that… ah… it's just like I realized that I was thinking I was alone and in a sense I am alone, but I'm also a part of just an overwhelming control of spirits everywhere that just came just immediately, just even though they weren't ..there was nothing to see, they were all right there, just saying that… and of course there was no language, they were just there, saying that… saying there is so much more that we will never, never understand but it's just part of this world of (sigh)… you could call it God, I don't mean it as God, but I just, there's a whole world, there is more… way more than the world, just everywhere is just filled with power and spirits, and at the moment I'm not part of them and yet I am part of them, and they're just saying that I'm perfectly content and happy and part of something that is so much larger that I don't need to worry about being… being in any way concerned about what I do. It's just – I'm just part of something that's… even though I'm by myself now, the power and presence of every… of all this energy around me makes me look kind of… (laughing) kind of puny!
MK: Wow. Well, I'd like you to experience this some more… so I will be silent again, and you will experience this… just immerse yourself in this, ok? This is who you really are… this is the gift for today. And imagine it and just let it talk to you telepathically, and answer some of your questions. I may not even need to ask them… so I'll be silent and I'll ask you questions later. Just experience… (Long pause)
W: (Very peaceful look on face, some body twitching again, tears) I think… I think it's just, I think I've just been kind of made to believe that everything I was worried about is just so… meaningless, that it was kind of humorous because I worried about things that have essentially no significance in the scope of things, and I… I just have a feeling that, at least for the moment that everything…

I'm just realizing that my little concerns just don't… don't amount to anything! That I just (sigh) probably should just continue doing what I am doing and in the end, it's going to… things are, there is so much beyond me, that it's kind of pointless to be worried about things. Things will happen that are so far beyond me that my concerns and my selfishness, actually, is just kind of, it is humorous because in the scope of things, whatever happens to me is totally meaningless anyhow – and I might as well just… I mean, in the scope of things it just doesn't amount to… literally, like I'm like some grain of sand on a beach someplace, trying to worry about what in the hell I'm supposed to be doing! (laughing) It doesn't make much sense! (laughing)

MK: Is it also like everything will just unfold, then? If you are a grain of sand, then… you just go along with whatever…?

W: I think I'll just, you know, if the current wants to sweep me out to sea, I'll look at the sea fish and everything and have a good time! Because I feel like I've been sort of put in my place, and far to my advantage because I don't HAVE to worry about these things!

MK: Yeah. You just are part of the whole, and "go with the flow" kind of thing?

W: Yeah. Humph. Yeah.

MK: Well, I think you should have more of this experience then, because you may as well, to really confirm, so you don't think you are just making this up, because you can't make this up!

W: No, I don't think I made this up! (laughing)

MK: I know, and I've had similar, and have wanted to be in it for awhile, so… this is really, and I don't mean to suggest this, but that you are in the presence of God.

W: I think I am. (sobbing) I think I am!

MK: So just enjoy this, okay? And remember… I will be silent again. Just experience… (Short pause)

W: I don't… I don't think there's anymore to experience because I think that I've… it's almost as if God… when you said that, that God had come just to say that it IS, that I don't have to be concerned about it, and I think I've learned a huge lesson. I don't… I think that I GOT it! I don't think that I can feel anymore positive about it! (Laughs)

MK: Okay! I'm going to suggest that you will remember this always, which I know you will, but to remember it in every cell of your being, and now you see who that being is, that you are far more... far more than you ever thought. Congratulations!

W: Thank you!

MK: Welcome home!

W: Thank you very much!

MK: I'm going to gently call you back now, knowing that you really are this, no matter whether you are in a trance or whenever, this is who you really are... and you will always remember this, and it will help you in every moment of your being-ness. Now, only as in your human form, but as you go onward, and this experience has changed everything now... (count back).

End of PLR

Madonna J. Kettler, PhD

<u>Summary</u>

While in his regression experience, William couldn't have cared less about whether he should move to a new location, or if he was on track with his life purpose, or whether to pay for another year of college—he "knew" it was all good, all in Divine Order, and that all that mattered was his remembering who he really was.

When we allow ourselves to achieve such a profoundly deep trance state, either through meditation, hypnosis, dance, breath, walks in nature, etc., our lives change. When we remember who we really are—LOVE—*everything* changes.

William's session is a perfect example of the Spirit-Directives listed above, and I feel are the perfect inspiration for the final two weeks of the Program. When we have the experience of our Divine Self, a Creator/God-connection, we know we have whatever we need in order to complete the rest of our Earth life. We are able to maintain a more constant ability to live in the moment and adjust to any *opportunity* that may come into our experience. We are like the lion in the Wizard of Oz—courageous beyond anything we have consciously remembered. As the rest of William's life on Earth is lived, he may again be drawn into the chaos and drama, yet as he himself said during the session, "I am forever changed. My life will never be the same."

Be courageous in your life. Commit to a life of adventure, since change happens anyway. Break through your safety net and choose freedom from anything that could be holding you back from living fully and consciously. This is not always the easiest or most direct route, but it is worth it. You are worth it. You are WORTHY OF WHATEVER EMPOWERMENT DESIRED!

Chapter 14
Love Research

Ode to the Old Me
by Madonna J. Kettler

Loves lost, not forgotten—now released.
Pain suffered, held onto—now released.
Worry and guilt overwhelmed me—now love and peace engulf my life.
Allowing people to "reduce" me—no longer works.
Boundaries once non-existent—now healthy and productive.
Habits that saddened me—left behind, no longer needed.
Beliefs that kept me rigid, controlled—blown
away in a gesture of freedom.
Fears of death, pain, suffering or confrontation—
nearly gone, replaced with love.
Devotion to myself. No matter what.
Loving myself. No matter what.
Honoring my Body, Mind, and Spirit. No matter what.
Always moving forward.
Always *in love*—with All That Is.
Always *in love*—with my self and my Self.
Being in Love—the only way for ME!

Over the past 20 years while seeing clients for clinical transpersonal self-hypnosis, regression therapy and Life Between Lives spiritual regression as well as Hands-on and Reiki healings and intuitive readings, it has been proven to me, over and over again, that the client will have a far better outcome when they come to an *acceptance of what is*. This includes accepting themselves for who they are in that moment. It includes loving themselves as their Creator loves them, and it includes having confidence in who they are because they *remember who they really are*.

In Chapters 2 through 13 you have read stories and case studies that show nearly instantaneous healing outcomes. These are only a handful of the clients with whom I have had the privilege of working who have released fears and anger, overcome horrendous obstacles, then moved into a place of peace, joy, and excitement for life *as it is*. In this chapter you will also see the results of a controlled double-blind study that I conducted with 44 volunteer participants that further validates the positive results—including the tangible reward of physical weight loss—from shifting into a positive place of Being.

When we can come to remember we are spiritual beings *first*, when we recognize our Soul Self, our Divine Self—when we know and understand that we are God—that we are a part of the Divine—part of our Creator—*everything* works better. Our mind comes into an acceptance of ourselves in every moment, *as we are* in that moment, and from that we discover we are worthy of whatever we may desire. Then we are willing and able to take steps to accommodate that worthiness and to begin living more fully.

My intention for the following research was to show that through the practice of regression therapy **in addition to** *clinical hypnosis, primarily focused on loving themselves unconditionally, people can release weight even more easily and effectively than with clinical self-hypnosis alone.*

The guidelines for the participants in the "Love Research" were as follows:

Each participant needed to be:

- Female between the ages of 25-60
- 30 pounds overweight or more
- Have had this weight on for over one year
- In average health (no major illness)

All the volunteers received a self-hypnosis CD that focused on weight release and loving themselves. In accordance with controlled double-blind study methods, half of the volunteers also randomly received a regression CD that guided them to a memory (conscious or unconscious) of when they were loved unconditionally.

The participants were required to agree to the following:

- Listen to a self-hypnosis CD (provided to them) daily for 28 days
- Walk briskly or do 20 minutes of some sort of movement a minimum of four times weekly
- Keep a journal and commit to writing a minimum of three sentences daily.

Each person signed a Consent and Release form and was given a checklist and journal sheet to keep track of her progress.

Initially, there were 44 volunteer participants. Five participants dropped out of the study before completion because of personal/family issues that arose. When the final/exit questionnaire was emailed, 22 responded. Seventy-five per cent of the 22 respondents had received the second (regression) CD. The following results were compiled using the information gathered from these 22 respondents.

The participants were not told that this was a double-blind study, but only that it was for research relating to a program I had designed to help people release weight. The official I AM WOWED™ Program was neither completed nor available for the participants. The Be In Love Oracle Deck and this book also were not yet available. I would like to note that even more significant positive results are being reported after participating in the "official" program.

After 28 days of this program, participants experienced an average weight loss of 3.2 lbs. The subjects gave positive feedback on their weight loss and their experience with the program in general.

Below are some of the responses:

- I feel more at ease with myself, more loved and more loving.

- I became aware of my distractions and my newfound ability to "cancel/clear" any self-sabotaging talk.
- I am more honest and forgiving of myself.
- I liked committing to myself and having support, though would like to have more support either through weekly groups or online.
- I liked the feeling of losing 4 pounds!
- I am more empowered.
- I liked the CDs and daily walks.
- I am more comfortable in my own skin.
- My health improved overall.
- I became aware of my resistance, learned to comfort myself, and discovered I used food to do that. I released a lot of anger.
- I have realized how hard I am on myself and am looking at my core beliefs.
- I noticed positive behavioral changes relating to food and exercise.
- It was fun and made me feel good about myself.
- I actually began to *enjoy* walking regularly, and missed it if I didn't walk!
- I learned self-love is key to any intention.
- Every time I do it (for four or six weeks each time) life just gets better and better!
- It is holistic and positive.
- I liked committing to a daily program of listening, processing, and walking. It changed my life for the better.
- I was surprised that I *wanted* to start it again with a different specific goal in mind!

And finally, one of the most profound statements:

- I got a surprise benefit from the healing suggestions on the CD. Lung nodes were discovered in May, so I used the healing ribbons of light you channeled on your CD, and focused my attention on them. My 3-month CT scan taken during week 3 of my 28 days revealed no growth—great news! The other benefit was being conscious of my thinking and using the cancel/clear technique. While my interior mind is usually clear and uncluttered, it was helpful to deal with what appeared immediately—especially those untruths we believe from others.

Most participants wanted more. They wanted more weeks of the program, more support, both in weekly classes and/or online. They suggested having a variety of CDs to choose from, and the ability to connect with others who had taken the program.

Before I set up the guidelines for this research, I was sincerely questioning whether or not to go through with a project that seemed a bit more than I could handle. In a moment of intense doubt I asked the Universe, "Am I *really* supposed to go forward with this program? And if so, please give me a clear sign, *right away!*"

I didn't have to wait long. Immediately after making this request (demand), I went into a deep meditative state. Fifteen minutes into the meditation, a friend I had not heard from since moving to New Mexico called me. She had been one of the very first participants in the program and she said she just *had to call me right now* to share how very much the program had helped her. She also said if there was anything she could do to help promote it, to let her know. I told her she had done just that!

The completed program, many more satisfied participants, and *this very book* are the result of that enthusiastic affirmation.

Chapter 15

The I AM WOWED™ Program

The I AM WOWED™ (I AM Worthy of Whatever Empowerment Desired) Program is a four to twenty-four week program designed to help you permanently release any distractions, addictions, fears or blocks that are preventing you from living fully and consciously. Examples of this would include food/eating, worry, lack of self-confidence, alcohol/drugs, gaming, gambling, smoking, fears, unworthiness, anger, work, TV, abuse, codependency, perfectionism, negativity, judgment, etc. It can also help you, depending upon where you are in your life, go to the next level of awareness; for instance, it can help you open up psychically, remove creative blocks, and enhance any part of your life you feel could be improved, *all the while remembering you are always loved unconditionally—no matter what!*

This comprehensive, empowering program is based in hypnosis and hypnotherapy, yet throughout the program you are introduced to various other holistic modalities such as yoga, journaling, fitness, massage, exercise, nutrition, acupuncture, art and healing—which can assist you in developing a program that works specifically for you, based upon your goals and intentions, likes and dislikes. We all have specific needs and preferences, and what works for one person may not work for another. Weekly inspirational lessons with online support lead us closer to our ultimate dreams, until we create a more fulfilled life of our design.

To begin, there are three primary commitments you make *to yourself*. You commit to:

1) Listening to a self-hypnosis CD a minimum of four times a

week until you listen to each CD a total of 28 times. (The list of available CDs on my website.)
2) Some type of fitness and/or movement (yoga, walking, strength training, Pilates) for a minimum of 20 minutes four times a week, and,
3) Journaling *at least* three sentences daily.

If you are meeting in a group setting (certified facilitators are listed on my website), different holistic modalities that can optimize your program will be discussed in class. Because of our uniqueness, these additional supportive practices can help facilitate our personal process faster. For instance, it is proven that acupuncture can assist with trying to quit smoking or for appetite suppression, so it would be a likely adjunct to the program, if that is your goal. If your budget allows, try one of these modalities from time to time to see how it works for you. I suggest you use your intuition to find what interests you. The program is all about self-empowerment and self-acceptance. When we realize we are worthy of some of these little "extras," our attitude toward ourselves, and life in general, can be enhanced exponentially.

There is a companion workbook that has everything you need to begin the I AM WOWED™ Program, including a daily journal, weekly checklist with thought-provoking questions, and positive thoughts and inspirations. It also includes several forms including a Letter of Intent and Commitment, a sample Commitment Ceremony, CDs Selection List, Potential Healing Modalities, Possible Distractions/Addictions/Blocks/Fears List, and more. If you wish to enhance your life without the workbook, this book may be sufficient for your needs—simply reread one chapter (2 through 13) every two weeks, follow the suggestions of the Spirit-Directives included in that chapter, and agree to the three primary commitments listed above. If you do not choose to purchase the workbook, you will want to purchase a notebook for your daily journaling; however, for your ultimate success, the workbook is highly recommended. Because it includes everything necessary for the program (with the exception of purchasing a CD of your choice), it keeps you on task and eliminates any reason (excuse?) you may have to postpone moving forward!

There is also a companion *Be In Love* Oracle Deck that offers daily guidance, inspirations and affirmations that can assist you in maintaining your focus and staying on track with your goals throughout the program. The forty-four cards in this deck are the forty-four Spirit-Directives described throughout this book. The oracle deck is a fun and helpful self-empowerment tool even if you are not in the program! To learn more about this oracle deck or how to use any deck, go to: http://www.youtube.com/watch?v=W4w3uERCWVM

I have never personally stayed with the "official" program for more than eight weeks at a time. However, the basics (movement, journaling, and meditation) have become a regular part of my life. Many people have done it for four to eight weeks, taken a short break, then committed again, but starting with week nine instead of repeating the first eight weeks. How you decide to work *your* program is entirely up to you, but it works best *when you are committed to yourself.* You can enjoy the program as many times as you desire and it will be different every time. Each time, something amazing happens: you begin seeing things differently, living more easily, and loving yourself and others naturally and unconditionally. It has become my Tao (way) of living.

If you choose to continue with the program after the initial four weeks, it is highly recommended that you chart your progress from the first four weeks. It will be much easier the second time around, and beneficial to a highly successful outcome. After week four, or after you have listened to the first CD for at least 28 times, you will want to listen to a different CD based upon your particular intentions.

So, what is considered a successful outcome? This will be different for each person, each time they do the program. As the research in Chapter 14 shows, this has worked for many people by assisting them toward a deeper understanding of who they really are. When we start to remember our Divine Self, when we know we are a part of something much bigger, we begin to treat ourselves and others differently—with respect and non-judgment. We begin to truly love ourselves from the inside out. Not in an egoic way, but the way our Creator loves us—unconditionally. This, to me, is a successful outcome.

Throughout the program, as you listen to different CDs, you change your beliefs to ones that really work for *you*. Through the process of repetition, reaffirming things we do not necessarily believe when relating to ourselves, that repetition leads to beliefs we CHOOSE to accept. Remember the Three Levels of Thought described in Chapter 4? In relation to this program, while in the First Level of Thought, a state we would usually classify as an "average" state of being, we listen to TV, see advertisements, and hear political officials and we think, "this doesn't seem right with what I'm feeling…" Yet we continue to listen and often times accept what is being said, because, with the constant inundation of this type of propaganda, it seems easier to accept the fear-based thinking instead of staying with our first, inner thought. At the other end of the spectrum, the Third Level of Thought, we find the unconscious self that knows beyond a shadow of a doubt that we are Divine, and that this "stuff" being thrown at us is not true. In between these two levels of thought, the Second Level, is the "Yeah, but" level, (ego) that continually argues with what is *said* to be right and what we *know* to be right. What self-hypnosis and this program do, is balance the conscious will—with the unconscious knowing—creating a balanced process of be-ing that allows us to live peacefully. It's that simple. The other holistic processes introduced in the Supplemental Information section of this book can assist in the overall success, but the initial research used self-hypnosis, hypnotic regression, movement, and journaling in order to replace any negative thoughts or fears with positive thoughts that affirm our Divinity and our worthiness.

Over the past twenty-plus years, the primary complaint clients and students present with when they come into my office has been some version of "I have never felt that I am enough." We are constantly inundated with messages that we are not good enough, tall enough, thin enough, smart enough, fit enough, young enough, pretty enough, creative enough, strong enough… and this program reframes or rescripts those negative, unworthy thoughts into positive, self-affirming beliefs.

The first I AM WOWED™ Program had three participants. It was a six week program, and the guidelines were the same as they are now, only there was no workbook, and we each used our own journal. We met weekly to discuss where we were in relation to our intentions. One student set the intention of increasing her client base by 25%, to accept abundance into her life and improve her self-confidence. The second student wanted to release a creative block that had plagued her for many months. The third person wanted to get healthier and like herself more. A few weeks after the program concluded, the first student moved to a studio space three times larger than the one she had occupied and her business has flourished ever since. The artist released the blocks to her creativity and since the program has not only had many articles published in major art journals, but her art has been on the cover of one, and she in the process of writing her own art book. The third created a health regime that has stayed with her to this day. She is fitter than she has ever been, and she continues to cherish herself and her life more every day. Two of the students primarily released fears and blocks, while the third student focused on increasing her sense of worthiness. After these positive results, I was determined and guided to build an even better program—and the current official, I AM WOWED™ program is the result.

It has been proven scientifically that anything we do or say that brings us to a place of peace, helps the whole. If I am feeling rage or fear, say on a scale of 6 (which thankfully seldom happens), and I bring it down only 2 notches, to 4, it helps the whole. If I am in a blissful and peaceful place as I am while meditating or walking in nature, that also affects the whole. What effect do you prefer to have on the whole? It is said that even one person meditating, praying, or thinking positive thoughts, can change how it is for thousands of others. I personally feel it is part of my dharma to be in a place of peace whenever possible.

By committing to the I AM WOWED™ Program, we are birthing a new way of be-ing. With any rebirth, there is death. Before we can be born into our new beginnings, some part of us dies—a part of us we no longer relate to, or an aspect of our life that no longer works for us. Somewhere in the process of shedding the old and welcoming the new, we realize our Divine birthright. It is in these moments of remembering who we really are, that shedding the old becomes the norm. Though we are perfect in every moment, this program can bring us closer to that place of *loving what is*—relishing every moment. When this becomes our experience, *"it's all good!"*

Some of the ways people have empowered themselves include:

enhancing creativity, removing blocks to success, releasing weight, building self-confidence and self-image, releasing an array of fears and phobias, increasing psychic abilities, enhancing relationships (including with self), and manifesting most any intention desired, particularly guiding the participant to a place of gratitude and peace that resulted in a positive sensation of worthiness.

For the first part of my life, I used to compare myself to Charlie Brown—kind of wishy-washy, not knowing what I wanted, being what I thought *others* wanted me to be. Although I thought I was okay with this comparison, at some point (around age 40), I realized that way of living was not working—not working for me or most anyone associated with me. Now, after many, many years of inner reflection and spiritual work, I would say I'm a modified Lucy. Strong in who I am, a little opinionated, though not QUITE as bossy—or at least I'd like to think so! (Remember, these are MY perceptions!)

The I AM WOWED™ Program helped me in this transition from wishy-washy to standing up for myself, balancing both my masculine and feminine strengths, walking my talk, living in the NOW, enhancing my creativity, and having gratitude and acceptance of myself and others in the most loving, gentle way. *It is a most splendid way to BE.* It is proven that with clinical hypnosis a habit can be changed in about 21 days. Based on this program and the research done around it, I would say it is more like 28 days to change any one fear or habit. If the fear or block is minor, there can be several changes over that time; however, if the habit is a long-running addiction, it is wise to "cut yourself some slack" and give yourself the gift of more time to adjust to your new way of living. There is a lot that can happen in the four to twenty-four weeks of this program, should you choose to accept it into your life.

May I suggest that you are perfect and loved unconditionally in this moment, no matter what? When we accept ourselves unconditionally, that death-birth cycle begins, and things begin to change from within. I don't know exactly *how* this happens, but it *does* happen. My experience and the research results in this book show how it has worked for me and for many others. Our minds are amazing things, and we are amazing beings. Through the power of committing to yourself, by balancing your unconscious desires with your conscious intentions, we can come to a place of loving ourselves as our Creator loves us. We are all worthy of anything that brings us to a place of peace. We are worthy of love. I believe our primary life purpose is to realize, intimately and completely, that *we are LOVE.*

Chapter 16

Grace, the Tao, and NOW
Remembering Who We *REALLY* Are

We are human BEINGS, not human DOINGS.
The message on Bear Butte was to BE In Love, not DO love.

Grace

In the preceding chapters I shared case studies and stories that showed how karma pretty much dictates the continuing saga of our lives. The adages "you reap what you sew" and "what goes around comes around" are perfect examples of karma. Many scientists say that for every action there is an equal and opposite reaction. There isn't "good" and "bad" karma—it's all good and it follows the Universal Law of Cause and Effect.

I also have shared how our souls sometimes choose extremely challenging life experiences in order for us to evolve faster than average, and that this is one reason we never want to judge other people, ourselves, or the situations in which we are involved.

Edgar Cayce, one of the pre-eminent psychics of our time (www.edgarcayce.com) said that "Karma supersedes Grace." Our free will as a soul allows us to chart our lives. This plan may include karmic retribution from previous incarnations, our soul's highest aspiration, and our soul group's intention. Together with guidance from higher beings, we make arrangements for the primary purpose of soul evolution.

Grace includes the acts of the spirit: kindness, love, patience, forgiveness, understanding, gentleness, fellowship and long-suffering—and of these, the greatest is love. Any of these acts done from a place of loving intent and not from ego, takes the place of karmic justice.

For instance, life after life, there has been a triangle of jealousy and ill-doing, even murder. Then one of the souls in this triangle decides, instead of retribution, to forgive the other two souls. That act of forgiveness is grace, and it allows the forgiving soul to relinquish any and all previous karma. Although forgiveness can be extremely difficult, it is possible and is a quicker path to enlightenment.

Cayce also said, "God is Law, and the Law is Love." We do NOT have to suffer for our discretions. Our Creator does not ask this of us. Our Creator asks us to love another as we love ourselves. When we remember we are of our Creator, that we are love, we can abide in that love. Grace offers us another option—the option to end the struggle and BE LOVE.

The Tao

The Tao Te Ching is the second most translated piece of writing after the Bible. Written by Lao-tzu, a Chinese prophet who lived over 25 centuries ago, it contains 81 amazing verses. No matter which translation you choose, it speaks directly to the soul.

Loosely translated, *Tao* means "The Way." It guides our thinking in ways that can open our hearts and challenge our every observation. The Tao contains all the truth of the universe, yet in the very first verse Lao-tzu says, "The Tao that can be talked about is not the Eternal Tao." Throughout the 81 verses your way of thinking is challenged *and* soothed. It can feel as though your mind is being played upon, yet, little by little, you *get it*. I've only read four versions so far; I suggest that if you wish to adjust "The Way" you think and live, this is "One Way" that can help.

Now

You've probably read "The Power of Now" by Eckhart Tolle, or heard comments about living in the now. I have found that through practicing mindfulness, being present in the moment, focusing on *what is* instead of what *could be* has helped every aspect of my life. In my younger years I tremendously enjoyed planning an annual two week vacation. I reveled in

Birth, Death and the Afterlife

every detail and for months, enjoyed the anticipation of the upcoming event. Then, the closer it came to the actual occasion depression wormed its way in. My husband at the time dreaded those days and could not understand my increasing trepidation [that soon the vacation would be over]. I barely enjoyed the two weeks because once it was happening, it was over for me. The mood lightened once I could begin planning again. What a crazy way to *not* live! Yes, it's fun to plan, but I no longer leave the present moment in order to do so. Now I practice mindfulness which is my version of living consciously, with an awareness of the moment (most of the time).

The other day I watched George Burns singing "I Wish I was 18 Again" on YouTube. It's a very poignant song, yet even as I teared up while watching and listening, I knew I most certainly did *not* wish I were 18 again! Each of my wrinkles holds a story, every scar triggers a memory, and this body holds a mystery beyond mysteries—my eternal being. I didn't know (remember) this at age 18, and I only now am scratching the surface of *who I really am*. So I choose, as much as possible, to be present—in the Eternal Now.

Remembering

As I was writing this last chapter, I asked the Universe to help me find the appropriate final client session that would sum up what the most important message was for us to know at this time. A few days later, "Kay" called for an appointment. We had never met, but we did have a mutual friend. "Kay" knew nothing about the book, oracle deck, or I AM WOWED™ Program. She presented for a PLR with a few questions she wanted answered, yet she had no clear expectations or attachments to a specific outcome. Her session is a prime example of how our guides are working hard in order to help us remember. Following are excerpts from her session.

> MK: (Used my most common method of regression. She soon found herself in a tunnel that she described as more of a wormhole. She said she was traveling when I asked her if she sensed any guides or energies around her.
> Kay: I feel love. It's a feeling. Acceptance… welcome… undefined… special… and I'm traveling… very beautiful. This is what I kind of feel like the real reality is, not 3Dimensional.

MK: So just go deep and immerse yourself in it. As you are able, just share what you are experiencing so you are able to really remember this.

K: On my right hand is a darker, denser… on my left it's more bright, like sunlight rays, only not quite. Maybe it's a welcoming. I come out here and ask myself, "Who am I?" And it just waits for me. It's like traveling through space only it's not dark, it's very light. I am moving, but I'm floating. Just like a filament of color that breaks apart and it's getting thinner.

MK: (I ask the consciousness she is aware of if it would answer some of her questions.)

K: It's like it doesn't want to do that—it wants to stay above it as an observer… that those questions aren't important. It says it's important just to be. Strange. It's like I work too hard at it. That be-ing is not that hard.

MK: Can it share with you, ways to BE more? I would understand this as being in the present moment and yet… and I understand the experience that you're having, but when you come back to this 3D Earth, how do we bring this experience back with you in order to live…

K: It's like it's a door out of the 3D… that there's more than the 3D… that this… I should be doing more of this and move beyond. Strange.

MK: You should do more of this in order to move beyond or do more of this *and* move beyond what you are now experiencing?

K: *AND* move beyond.

MK: And "this" being meditation? Or getting into this type of experience, or what?

K: It's the feeling "being in love." Not being in love—being and loved, that… relax and let go, I guess, is what I'm getting. It's okay! I can let go. That's what it says to me—let go—just come out here, you'll see—there's lots of love, there's lots of light! No worry! I'm tripping on some small stuff. It's a very strange experience. Maybe this is my Higher Self.

MK: See what else you get. What is this? I'm asking too, to this consciousness that you are experiencing or whatever it is, that if we can give it a name or a tag, then we can recall it more easily while we're in this human form.

K: Well, what comes into my mind, if I'm relating to it when I'm human, it's being in space. Only I'm not human out here. I just float and travel and relax, and there's light that comes. It's like a kiss on the forehead and away it goes! I wonder if this is what death is like? If it is, it's going to be very nice! I've not know this before. It doesn't want to deal with little questions.

MK: He?

K: It.

MK: It, okay. Well, maybe after this is done, it can guide you to where you can get some answers?

K: Yes. And maybe what I need to do is soak up love. It's a definitely wonderful medium-rich blue, with white light coming through it.

MK: And how are you in this experience? What color are you, or what is your essence?

K: Invisible. I am "it."

MK: Okay! So this is who you are? Is this who you really are?

K: Yes, I am this. But I'm not just me, I'm with all of it. It isn't lonely out there at all. I'm not alone! But they are not people I know, I can't say there's [name] and there's [name] and there's… it's just like we *are*. And I would have to make a conscious decision to form an identity. (Long pause)

MK: Okay. Wow. Remember all of this… even if there is something you cannot explain verbally… remember this experience… bring it into your conscious awareness… remember… What's happening?

K: There are little lights, blocks, that flicker, and I'm trying to get one of them to come in and talk to me. I'm trying to find an identity.

MK: Okay. You can see if one of them can take you to a place where you can get some of your questions answered. Or they can take you to a past life that will answer some of your questions about your current life and why you are here.

K: What is says is I'm asking the wrong questions. But I don't know what to ask.

MK: I'd like to ask, "What is most important for you to know at this time?"

K: I am loved.

MK: Can they share, possibly, what happens when you get angry or you eat when you don't want to eat? Where does that come from?

K: Not right now! (Laughs) He doesn't want to do that right now.

MK: For another time then?

K: I guess so! I got the feeling that isn't where I'm going right now.

MK: Okay. Okay, well we don't want to push the envelope here… so just really enjoy this experience… and even while you're enjoying it, I'd like you to open up to the suggestion that when you do practice this experience, over the next part of your life, that all of these questions [answers] will just automatically be revealed to you… that this information will come to you naturally. You will just know. Just like you are having in this experience…

K: You know, I have the feeling that knowing this, those questions don't become important. That's what it's saying. Don't get stuck in the little things. There is no anger out there. Let go and enjoy.

MK: (More suggesting to the client that she get totally into the experience and that she will remember it… long pause.)

K: Another question I ask myself, is "Who am I?" Well, maybe this is who I am. I have the feelings and the emotions that I have accumulated over a lifetime… but out here, I'm at peace… I'm surrounded by love.

MK: Then why do we incarnate? If this is what we are to remember, why do we incarnate with these issues?

K: That's how I gain knowledge. I'm out here and it's always here for me… but I chose to come back into a… this is limitless!

MK: Your experience or the Earth plane?

K: My experience today—where I am. The Earth has limits. But I think my job… I don't know this but I think maybe my job is to not forget.

MK: Okay. So really remember… bring this experience into every cell… even into your muscles and your bones and your heart and your skin and your hair and your eyes. Let every cell and fiber and tissue of your being, including your human self, remember this now…

K: I don't ever remember being here. I do now! I walk every day and ask, "Who am I?" And now I know, this is who I am! My blue field is leaving now. Now I'm waiting. Waiting. It's waiting for my question! It told me who I am… I'm asking why I get angry. I think it's saying to me… it took me up because I do this, because I don't understand how much I am loved, and how I love. I went into future, not past! I have a mild headache, like my brain is rearranging parts of itself to put this in. Kind of strange. I have walked away from time and space as I live it.

MK: Do you have a deeper understanding now, that you do have guides, that you are helped?

K: Yes.

MK: Okay. Do your guides have anything where they could introduce themselves? Do they have names?

K: They come by color and space.

MK: Are there many different colors, or…?

K: These are all shades of blue and white. On other times I've had a gold one. Yeah, they're there now. Oh, I had an orange one streak by! Playful. I asked what it says to me—I asked my Higher Self to answer questions and it chose the question of, "Who am I?" Because that's been an old question with me. And the ones I wrote down aren't the ones it wants me to worry about… today. It's a nice thing, who I am!

MK: Yes, it is, isn't it!

K: If I know there is so much more beyond what is a physical body, I think I should love my physical body while I'm here, and not worry about it. Because when you worry about all that, you lose who you really are. I came to have these experiences—enjoy them—don't get lost! It says I'm doing it right. Huh, I never would have gotten here by myself. Thank you, Higher Self, thank you for taking me out and showing me. I know who I am! Oh, it's all bright now! (Chuckle)

MK: Sort of like a light bulb going off, huh?

K: Well, sorta like saying, "You did the right thing, kid." It's leaving.

Thank you. Thank you. Thank you for bringing me to a place where that question is answered. Now when I have that question, I can come back here.

MK: Yes. You will be instantly back here, when you ask that question. It is imprinted in every part of your being.

K: It feels in every part of my being, I can feel it. And maybe the other questions will be answered some other day, but that wasn't what today was about.

MK: If they're even important!

K: Oh, wow! (Laughing) Wow!

MK: Okay, I'll be bringing you back now… just bring yourself back now, just like you do from meditation… thanking your Higher Self and all the beautiful beings that are one with us…

K: Thank you!

MK: (Final suggestions that the client will remember this experience of remembering who she really is, that she will remember more about the session in days and months to come, and that she will also have a deeper understanding of any other questions she may have, then the count back.)

Summary

Do you know who you are? How do you describe yourself when first meeting someone? Do you say your name and where you live and what you do for a living? Does this describe who you are? Are you ready to get past all that and to the heart, the core, of your Divine Essence that is love?

We are spiritual beings who have chosen—on some level—to incarnate into a physical body and have a physical experience on this Earth school. Once we begin to remember that we are both human and spirit, we become conscious beings. As conscious beings, we can choose to be in harmony with or combative to life. Most of us have chosen to learn and evolve while here. It is a great honor to be human during these times of consciousness shifting, though often it certainly doesn't feel that way! When we forget who we really are, we experience blocks, addictions, fears or distractions that keep us in a kind of void, or holding pattern, until we discover ways to remember *we are so very much more than we think we are.*

There are no concrete answers in this book—only ways to guide you to your own answers—methods that worked for others, that could also work for you, and suggestions on how to find your personal Dharma, your core passion, your Tao.

Love.

Finally, on the last day of writing for this project, I went to the *Be In Love* Oracle Deck and asked the question, "What is the most important message from this book?"

I'm shuffling… shuffling… shuffling… one card *flies* out:

"Unconditional Love"

And so it is.

Supplemental Information
Contributing Authors

The modalities and the beliefs expressed in the following articles are those of the contributors and are not necessarily mine or the publishers. They may, however, be reflective of your beliefs and what you desire at this time. This chapter is about finding what could work best for *you*.

When I initially asked for contributors to the book, I was inundated with offerings from passionate professionals wishing to share how their modality can help in remembering who you really are; how their work could help you release blocks, addictions, fears or distractions that are holding you back from living fully. The holistic modalities are listed in alphabetical order. Each contributor volunteered his or her time and talents to write about their passion and how it can help you. I, or someone I trust implicitly, knows the contributors personally, and would highly recommend them as qualified professionals in their field.

The articles that follow have been reduced/edited down due to the length of this book. They have been printed in their entirety in the I AM WOWED™ Workbook, and should you require more information about any of these practices, please either purchase the workbook or contact the author of the article directly.

In addition to the contents of this section, there are a many other holistic practices not written about here that I have experienced and that you could check into in your area or on the web including, but not limited to: intestinal cleanses, fasting, detoxification, walking, Pilates, dancing (Nia, Trance, etc.), stretching, physical therapy, dreaming, kinesiology/muscle testing, pendulum, vision quest, drumming, writing, singing, Chi Gong, Tai Chi, Matrix Energetics, Rolfing, bicycling, running, jogging, and many other forms of fitness. Anything that you feel could feed your body, mind, or spirit in a positive, fulfilling manner, will assist in your process of enlightenment.

Also, notice anything you hear about or read about three times within a few days or weeks and check it out—it could be a sign from the Universe that it is something from which you would benefit and enjoy.

Always listen to your intuition, (your inner self), to discover which practices feel right for you. We are each unique in our destinies and in our personal needs. Each of you may be guided to experiment with different modalities to work in conjunction with your participating in the I AM WOWED™ Program. Some of you may wish only to work with the Program. Still others will wish only to learn about these practices—you will know what is best for you.

Appendix A lists each contributor by name, title, and contact information. If they are unable to help you, they may be able to refer you to a qualified practitioner in your area. In any case, read, listen and enjoy!

Art/Creativity
Karen J. Lauseng

When we open ourselves to our creativity, we not only gain more control of our life, but also develop an inner sense of peace. Neurophysiologists tell us that both Art and Healing originate from the same source in the body. Art and Healing are associated with similar brain wave patterns and are deeply connected. Art affects every cell in the body instantly to create a healing physiology that changes the immune system and blood flow to all the organs.

We are Creative Beings. For many of us our creativity was suppressed at an early age. Rigid educational systems, behavioral expectations, competition, and the hurried nature of our society have negatively affected our creative spirits. Most people, over the age of 10, no longer believe in their immense creative capacity. Ingrained self-judgments have hampered the development of our natural talents and curtailed our desire to go inward and express our creativity in unique and fulfilling ways.

GOOD NEWS—This is an easy state to remedy and can be accomplished with little effort. Creating art can be as simple as adding a sprig of parsley to your dinner plate, choosing a new hair style, displaying colorful dishtowels in the kitchen or rearranging your living room furniture. By being present in your daily life, the opportunity to be creative is omnipresent.

Focusing on ways to enhance the beauty and meaning of those everyday things you do will strengthen your creative spirit and open the door for more formalized artistic practices.

Appreciating Art is equally rewarding. Whether you listen to music, read poetry, visit an art gallery, attend a dance recital or allow your mind to float through the cumulous clouds on your morning walk, your outlook and way of being in the world will be transformed. The search is not for new sunsets, mountain views or landscapes but rather to focus on seeing (actually *seeing*) your existing world through the eyes of your soul and rediscovering the immense beauty that surrounds you.

By spending as little as a minute per day looking at a rose blossom, the colorful bug on your window sill or the snow on the treetops, benefits to your creative spirit and sense of peace will be profound as you open yourself to your creativity. I have found that as my spirit travels to its inner world of visions and emotions, my artistic and healing energies are enhanced. My stress level becomes relaxed. My attitude, creativity and inspirational thoughts are heightened and my overall sense of well being improves. This is how I feed my spirit—with a tranquil feeling.

Brain State Technologies

Donna Clayton Walter, editor, writer, nonprofit organization manager

Brain State Conditioning is an effective, holistic and non-invasive method of treatment that guides the client's brain back to its natural, healthy and balanced state. This pain-free modality is the product of a Scottsdale, Arizona-based company called Brain State Technologies (BST). The company's Web site (www.brainstatetech.com) says the treatments can bring about positive change in a wide range of areas, from enhancing sports performance and deepening meditation to overcoming addiction and post-traumatic stress disorder (PTSD).

The brain is the control center for our entire body. It controls every cell, every organ, every tissue and the entire autonomic nervous system, as well as reactions to stress and behaviors. For the brain to work well, it needs to be in a balanced state, with its complex sympathetic and parasympathetic nervous system in harmony.

While the brain is strong, enabling our very survival, it also is complex and fragile. "Trauma"—whether physical or emotional—impacts the brain. It isn't possible for any of us to go through life without experiencing some measure of trauma—the death of a loved one, a physical injury, being in or witnessing a car accident, experiencing the pain of the end of a relationship—things come our way every day, in ways large and small.

Brain conditioning treatment, also called "brain re-training," consists of reclining in a quiet, softly lit room in a comfortable zero-gravity chair for an assessment and (usually) ten treatment sessions about 1-1/2 hours long. A technician pastes electrodes to the client's scalp and the client relaxes. Sometimes the technician gives instructions to visualize a relaxing scene, but mostly the experience is like sitting in quiet meditation.

The client listens to a pleasing series of tones and the electrodes send the brain's response back to a computer. The program of tones, called a "design," is actually the client's own brainwaves converted into musical notes, as well as other sounds meant to encourage the brain towards a more balanced state. The computer program customizes to what that individual's brain needs to hear in order to make positive changes and free up the neural pathways so that they function clearly.

In most cases, clients set up a block of appointments, getting two re-training sessions per day, for five days running. This accomplishes all 10 sessions within one business week.

While many clients notice changes throughout the course of their treatment, most people note the most significant changes two to three weeks after completing their training. Results are generally subtle at first, and then build over time.

Brain re-training is like pushing the "reset" button on your brain. It removes the hindrances and "static" that resulted from trauma. The cleared neural pathways allow information to flow unimpeded, the brain restored to its original state of balance—that brain's own "personal best." Clients often report more joy and a greater sense of moving through life with ease—and that's certainly been my experience!

Chakra Clearing
Professor Debra L. Yeager, Madame Mystic

Releasing blocks is something we all can do. But unless we understand why they are there, or we have "paid off" the karma from them or there was some lesson learned from them, no one ever will be able to release them—neither yourself nor any other healer.

Did you know that your skin is the largest organ with regards to your body? Skin cells are being created all the time and are rising up into the dermis, the inside layer of skin and finally surfacing into the epidermis level, the top layer of skin. So why is it that we continue to have a scar on our leg from many years ago? Do the new skin cells being generated have this pre-programmed 'thought' that they are to mutate before they reach the surface? Now those would be some pretty smart cells!

In reality, it is a cord—or an "attachment"—to that past event that created the scar. This event must be worked through, and then released, for the scar to go away. So in your next meditation take the time to 'see' that past event, ask the guides for resolution, and then cut the cords that are attached to the event. The scars don't magically heal—this is a process that will take many times to go through before it is finally, completely released.

If a scar has been on your body for 30 years, it just might take that long to release it. However, if you are done with that pain, fear and scarring on any level, it may not take very long. How emotional are you about this event? If there still are emotions connected to this event, then it shall take longer.

Some people can drop into a meditation and start working on releasing the first day: others will take years to feel comfortable enough to get into a meditation to even start releasing. The goal is to get you into a meditation and collaborate with the guides to work on cutting the cords.

Remember that this is about the person who needs the healing: Are they ready? Do they want to release things out of their life? If they are, the process can start. If they are not ready, it does not matter how many healers you bring into the room—it will not make a difference or be effective on the one who needs help.

All change will cause an adjustment to the body. Continue to tell yourself that you are at peace with the changes that are happening in your body as you move through your healing process either on your own or with the help of a healer.

Working in collaboration with the guides, all things are possible—from finding out what lies ahead in your future to past lives you have not yet worked through. Working with the guides is akin to connecting to the universe with all knowledge and abilities to make changes not only in your own world, but in the world of others.

After working with guides for many years, I can tell you one thing about illness that is rather interesting. Many times we write an illness into our lesson plan so we can go through the process of healing ourself. Then we move on to the next level, helping to heal others of the same thing. So pay attention to how you feel, and how you feel changes affecting you. This information will come in handy at some point of your future.

Remember that your guides/angels are always with you—all the time, every moment, every day—to help you through your life. It is in your "contract" with them, and they with you. The guides come here to work with us as part of their agreement to become greater connected beings. So the better we turn out, the better they look to their higher power. All you have to do is ask, and they are there to help you.

I wish you blessings as you move forward in this!

Chiropractic
Louise Cash, D.C., C.A.C.

Chiropractic deals essentially with clearing the Nerve System of interference. In doing so, all systems of the body/mind are re-booted and function at a higher level. Life is a series of experiences which enter the body as subtle energy information. The tissues of the body must fully integrate this incoming energy information in order for the body/mind to grow, mature and have optimal health and well-being. When the body cannot fully integrate some incoming subtle energy information this energy gets stuck in the tissues, whether it be the connective tissues, the joints or the muscles. The chiropractic adjustment assists the body to fully integrate this non-integrated subtle energy from a life experience. This allows freedom and expansion of the body/mind. When non-integrated subtle energies are hanging out in the tissues, symptoms such as discomfort, inflammation, lack of energy, swelling, dis-ease, difficulty focusing or thinking, addictions, anxiety/depression, victim mentality and myriad others interfere with the flow of the Innate Life Force in the body/mind. The chiropractic adjustment allows the body's own Innate Life Force to build, flow and heal as well as bring forth the opportunity for us to be the fabulous creators we are intended to be.

Along with the gentle and specific chiropractic adjustments, I use cold LASER for emotional release and re-setting neurology; sound therapy through Tibetan Singing Bowls which help the body to adjust to the new way of being; color therapy in and around the major seven chakras, and percussive massage to help release the fascia's tight grip around the muscles. This package of therapies used with the chiropractic adjustment works very well and continues to evolve as times change.

A chiropractic adjustment is the beginning of the healing process. It has taken time for the body to get to the interfered state that it is in, and so it will take time for it to come around again to new health. The body's nerve system is the slowest to heal and the supporting ligaments are second slowest to heal. When I work with a patient, I am working toward stability of structure. Symptoms are often gone before true stability occurs. Full recovery and the speed of recovery depend on many factors, such as: how long it has been since this all started; the basic condition of the person—eating, drinking, exercise habits; the damage involved to the nerve tissue, organs, muscles, and mind; compliance of patient—compliant patients, I have found, have the greatest recovery rate. There is no standard for length of time this process can take. In my office, I suggest new patients schedule six visits, initially, to enable moving through the basic neurological muscle tests and chiropractic adjustments. In my clinical experience I have found that these visits give a patient a very good foundation for improved health and the ability to decide how to proceed with care.

Interferences can slow or stop progression to stability and deflammation. The most common are continuing to sit in a recliner—this "stoves up" the sacrum and shuts down your breath; eating foods and herbs that one is sensitive to, creating inflammation—I offer the Alcat blood test in my office to determinate what foods one tolerates; if there has been exposure to molds, mildews, environmental chemicals: what food additives and colorings one is sensitive to. Over-or under-exercising and stretching; negative thought and speaking patterns—these are things that can weaken the body/mind.

Chiropractic is holistic. It treats the whole body and mind. Some folks come in for neck pain, back pain, sciatic, numbness/tingling, weak muscles, digestive problems, menstrual disorders or headaches, but what they all receive is a full body workup. Everything is connected. Leave some one thing untreated and the whole will be weakened. The techniques that I use in my office are gentle and patients find them very relaxing. Some consider pain a bad thing. On the contrary, pain is a wonderful sign that something is amiss in the body. My patients and I work with their pain, using it as a touchstone to help us to get to the core issue involved. I am not a "fix-it" doctor. I am a facilitating physician who coaches and assist patients in all ways that I am professionally able to clear and heal the body to the level desired. At my practice: There is no special preparation needed for the first chiropractic examination and treatment. I ask only that you wear comfortable clothes. I do treat on the first visit after taking a complete history and discussing your goals for your health. Some find they are sore the morning after the first treatment. I explain that the expression of many nerves was turned down, much like a dimmer switch being turned down on a dining room chandelier. After the treatment, the dimmer switch is again turned fully on in the nerves and the muscles that receive the nerve flow are working to their full capability. This is what creates the soreness—much like an athlete that has been out of practice often gets sore when he or she returns to working out.

No matter what reason one may initially come in to begin chiropractic treatment, I have found that *lives change*. The process of getting chiropractic adjustments changes the vibratory signal or tone in the body… the music of the body/mind changes and since the body/mind cannot be separated: what changes is one affects the other. This invites new opportunities into your life. I have seen this again and again in my office as well as my own life.

Madonna J. Kettler, PhD

Crystals and Rocks
Cindy Bann

The Healing Benefit of Stones

As a young child, I was always fascinated by the shape and colors of stones I saw in my neighborhood and during family vacation travels. There always seemed to be more to the stones that I was fascinated with than just their color and sparkle. As I expanded my adventures to include the discovery of spiritual and healing modalities, stones became more and more a partner in my experiences.

There have been numerous studies and papers written on the vibrational frequency of the Earth. Everything within the universe, including this planet, resonates at its own frequency. We've become so accustomed to these vibrations that we don't notice them until their vibration changes in frequency or intensity. Since stones also vibrate—remember the old commercials for a wristwatch with quartz accuracy?—it stands to reason that they can be used to aid in healing work.

There are a number of wonderful books currently in the market, including 'Love is in the Earth,' by Melody, that provide detailed information on the healing properties of stones. This information includes the astrological sign, vibrational number, associated chakra and associated body part for each stone and gem. Some books also provide detailed information on the physical and emotional levels of healing that each stone can aid along with full body layouts using stones.

I had often used stones when mediating or grounding and carried favorite stones in my pocket during stressful meetings at work. I have seen and felt the vibrational power of these stones during very stressful and very peaceful situations. It was during some practice healing sessions I was facilitating that I first became acquainted with the vibrational healing power of stones.

As a healing practitioner, I've placed stones under the body, on chakra points and on body positions of a client. Stones used in healing sessions not only help to maintain but also enhance vibrational and healing energy levels. Stones such as Laser Quartz aid in breaking and dissolving blockages. Grounding stones such as Mary Ellen Jasper or Hematite can be placed at a client's feet to keep the client grounded and in their body during a healing session. A pair of Concretions can be a great help when working on organs and emotional issues. Other stones such as Fluorite or Selenite can be used to calm and balance areas of 'dis-ease'. Stones can be integrated into any other healing modality to enhance the healing session.

It is always important for a practitioner utilizing stones in a healing session to keep the client safe and comfortable. Sharp or heavy stones that could cut or cause the client physical discomfort during a session should not be used. Also, it is important to follow one's intuition when using stones in a healing session. Just because a book indicates that a particular stone should be used on a particular part of the body doesn't mean that the stone can't be used somewhere else on the body to aid healing. The vibrations of the practitioner, the client and the stone all integrate and work together to provide the healing experience.

In healing sessions where I utilize stones, I encourage my clients to communicate if the stone isn't working for them, or if they would like a different stone used or to change the focus/position for the stones used. I encourage anyone participating in a healing session as a client to bring his or her own stones. You can use these stones later to help integrate healing energies from your healing session.

Integrating stones in your healing and spiritual practices is a great way to connect to Earth energies and, in return, a way to send healing energies back to the Earth.

EFT (Emotional Freedom Technique)
Valerie Lis, MA, EFT-CERT-II, EFT-ADV

Emotional Freedom Techniques (EFT) for Addictions

EMOTIONAL FREEDOM TECHNIQUES (EFT) is an effective self-tool to release blocks and distractions, and to support recovery from addictions. It was created in the 1990s by Stanford engineer Gary Craig as a shortened form of Thought Field Therapy (TFT). It involves tapping with fingertips on specified points of the face and upper body while mentally focusing on a distressful memory or thought. It is based on acupuncture principles and often works in minutes. While relaxation methods are usually temporary, EFT offers a more permanent solution.

EFT is used in many ways to support universal emotional healing. It dissolves stress reactions associated with trauma and phobia. It reduces chronic pain and resolves minor physical complaints such as headaches and acid indigestion. It eliminates food and chemical sensitivities, and it improves sports and physical performance.

EFT is used in the following ways to support the recovery process from addictions:

- To eliminate cravings and reduce withdrawal symptoms
- To heal from traumatic events from the past and resolve anxiety over the future
- To neutralize emotional pain such as anger, fear, sadness, and shame
- To correct self-sabotaging thought patterns
- To reduce stress, helping to prevent relapse
- To provide a sense of personal control and self-empowerment
- To rid sensitivity reactions to sugar, B vitamins, and amino acids, which are often associated with addictive patterns
- To release emotional blocks in co-dependent individuals, leading to stronger relationships and support systems for the addict

The recovery process from addictions is challenging, and few self-tools have been available. EFT effectively supports recovery in many ways, and is a highly beneficial practice for addicts in recovery, co-dependents- and just about everyone else.

This short exercise has been included to take you through the simple—yet powerful—process of EFT.

Begin by focusing on a specific bothersome memory. Notice how much stress you feel and where you feel it in your body. While continuing to focus on the memory, gently tap with your fingertips 4-5 times on each of the following locations: top of the head, inside of the eyebrow, side of the eye, under the eye, under the nose, on the chin, on the collarbone, 4-5" below the armpit. Repeat (tap again). Now evaluate your stress level. If you notice a shift, adjust your focus and start over. For example, if your emotion changes from stress to fear, now focus on fear and tap again. If the craving moves from your stomach to your throat, now focus on your throat and tap again. Continue to tap, readjusting your focus as symptoms change, until your distress is gone. This short exercise allows you the opportunity to experience and understand the process of EFT. You will find the standard version substantially more effective. You may also want to work with an experienced practitioner.

For addicts and co-dependants, EFT is used to release blocks that support recovery. It can actually be used by *anyone* to release blocks that support emotional and physical health and wellbeing. Best of all, EFT is a self-tool. You choose when to use it. It is always there when you need it.

Energetic Resonance Encoding (ERE)
Sandee Traeger, CMT, Reiki Master,
IET Practitioner, Inter-Faith Priestess

This healing modality involves the use and transfer of Sacred Geometric Frequencies or Vibrations to aid in clearing blocks, releasing limiting cellular memories, and balancing the electromagnetic energy field. Depending upon an individual's soul purpose, results can vary from instantaneous transformation to simply aiding in the healing or transition process. Effects vary within individuals as well. Some people feel or experience a physical, or emotional release, a burst of energy or a great sense of freedom and restoration or balance.

ERE can be used on its own or combined with any other healing modality. While ERE encoding occurs on both cellular and energetic levels, it is a non-invasive healing modality. The process involves stimulating the conscious mind, or distracting it, so that the subconscious mind, emotional, physical and spiritual bodies can be free to receive the ERE vibrational frequencies.

When I am speaking with someone or conversing online, either in session or out, I am aware of the energy vibration of each word that I speak or write. Each word has a resonance and I am divinely guided as to which word to select, based upon the energy vibration that is needed by that individual person at the time.

Stepping away from the daily distractions, retreating to my own safe sanctuary for meditation and rebalancing of my energies is what helps me stay in touch with my inner "I AM" presence.

Feng-Shui
Paula Geisler

Feng-shui is a lifetime quest. It only gets better, something that cannot be said for many lifestyles. Because feng-shui creates order in a seemingly chaotic world it has a calming effect thereby allowing a person to live their life more fully. It does not interfere with any other healing modalities. A cleansing ritual is an appropriate preparation for feng-shui living. A bodily feeling of improved well-being is the goal of practicing feng-shui. The number one concept to be grasped in feng-shui is that "everything becomes its opposite.

Natural forces and drives like gravity, magnetism, wind, water, hunger, heat (including desire), coldness, sleepiness, awe, mystery, curiosity, tenderness, anger and reverence (for starters) affect all sentient life, plant as well as animal. We are all in this together. There is much spiritual nourishment in feng-shui but gluttony is not auspicious. Only a measured, controlled application of its principles creates the desired effect: a sense of increased well-being. We are dealing with the conscious manipulation of "chi," or élan-vital, with the intention to increase its efficacious effects upon ourselves, others, and—if the Butterfly Effect is real—perhaps the entire world. The study of wind and water is a worthwhile endeavor for a lifetime. And here is more good news: feng-shui is simple, yet profound, free and readily available... if you only know where to look.

Healing/Energy Work

Healing Breath
Cindy Bann

The idea behind Quantum-Touch® is to bring the area of 'dis-ease' up to the practitioner's vibration level and maintain that energy and vibration level through the use of breathing and energy focusing techniques.

Healing practitioners using this method can be certified as a Quantum-Touch practitioner after completing specified coursework and performing a required amount of practice hours. A practitioner of Quantum-Touch will use a number of breathing techniques including 'Fire Breath' to maintain the vibrational level and to focus the energy during a session. Energy focusing methods that may be used could include the use of chakras, color, vortexing, visualization and hands-on healing techniques.

Quantum-Touch techniques are so versatile that they can easily be used in conjunction with other healing modalities. The breathing and energy focusing methods can easily be incorporated with and compliment other healing techniques such as Reiki, massage and healing touch.

During a healing session utilizing Quantum-Touch a client may be standing, seated or reclined. The practitioner may start a session by performing an energy body scan using his or her hands and/or a pendulum. Session expectations and desires should be discussed between the practitioner and the client to identify specific areas requiring healing focus. Then, using breathing and energy focusing techniques, the practitioner will facilitate a healing session.

During this session the client may be directly or indirectly touched when 'hands-on' techniques are used by the practitioner to focus the energy work. It is important to remember that in any healing session, you as the client are also an active participant in your healing session. As a client, always indicate to the practitioner whether or not you want to be directly touched. There are healing touch techniques that can be done within the various levels of the body's aura, energy fields around the body, that do not require direct physical touching. You may feel heat, body sensations and intense emotions. You may experience discomfort and notice that this discomfort travels to other parts of your body during the session. You, as the client may also feel peaceful, pain-free and fall asleep. In some instances, you may not feel anything until well after the session has completed. As an active participant in your healing, communicate any sensations you experience during your session to the healing session practitioner so that appropriate focus and energy techniques can be utilized to aid and enhance your healing session.

Also during a session the practitioner may psychically receive information which could help your healing process. Some of this information could be very personal or disturbing to you. You have the right to communicate to the healing session practitioner whether or not you want to be told this information. Any information received by the healing session practitioner will be kept confidential. You have a right to make your healing experience comfortable and safe.

For more information on Quantum-Touch® and a list of certified Quantum-Touch facilitators in your area, please see the web site at www.quantumtouch.com

Reiki
Sherri and Steve Ingvarsson

Reiki is an ancient healing art that channels universal life energy through the hands of a Reiki Practitioner into the body of the receiver.

Reiki is a wonderful tool for relaxation which helps the body, mind, and spirit. It helps disperse blocks, both physically and emotionally. Reiki is also a great grounding energy. It helps you become more based in reality which will help you deal with your life throughout the day.

All modalities work with Reiki, especially Hypnosis and IET (Integrated Energy Therapy). They are very compatible with the Reiki energy.

A Reiki session takes about an hour. The process to help with the issue/issues can take just one session or many. You can learn and be attuned to the three/master levels of Reiki. When someone is attuned to the first level of Reiki they can self-heal. This is a great way to continue with your own healing.

There are a few things that can interfere with Reiki. Drugs (not prescription drugs, but "recreational") and alcohol do interfere with the energy. Also, sometimes someone simply does not want the energy, for whatever reason. In this case, the energy given to the receiver just goes into the universe and is dispersed where it is needed.

No special preparation is needed for a Reiki session. During the session you will become very relaxed. You may experience an emotional release. Some people do shed some tears when this happens. They usually are very surprised at this, but feel so much better due to the release of emotion. After a session you may feel like you have a cold. Some people get a little upset stomach. Most people, however, have no physical after effects. You may notice a heightened intuition or insight. Drinking water after a session is always recommended. Reiki and water seem to interact with one another. The water seems to retain the Reiki energy.

Reiki is a beautiful energy that is natural. It is not exotic or far-fetched. It is a very realistic energy. The energy not only helps with physical ailments and emotional well-being, but can enhance your sense of respect for self and others.

Another part of Reiki is Distant Healing. You can contact your Reiki Practitioner and ask for healing that is sent to you. When someone is attuned to the second level of Reiki they are able to send Distant Reiki. This is wonderful when you want to help someone who is far away or simply can't get to a Reiki Practitioner for a one-on-one session.

Simply put, Reiki is a universal energy that works with all healing modalities and the recipient feels relaxed and loved. It is an energy that can be given to people, animals, and even inanimate objects—like an old car that you just want to keep working.

Health Coach, Life Coaching, Integrative Coaching

Do you need a Health Coach?
Maggie Christopher, CHNC

Would you like to eat natural wholesome foods, but think it takes too much time or money? Worried that the foods you love will be replaced with bland, tasteless food choices? Many people suffer from these thoughts when contemplating a way to improve their health. Usually, they embark on a short-term solution called a 'diet' to lose some weight; but unfortunately, this seldom brings them the long-term results they crave.

Studies show that people increase their success rates when they enlist support to attain their health goals. A Health Coach (aka Holistic Nutrition Counselor) is trained to educate, inspire and support you to achieve your health objectives. A Health Coach *listens* in order to understand your background, life challenges and expectations concerning your vision for optimum well-being. Then they formulate a personalized plan that guides you, step by step, toward healthier food choices and better lifestyle habits. This is important because just as there are no two people alike, there is also no such thing as one "diet" fits all. Just look at how many fad "diets" have come and gone!

Another advantage of teaming up with a Health Coach is the coach's ability to create a structure for your success. In addition, you don't need to spend years studying the proper combinations of foods to maximize nutrition because Nutrition Counselors know and understand how to gently and comfortably "step" you into enjoying these power foods. Over time, these new habits will bring your health goals and lifestyle changes into reality.

The Institute for Integrative Nutrition focuses on 'primary food.' Primary food encompasses: career, exercise, relationships and spirituality. Have you noticed that if one or more of these areas in your life isn't running smoothly, you are more likely to use food as a coping mechanism? Lifestyle and emotions not only play a significant role in your health, but also your ability to maintain your new "mindful" eating habits.

Another critical component of mindful eating is fine tuning your life so that you really enjoy your food instead of using it as an emotional crutch. We've all been there. There's an argument or breakup with a significant other and suddenly an entire sleeve of Girl Scout cookies is gone. Or your job is no longer satisfying so you're a regular at the vending machine hoping the diet soda or M&M's will get you through another day. A Health Coach guides you through these challenges in a way that lessens your reliance on food as a coping mechanism. He/She can introduce alternatives to food in times of stress.

A Health Coach or Holistic Nutrition Counselor gives you an intimate understanding of food and how to incorporate foods to create high energy and stable moods. You'll learn ways to combine natural foods to significantly reduce or eliminate cravings. You'll also discover new ways to manage your emotions which will increase your ability to comfortably maintain your weight.

Another key to a successful health plan is discovering your body's personal food choices so that they're enjoyable, flexible and sustainable. A Health Coach can assist you in this process by balancing not only your foods but the reasons *why* you eat *what* you eat.

Finding the right Health Coach is much like finding the right therapist. Many will offer a 60-minute complimentary nutrition consultation so you can get a flavor of the work they do. Most have an area or two that they specialize in such as diabetes, celiac disease, emotional eating, etc. Formulate a list of questions that you can easily compare and invite them to share their perspective on your personal requirements.

A Health Coach can take your life to new heights by teaching you how to care for yourself in a loving way through food combined with a healthy lifestyle.

Why Explore Integrative Coaching?
Lori Shin, CHT, CR

There has never been a more powerful or critical time to explore your life purpose than right now. To evolve as a collective community, we need people who walk their talk, and bring to the table the tools, practices, and processes to shift and transform both their lives and the lives of others. We see what the costs are every single day, all around the world. Revolution, upheaval, dissention; citizens of the world are willing to make the shift, and some pay with their very lives. People are not accepting the status quo any more, because "what is" isn't working for them.

What can open up for you when you explore the very things that keep you from where you want your life to be? Each day I'm reminded of this quote by Mahatma Gandhi: "My life is my message." What is your life saying about you? What is *your* message?

In my practice, I work with clients for either 6 weeks or 14 weeks in a specific method, uncovering both the conscious and unconscious beliefs, patterns, and habits that kept them from becoming who they came to be in this life. It's important for clients to embrace all of who they are, even the aspects of themselves they consider or deem bad or wrong, what Carl Jung coined as the "shadow" aspect of humans. I work with clients one-on-one over the phone, they have weekly action steps they come up with using their inner wisdom, they have a measure of accountability, and they see results from their work.

For clients who are so inclined, hypnotherapy would be very compatible with this modality. Any person willing to focus on self-inquiry is encouraged to explore all of who they are. Also, coaching encourages people to take 100% responsibility for their lives, and all modalities involving self-care are encouraged.

Self-inquiry and shadow work is for the warrior of the heart. To look at something one has denied or ignored in their life involves some risk of pain. It will also set a person free when he or she can become transparent.

Hypnosis and Hypnotherapy
Eric Christopher, MSMFT, CHT

Hypnotherapy has many faces. There are numerous therapy methods that use hypnosis to access the mind's vast potential to heal. One very effective way is to use hypnotherapy as though it were a giant microscope on an emotional issue or problem. It's a fast way of becoming aware of the subtle subconscious thoughts and beliefs that underlie and form anxiety, depression or other stuck feelings. Often we are not consciously aware of these limiting mental blocks, yet our lives are governed by them. The first step in overcoming any issue is to simply be aware of what you most want to move past or get rid of. That is why Carl Jung said that we cannot heal until that which is unconscious is brought into conscious awareness. Hypnotherapy dissects the problem, revealing it to be a knot of old thoughts and beliefs that carry an emotional energy charge. As that knot is untangled, the repressed emotional charges that come with it can be released, and the lightness and freedom of your soul essence (that which you were before the negative thoughts took hold) can take its place. This healing can occur in one to three sessions, depending on the issue.

There's a saying, "What you resist will persist." We often go through our lives subtly resisting uncomfortable emotions, or trying to get away from anxieties. Addictions have been called 'a strategy of avoidance' because they are often "emotion stuffers." Ironically, the way to erase the emotional charge of any uncomfortable feeling or block is to fully place the spotlight of your attention on it using hypnotherapy.

When the mind is focused under hypnosis, you can feel where in the body you are storing the negative emotion or stuck feeling. That is the past you are carrying with you. It exists as a memory, or stuck thought-form energy in your body/mind system. As you focus on that feeling further, you notice that it is made up of tiny, subtle subconscious thoughts. For instance, under a recent client's chronic anxiety was the belief, "I can't make a mistake… because if I do, I'll be criticized… and then I'll be unwanted and alone."

He felt that anxiety in his gut. His inner mind showed him some situations with his parents when that belief took root. Then, in his mind's eye and with his conscious will and intent, he sent the emotional energy charge of that feeling in his gut back to whoever gave it to him, instructing them that they, in turn, can give it back to whoever gave it to them, but he's not going to hang onto it anymore. It is amazing how one can always clearly feel the sensation of that energy leaving the body when they focus on it. Then he brought back into his body the energy of confidence, enthusiasm and liveliness that he had lost when he took on those old beliefs. A feeling of lightness, strength and joy always replace a heavy fear-based feeling. The result will be a feeling of great freedom, and a noticeable shift toward healing, which means becoming more whole and complete. The shift tends to be lasting because it is done at the subconscious level, where the problem was rooted.

Often deep wounds and our stuck points in life can be traced back to a chronic feeling of unworthiness in some aspect of our lives. If left unexamined, these false beliefs will act as a magnet that draws life situations that reinforce this belief, due to the law of attraction. For instance, you cannot experience true love if you have an unconscious mind program that says you are unworthy of love. Life is often like a giant copy machine that hands us a copy of our unconscious beliefs. However, if these unworthy feelings are deeply examined, it will be seen that they are simply mind programs that were given to you by some hurt caregivers early in life who were unable to be fully present with you, or else passed on their own hurt and anger onto the safe targets of their children. Thus, all stuck, negative feelings can be reduced to a subconscious mind program that was given to you by a hurt person or an unfortunate situation. Like a faulty computer program that creates havoc, once the problematic mind program is made aware of, it can be released and replaced with an empowering feeling that is more in tune with the truth of who and what you are. You are *in fact* an amazing, eternal and indestructible soul being that is using a body to let its essence of gifts, strengths and passions shine through, unobstructed by false mind programs.

Hypnotherapy creates a gap between you and your limiting, subconscious mind programs that create negative feelings. In truth, we are beings which transcend not only the body, but also the mind programs that formed as we grew up. The potency of hypnotherapy comes when you can deeply *feel* the freedom and power of the truth of your being when you release the heavy, fear-based energy of false beliefs that you have been accustomed to. Truth is felt. When you KNOW you are worthy of love at the deepest level, you no longer believe any habitual thoughts that contradict who and what you really are. You then feel lighter and more complete because the 'mental dirt' of false beliefs has been washed clean from your true essence.

Most sessions are two hours in length, sometimes a bit longer. When clients see me for a particular issue with which they are struggling, such as anxiety, they will feel a deep shift in just one session because Releasement Hypnotherapy works at the level of the body and the subconscious mind, not just intellectually. Depending on the severity of the issue and the motivation level of the client, one or two additional sessions could be needed for a deeper, more permanent shift.

Clients do need to be fully ready and want to heal. If part of them is afraid of healing and moving to the next 'level,' we have to work on the roots of that fear first. But as Joseph Campbell said, "The cave you fear to enter holds the treasure you seek."

Journaling
Allison E. Oja

From the moment I could string two words together, I have kept a journal. The act of keeping a journal is very personal—it's a conversation you have with yourself. Being a visual person, journaling was always something I saw in broad terms. The pages of my numerous diaries are not just filled with writing, but rather a mix of lists, drawings, newspaper clippings, paintings, pictures and a few interesting mementos.

Some people write every day to reap the restorative benefits. Others, like me, tend to journal when they feel the need to work through an issue, de-stress or make important choices. There's a freedom about emptying your mind onto a blank page—it allows you to sort out and organize your thoughts and ideas—letting go of what you no longer want, and making a place for forgiveness and healing to grow. Always remember, change can be incredibly hard and painful, and it does not happen overnight. Change is a process. A journey. Journaling is about documenting your soul's course through life.

The joy of journaling can be experienced by anyone, anywhere, at any time. There are no rules—no right or wrong way. It can be as simple and inexpensive as a notebook, or as personal and creative as a hand-bound book you make yourself. How you choose to express yourself isn't important. It's the act of expressing yourself, having an honest conversation with your soul—that's the point of journaling. Creating allows you to access your Higher Self, and for many, journaling is the perfect medium for communicating more clearly with the Universe. Handwriting, spelling and grammar don't matter. The ability to paint or draw doesn't matter. Allow yourself to explore! Buy a pack of color crayons, or markers, or a fountain pen—use what makes you feel happy, fits your mood or you just happen to have on hand. As you become more in touch with your whole being through journaling, you are often able to make better choices because you are more in tune with yourself—who you are, the world, and your place in it. Experiment. Play. Have fun. It's about self-discovery.

Give yourself permission to say whatever you want in your journal. Don't censor yourself. Granted, that may be difficult if you are worried about someone else reading your innermost thoughts, so be sure to store your journal in a secure place. If you know no one else can access your journal, you are much more likely to be truthful about what you really think and feel. Candor, especially with yourself, is of utmost importance.

Journaling often works in conjunction with other holistic healing modalities to enhance their efficacy. Psychotherapy, dreaming, numerology, astrology, hypnosis, prayer, guidance cards, rocks or crystals, art and creativity are just a few of the numerous approaches that tend to lend themselves naturally toward journaling. Used alone or in combination with other methods, journaling is a powerful tool for assisting people in achieving emotional, physical and spiritual release and healing. So sit down, pick up a pen, and listen carefully. Your soul is waiting to have a conversation with you!

Life Between Lives Spiritual Regression
Eric Christopher, MSMFT, CHT

We are all far more than our bodies and what we think about ourselves. We are magnificent, eternal soul beings with far more creative potential than our minds would ever allow ourselves to believe. One of the most efficient ways of directly experiencing who and what we really are is through a Life Between Lives session.

Life Between Lives Regression (LBL) officially began with Dr. Michael Newton's research in regressing 3,500 people to their existence between lives. While documenting the amazing consistencies that they reported in his book, *Journey of Souls*, he also noticed that as a by-product, the sessions were profoundly beneficial. Sessions brought a sense of solid clarity, peace and wisdom that resulted from basking in the 'clearer seeing' of what Newton terms a super-conscious state of mind. He discovered that just as a person may have certain agendas in life such as growing up, going to school, finding a vocation, having a family, retiring, etc., so the soul has its own agendas—to grow, develop and blossom into expressing its full, enormous potential.

Since you're already an eternal being using a body, you can tune into this aspect of yourself that transcends the material realm of time and space.

LBL offers an efficient, steady and systematic method to accomplish this. First, you begin by withdrawing your focus and attention from the outside, material world and turning it inward. Hypnosis is a great tool to achieve this because it quickly creates the effect of an extremely deep meditation. Inherent in the LBL process is a continual deepening of the hypnotic trance depth which may enable you to unlock soul memories, meet soul guides, become aware of the agendas in this life that you planned for yourself as a soul, as well as obtain other glimpses of your life as a soul.

In the beginning of the LBL process, you 'un-identify' with the dominant thoughts surrounding your current body, replacing them with impressions and information about a past life identity. As you proceed through the stages of your most recent life identity, you ultimately transition through the death scene and into the transcendent part of you that never dies, free of body attachment and its inherent limitations. Then you begin to identify with the higher dimension of your soul-being that has lived a variety of lives for its own journey of growth, evolution and awakening.

As you continue to focus your full attention on the experience of tuning into and moving deeper into soul identification, you will notice an intense sense of well-being. The incessant chatter in the back of your mind completely stops and is replaced with a vast, expansive, calm awareness that feels like 'you.' Information 'drops into' you in a very different manner than usual... words cannot describe it easily because words belong to the realm of our senses. Information comes from beyond the mind in what can best be described as a 'telepathic download' of simultaneously occurring pictures, sense impressions, insights and/or instantaneous intuitive 'inner knowing.' You become aware that words feel inadequate to describe what you are experiencing, as if they merely capture only the tip of the iceberg. As you continue to tune into and resonate increasingly more with this soul aspect of self, the above characteristics become more pronounced, and insights that drop into you are permeated with love, clarity, wisdom and selflessness. From this higher state of vibration, you have access to all the love, joy, peace, security and creativity that may have been lacking in your human experience, should you choose to place your focus and attention on it. Also, you may notice a profound sense that your 'real' self is never separate from these qualities. You experience 'home' in the deepest sense of the word. Although this description may be a common experience, each person's LBL journey varies according to what they most need to see, experience or learn in order to move ahead to the next level of growth, understanding, evolving or awakening.

Since we are multi-dimensional beings, LBL is ultimately an exercise in tuning into the spiritual aspect of self that is vibrating at a faster rate, a rate that allows you to move closer in resonance with the spiritual dimension of guides and the souls of departed loved ones, as well as accessing information regarding your more "permanent" life as a soul. It's an exercise in awakening to what feels like a more 'conscious' aspect of self. You gain a sense that each of your Earth lives offers opportunities for spiritual growth and evolution. From this vantage point, your current Earthly problems become learning opportunities, and resolutions can more easily be seen.

Usually, clients leave the session with multiple insights such as a feeling of rejuvenation, a clearer sense of direction and their purpose(s). Above all, they experience a more 'real' identity that transcends the fears and stresses of this life with awareness that they possess, and can access the clear guidance and understanding to more easily move through the challenging situations of their life.

For more information about Life Between Lives Hypnotherapy, visit http://www.newtoninstitute.org.

Massage Therapy
Victoria Lucas, LEST, MT, CHT, RM, Wellness Practitioner

The physical and psychological benefits of massage can change and improve one's life in so many ways. Massage can be magical; by using the right pressure and allowing the hands to read the patterns of the body it takes you to a safe place, eases mental stress, increases oxygen, lowers blood pressure, increases circulation, relaxes muscles, and can provide comfort in time of stress.

Massage can be compared to a Hypnotherapy session, relaxing you into the zone not asleep but not clearly awake, taking you on a journey to slay the dragons of your past, to help remove the untruths that are locked in the muscles and release the sickness that keeps the body captive. Massage can help you build a foundation for the future, can actually help you become more aware of what is going on inside your body and help release (block) the toxins that are attacking you. Massage can help lift the weight of the world off your shoulders and open and expand where you are, right down to your soul—allowing you to visit the very core of who you are and return to the here and now—refreshed, revived and awake.

If everything is energy, then massage is a great way to bring all the energy cycles in the body together—the physical, emotional, mental and spiritual—creating external and internal balance. Massage allows our bodies to go with the flow, from the top of the head to the tips of the toes.

I have been working as a Massage Therapist for more than 24 years and am passionate about my work and the effects that massage has on my clients.

Meditation

Mindful Mediation for Depression
Cindy Bann

Mindful mediation is based on the Buddhist tradition of mediation where the participant, the person practicing the technique, stays focused on the present moment. To practice mindful mediation the participant focuses on a predetermined focal point such as an object, breath, mantra or sound without ignoring internal or external body sensations. If a distraction or bodily discomfort occurs, the distraction or sensation is acknowledged and then attention is refocused back to the focal point. A participant can practice mindful mediation anytime of the day for as long as desired.

It has been found that persons suffering from depression will try to understand the cause of the discrepancy they are experiencing between their current state and their desired state by looking at what they believe is their weaknesses and inadequacies. A number of studies have identified this pondering process as rumination. The person suffering from depression focuses on their perceived inadequacies to order to reduce their experienced discrepancy. This process in dealing with depression has been found to actually maintain, if not exacerbate the depression due to the continuation of the perceived discrepancy between the current and desired states. People utilizing rumination or pondering as a way to deal with their depressed feelings can cause themselves to relapse back into depression or make their current depression worse.

Several adaptations of the Buddhist mindful mediation technique have been put into clinical programs such as 'Mindful-Based Stress Reduction' (MBSR) and 'Mindful-Based Cognitive Therapy' (MBCT). Both programs have been found to aid people dealing with depression and its reoccurrence. MBSR is a mindful mediation-based program where participants are trained in the concept of mindful mediation and taught to see emotions, thoughts and feelings without applying judgments to them thus remaining fixed in their perceived meaning and keeping emotional interpretations out. MBCT is a combination of practices where the participant focuses on aspects of the body and how its responds to internal and external stimuli such a sounds, thoughts, feelings and bodily sensations while performing every day activities and experiencing pleasant and unpleasant situations. Both programs involve formal and informal practices. Formal activities involve class-lead training for a prescribed amount of time. Informal practice requires a participant's commitment to practice the technique(s) for a specified period of time, either daily or weekly.

A conclusion that can be made from the various studies performed on these programs is that mindful mediation can be an effective low-cost program for reducing depression and its reoccurrence. The success of the therapy program, though, clearly is dependent upon the commitment and dedication of the participant.

Empowerment Through Meditation
Tracye J. Eppler, LBLt, MHt

> "Meditation is a state of mind that takes you deep inside yourself where you meet yourself face to face. It is the eye of the storm. The peace in the middle of the flowers. You sit with yourself and look into your own eyes." ~ Tracye J. Eppler

Imagine this: Your thoughts are quiet. Opening your hands, you sit peacefully grounded upon the Earth. Your mind is rising up through your heavenly connection, becoming one with the Source of All Things. As you sit in this posture, your inner light shines brighter and brighter. Notice that each time you sit in this space it is like a new day. Your heart is opening wider, and your thoughts are growing higher. The expanse of wisdom is becoming open to you. Whether sitting or going about your day, you are receiving wisdom in whatever form is needed for your life's journey. Sitting in this peace becomes the cornerstone of your life…

Wow! Does this sound like an impossible dream or what? You are probably thinking, "Well that is great for you, but I can't sit still, and my thoughts are everywhere." That may be right in the beginning, but the meditation experience is a practice—just like increasing your walking or running time. Don't give up! There are too many benefits unique to meditation that you will miss out on by quitting too soon. Ongoing meditation improves all areas of one's life. Physical and emotional health, better concentration and mental clarity, character growth, enhanced creativity, and positive life changes are all great motivations for beginning and continuing a meditation practice.

Considering why and how you want to meditate will help you decide where to start. In this modern day, anyone can learn to meditate, and there is something for everyone. You can learn to meditate sitting or engaged in movement. There is no need to have a religious affiliation or particular faith. Regardless of the route taken, the benefits will be far-reaching. Our life, as viewed from above the Earth, must look as if we are feverish… running around delirious and thrashing about. Our thoughts are cloudy and at the end of the day, where we have been and where we are going is still a mystery. When you begin meditating, the sense of peacefulness and relaxation that comes when you breathe, release tension, and focus may be what keeps you coming back for more.

If you commit yourself to a ten to twenty minute peaceful focus each day, you may begin to recognize yourself. You are more than that lovely woman or handsome man who stares back from the mirror each morning. The real questions come up when we sit quietly with ourselves. "Who am I and why am I here?" A benefit of ongoing meditation is fulfillment. We all innately want to know the answers to these questions. What is our life's purpose? How do we find the answers? Being in a world focused on the physical, we usually begin outside of ourselves. We read books, join community groups, or visit a therapist. These are very helpful, but we forget to look in the one place we actually put the answers before we arrived here… *inside ourselves.*

The truth is, we already know the answers. It is contained in that spark of light that we all have at the center of our being. One way to meditate is to focus on and grow this brilliant light. Since ancient times, meditation has been practiced as a means of spiritual en*light*enment… to connect to and become one with the All That Is. This is the end-all of meditation: empowerment.

When you sit in a space of love and peace, you are connected to the highest Source in a place of creation. It is a place of purification. Your heart opens wider allowing love to flow more freely. The quietness that overcomes your body and mind leads the way to a greater peace as you walk through your day. If your goal is to become less reactive and more lovingly proactive then this peace and "oneness" connection will help you. Mastering your meditation experience will allow you to become increasingly aware of what you are capable of. All that you are is already within you. Discover who you really are—a powerful being of infinite potential.

Mediumship
Marveena Meek, Clairvoyant/Psychic Medium

Mediumship is the art of receiving the communications from beings who do not have a physical body. The medium uses their higher senses to hear. We all have lower senses and higher senses. Most of us are set on using our physical senses to validate our experiences. A medium gives merit to the impressions she receives from her higher senses. The art is in the interpretation.

Our physical body has several layers or extended bodies that most people cannot see with their ordinary eyes. This is appropriate for this Earth experience. However, we have layers of energy bodies that have different functions. These layers are called our light bodies. The light bodies consist of our emotional body, mental body, soul body, soul emotional body, soul mental body and casual body. All of these bodies interconnect with each other and the physical body. At the time of death, the light bodies pull away from the physical body, taking the life force with them. The soul now exists in the astral body which is appropriate for the astral realm. The light body spirit still has feelings for the loved ones left behind and is still able to think and process thought. (Learn more about spirits and the process of transitioning on the Bardo page at www.marveena.com)

How does Psychic Mediumship work? For the spirit entity to connect with a medium, all they have to do is merge the aura of the medium and connect their mental field to the medium's. Now a mind-to-mind communication takes place. Symbolism is the language of the universe. The disincarnate spirit will impress a message of symbols through their mental field to the medium's mental field. The medium will often hear a combination of words, see images, and feel impressions from the disincarnate spirit. Usually the first thing the spirit will tell the medium is their name. If they ha an unusual name, for example, they might try to get their name across by using a song, like "Rocking Robin." I once had a young girl who was killed in a car accident come in with that song. The medium will hear the song over and over until they acknowledge it.

Sometimes, the spirit will say something about how they died or give names of surviving members of the family, or a special pet. They might show the medium scenes, symbols about their life. I try to describe them to my client exactly as they are being impressed to me. It is up to the spirit to project, and up to the medium to receive.

The amount of healing and peace people gain from a mediumship session really surprises them! Often times people come to me while deep in grief—they can barely function. They feel their life is in shambles. They may not be able to appreciate or care for the loved ones that are still on Earth. Suicides can hit families hard. There is often a lot of guilt for the family and friends left behind.

When loved ones get a concrete message from someone who has crossed over, the joy is over whelming and the tears flow! They know it isn't all over for them or for their relationship with them. Perspectives change, and the weight of the world is no longer on their shoulders. They can go on living in peace, knowing their loved one isn't far away, and they will reconnect in other life times. They have a more comforting understanding of life after death, and realize we really never die!

Madonna J. Kettler, PhD

Numerology

Rosemary Rohach, Certified Life Coach—Holistic Living and Life Strategies, Meditation teacher, Certified Qi Gong instructor

Numerology is an easy-to-understand method of getting to "know thyself." It is a tool that can assist you on the journey of self discovery through the study of the numerical values of your date of birth and the letters of your birth name. It provides a broad view of your strengths, natural talents and challenges and the lessons to be learned in this lifetime. It can be a tool to help you understand the pieces of the puzzle called "self" and assist you on your path to wholeness.

The study of numerology dates back to ancient history. Many historians believe it was a part of the very early Hindu, Greek, Egyptian and Chinese cultures. The Hebrew Kabala includes the study of the power and significance of numbers.

The method of numerology used in western cultures today was developed by the Greek philosopher and mathematician Pythagoras around 500 B.C.E. He believed that the secrets of the Universe could be discovered through the study of numbers. It is written that one of his core beliefs was "that at its deepest level, reality is mathematical in nature" and that "each number has its own personality." He believed that each number has its own vibration and that each letter of the alphabet resonated to a vibration related of a specific number.

Numerology consists of two sets of numbers. The first set is derived from your date of birth and the second set is determined by calculating the numerical values of the letters of your name as they appear on your birth certificate. Consider your numerology natal chart a personal code that can provide you with insights about your life and help you to discover your natural tendencies, challenges, strengths and abilities. When deciphered it may contain messages that will help you to understand why you experience success in some areas while experiencing difficulties or discomfort in others.

A *basic* numerology reading or natal chart will consist of four parts— the Life Path, the Expression or Destiny number, the Heart or Soul Urge number and the Personality number. These are described in the I AM WOWED™ Program Workbook.

The Basic Meaning of Numbers

All numbers have a positive aspect and a challenging nature. This list shows the positive aspects of each number and includes the Master Numbers which are not broken down into single digits.

1. Individuality, originality, leadership, determination, independence and new beginnings
2. Partnership, balance, peacemaker, harmony, diplomacy, gentle, mediator and team player
3. Self-Expression, communication, creativity, playful, joyful and optimistic
4. Worker, builder of new forms, order, stability, loyalty, practicality, planner and endurance
5. Freedom and change, curiosity, flexibility, progressive, spontaneous and open minded
6. Heart and hEarth, personal responsibility, home and family, beauty, service and truth
7. Knowledge and wisdom, thinker, intelligence, introspection, philosophical and spiritual inquiry
8. Material manifestation, achievement, power and authority, law of giving and receiving and fairness
9. Humanitarian, universal love, compassion, generosity, broadmindedness, tolerance and understanding

Master Numbers

11. Spiritual Messenger or Master Teacher
22. Spiritual Visionary or Master Builder
33. Spiritual Healer

A numerology reading can provide you with a personal blueprint of your life and may include some heartwarming surprises as you learn about the value of your own set of character traits and abilities. It cannot tell you what to do and cannot predict what you may or may not do in the future.

We have each been given the gift of free will and it is by exercising our freedom of choice that we develop our character.

Numerology works well with all other modalities to help release blocks and frustrations while determining the causes of stress in your life. A numerology reading usually takes about an hour. The client has to provide his or her birth date and the name that appears on the birth certificate as well as the name he or she uses today in advance of the session so that the numerologist can prepare the natal chart in advance.

One session provides an important overview of the client's strengths and challenges; however, follow-up sessions can be helpful when an individual is planning to make major life changes or to provide a resource in discovering the cause of reoccurring problems.

Numerology is an excellent resource that provides a broad view of your life while helping to pinpoint areas where changes need to be made to prevent the causes of stress and to experience personal growth. It is a single session and provides information that you take with you to guide you on your path.

Numerology is also a wonderful tool to help gain insights into the personalities of your children and spouse/partner and to help understand why they make some of choices that they do over and over. It is a wonderful gift for parents of newborns and provides them with an understanding of who this child is and in which areas they may excel or need special guidance. It can be equally helpful for us as adults to have a basic numerology reading done for our parents to help us understand them.

Oracle Decks

Healing with Cards
Jill Hendrickson, MHt

Using cards for guidance with daily life challenges has been around for hundreds of years. You can relieve stress and anxiety literally by the turn of a card.

As we know from the Law of Attraction, what we send into the world with our thoughts and feelings, we receive from the world. Our thoughts are reflected by what we get. Sometimes though, when we don't have a mirror, it is hard to see exactly what that reflection looks like. Cards are a great tool to give us that reflection. They are not judgmental and do not have a sense of right or wrong, good or bad. Cards are mirrors of truth. They help us see our current patterns and thoughts.

When choosing a deck, decide what kind of messages you want and use all your senses. Think about whether you want inspirational messages or symbolism. Do you want a deck that you will need to look up the meaning, or do you want a straightforward message? Where do you want your messages to come from? (Angels, Fairies, Animals, etc.) Do you want your cards to come from a specific intention? (Law of Attraction, Tao, Love, Health, etc.) As you are holding the deck in your hands, become aware of how the cards feel. Use all your senses to determine if the deck is right for you. The cards should make you feel good.

When we allow cards, whether traditional tarot or oracle, to give us a connection to our own inner wisdom, we release our attachments and open ourselves to new and better possibilities. It is valuable to ask yourself: Why is this card being shown to me at this time? What lessons can I learn from this? How do I feel about the card, the words, the pictures, and the numbers? Allow yourself time to explore every aspect of the card. Bring what the card has to offer into every aspect of your life. I find that there is always relevancy in every card I choose. You should never have to stretch to make it fit into your life. Just keep asking yourself questions about what the card means to you.

It is important to keep in mind that we always have freedom of choice. Card readings are for the present moment—as it is now. Cards reflect the thoughts and feelings you hold in the moment during the reading. When you do your best to find out why the card is being revealed to you without negativity or judgment, you will allow a new space to open that will expand your soul's potential for healing and truth.

Madonna J. Kettler, PhD

Past Life Regression
Crossing the Bridge of Time
An introduction to Past Life Regression Hypnotherapy
Jill Hendrickson

- ♦ Do you wonder why a certain place seems familiar even though you have never been there?
- ♦ Perhaps you met someone new and immediately feel like best friends?
- ♦ Have you had reoccurring dreams?
- ♦ Or dreams that felt so real that you're sure they were?

You don't have to believe in reincarnation to be intrigued by the concept of a past life.

Past life regression hypnotherapy is a tool to help you find purpose and clarity in your current life. You may have a simple fascination to experience a past life, be led to make life-altering choices, or to release negative patterns.

When you decide to have a past life hypnotherapy session, it is essential that you have an intention in mind. What do you want to learn from the experience? What do you want to learn about yourself? Then keep an open mind to whatever is revealed to you during the session.

I had a client that was at a turning point in his life and wanted to verify that he was making the right choice. His first past life impression was looking at a man that was behind bars in a dungeon. Although we tried to move on to another event, he could not get past the initial man in the dungeon. He soon observed the man's horrifying, grotesque death and felt it as his own. Because of the traumatic death, I used healing methods that called in white light, guides, angels, and ancestors. During the healing, I intuitively kept getting a push that someone else wanted to come through. As the figure approached, my client knew immediately who it was. It was his brother from this life who had died very young. His brother's messages of comfort and reassurance were clear. Although the intention wasn't to connect with the Other Side, it was the validation that my client needed.

Some people experience one past life during a hypnotherapy session, while others may review three or four. Some people understand the lesson in one life, while others need to see a pattern through many lives. Everyone's experience is unique. The main aspect is to allow yourself to go wherever you need to go for your highest good. The answer is simple—trust in yourself—for you already hold the answers.

People often ask me if their experience was 'real' or if they were just 'making it up.' I absolutely believe that what they experienced was real. After all, they had real visions and real feelings during their hypnotherapy session. It is like watching a movie with intense emotions. You become so connected with the characters and entranced in the scenes that you may cry, or get angry. Such it is, also, with hypnotherapy.

When you begin to experience a past life, bits and pieces of that life are slowly revealed to you. You can receive information by seeing, feeling, or hearing, telepathically, or just a deep sense of knowing. You might only see your environment, your shoes, or get a feeling in your body. Soon, like a movie, the camera begins to pan out and more of the scene is revealed.

As you move between the scenes, the life lessons begin to present themselves. Whether the past life was truly real or not becomes irrelevant. The past becomes a metaphor for what you need to learn in your current life. What lessons does this show me? What was the purpose of that life? How does it relate to my current life? I had a client who experienced a past life in the African savanna. She felt a tremendous heaviness in her chest. An elephant had trampled her. She could sense that her people were looking for her, but when she cried out, no one could hear her. Was it important that the elephant was real? No. Her story parallels her current life and clearly revealed her feelings of not being heard.

Often, the lessons are simple. How can they be anything else when we quiet our mind, body, and spirit and just listen? Our life on Earth is not meant to be innately complicated. We make it that way when we feel unconnected to our Source and our Spirit. Be conscious of the present moment and ask yourself, 'What do I need to learn today?' Then take a few slow deep breaths and listen.

Reflexology
Lori Shin, CHT, CR

The mechanics of reflexology are based on the concepts defined in 1909 by Dr. William Fitzgerald. Literally, reflexology encompasses the practice of applying pressure to the feet and hands utilizing specific thumb, finger and hand techniques without using oil, cream or lotion based on a system of zones and reflex areas reflecting the body systems and organs on the feet and hands. In working with these techniques, a change to balance the body takes place.

As humans, we all have an intrinsic need or desire to be safe, to feel at one time or another a state of relaxation and balance, and have our mind, body, and spirit tuned into the present moment, releasing any thoughts or concerns about the past or the future. I believe intention makes up a huge component in reflexology sessions, and the intent of providing a safe, clean, clear and comfortable environment for my client, as well as honoring who they are by listening to what they tell me through their intake form, their words, their body language, voice allow me to be fully present to them during our time together. Sometimes this time together is the only time they've experienced in quite a while where they or others aren't judging, projecting, or needing to do or be anything else but themselves receiving positive regard and positive energy. I also stay in a clear and present state while preparing and working with clients to avoid any transference issues.

One of the enormous benefits clients receive from a reflexology session, whether it's an integrative session of working on the ears, hands, and feet, or solely on the feet is the sense of deep well-being and deep relaxation. If that's the only benefit I can provide, it is a huge one

Some very well researched benefits of reflexology are:

- Reduces stress and induces relaxation
- Improves circulation
- Cleanses the body of toxins and impurities
- Brings balance to the whole body
- Revitalizes energy
- Preventative health care tool; A maintenance piece
- Best results when used before an emergency occurs

- Facilitates life style changes
- Stimulates creativity and productivity
- Nurtures relationships
- Oxygenates the body; Detoxifies
- Balances hormones in the body

A reflexology session can offer people a body-centric focus, which will both relax and invigorate. As clients allow their worries and stresses to fall away during a session, they naturally allow for new, creative pathways to open through them. Reflexology can allow distraction or mind chatter to quiet. They can also open themselves up to new possibilities when they can still their thoughts.

Empowerment With Shamanism
Mary Stoffel

Shamanism is the oldest spiritual practice known to mankind, practiced worldwide for the last 30,000 to 40,000 years. For many, the word "shaman" refers to a spiritual healer, medicine man or spirit doctor capable of accessing secret knowledge and healing powers. Throughout history, shamans have divined information for their community, and served as storytellers, spiritual leaders, counselors and healers. Those in the "shamanic state of consciousness" (SSC) are able to enter into and perceive "nonordinary reality" (NOR) by means of journeying. An important aspect of shamanism is that it provides a very practical means of solving everyday problems.

Many people in our culture experience varying degrees of chronic depression and illness, addiction, dissociation, post-traumatic stress syndrome, or just plain chronic bad luck. However, few of us would attribute these symptoms to spiritual imbalance or disharmony caused by traumatic or painful events. Left unresolved, this wounding of our life-force, or spirit, may lead to mental, emotional, and/or physical illness. I know this from personal experience, as my introduction to shamanic healing was literally a life-changing event. As my wounded spirit became whole and vibrant my life reflected a sense of increased harmony and general well-being. Life became worth living again! Even better, it became fun and fulfilling, with a renewed sense of purpose and direction.

Modern shamanic practice in our western culture co-exists peacefully with urban life, complex technology and mainstream religion. Basic techniques for seeing and journeying into the spirit world have been quickly learned and adopted by contemporary men and women seeking ways to reconnect with personal helping spirits in the form of animal or human teachers. These techniques illustrate that the core shamanic experience is really simple, timeless, and universal.

Shamanic practitioners address the spiritual aspects of illness on our behalf by working with compassionate helping spirits to restore balance, harmony, and life-essence vitality. It is their responsibility to alter their state of consciousness and perceive successfully what others do not. One of the distinguishing characteristics of the shamanic practitioner is the ability to move back and forth at will between ordinary reality (OR) and non-ordinary reality (NOR) with discipline and purpose in order to heal and help others. The shaman does a diagnostic journey to consult with the spirits to determine what type of healing is appropriate for the client. It may be a soul retrieval, a soul remembering, a power animal retrieval, shamanic counseling or general spiritual healing.

Shamanic healing is a wonderful support for medical care as it addresses the emotional and spiritual issues that may be blocking total healing. The intention is to bring all aspects of our being, physical, emotional, mental and spiritual, into balance. Harmony within creates harmony without. The easiest place to start is with a diagnostic journey to determine what type of healing would be most helpful for you at this time.

Soul Clearing
Marveena Meek

Soul Clearing clears off our hard drive patterns that are stuck, software that no longer applies to our lives, parasites and entities on our Golden Web. At any give moment, the average adult has at least 30 unresolved issues that are "stuck in the tissues." These issues are holding our energy and life force hostage. Soul clearing is a way of hitting the re-set button on our soul's mission.

You might have heard people say from time-to-time, "I was beside myself with fear" or "I just haven't been myself lately." This is how you feel when you have entity attachments. It can seriously de-rail a person and cause extreme damage on all levels of being. Ugly entities are experts at diverting our attention and stealing our life-force energy, even manipulating us into doing things we would never do otherwise.

I think of soul clearing like running spyware on your PC. I have a PC and two laptops. When they get really slow and start having malfunctions or glitches, I know I need to run a check, clean the cookies or cache. Actually, it's my husband who needs to do that. I just know something isn't the way it should be. "Please fix it honey!" LOL!

He'll then run spyware on my computers to see if they've been compromised. If one has been compromised, the spyware tells him how many issues there are, and it will make suggestions for curing them. My spyware finds the problem and destroys it. Then I usually have to restart my computer, and there are times I have to download my programs again.

Before a Soul Clearing our energy bodies are like a PC, we are vulnerable to entities, miasms, thought forms, and all sorts of psychic creeps—even watchers, stalkers and what I call Dark Lords. These creepy psychic entities make a living off our fears and negative emotions of any kind.

Negativity is their window into our space. If a person uses drugs or alcohol or even lives with someone who does, they can be attacked by them. The average person is more vulnerable than you might think.

After a Soul Clearing, you will have new shields to protect you. We could still be compromised by getting drunk or high. Even having surgery can cause us to drop our shields of protection. We sometimes have vulnerabilities; these can cause us to be susceptible to psychic attack and attachments of different sorts.

The more that we desire to be light workers, the more we have to protect our space. Dark spirits very much want to keep the light down. Knowledge is power. The more we learn techniques to help us clear, the better state of health and well-being we experience. We can be in a position to give back to mankind and do something to touch the world with beauty. When we are in our power in a balanced way we can manifest on a much bigger level.

Because Mother Earth is raising her vibrations, we need to do the same. We have to—otherwise we will have to go to another dimension to keep these old illusions. To move forward means letting go of our attachments to the old paradigm.

These clearings are called Divine Destiny Clearings. They help you step out of illusions and move forward into what you really came here to do. This is like syncing software updates. If you want the new info available, you have to sync it somehow. "How do I know if I have entities or viruses?" When we have viruses or entities, or our shields have been compromised, we will not feel able to make progress. We might feel like a dark cloud looms over us, maybe see ugly spirits. Our ability to prosper and earn could be greatly diminished. Even keep a job. We might feel like we are beating our head against the wall in life.

One of the clearings that I do is called An Abundance Diversion Valve Clearing. This re-sets your valves so you can channel the rightful soul energy you should have access to toward your dreams and goals. I also do the Divine Destiny Partner Clearing which helps us to connect to a partner who can complement us. Taking care of our personal space is an ongoing project and part of our responsibility. There are always more ways than one to get the job done; this is one that I have found to be consistent and powerful.

Traditional Chinese Medicine (including Acupuncture)
Cassandra Roberson, L.Ac, OMD

TCM (Traditional Chinese Medicine) is a modality that regulates the flow of Qi, i.e. "Life Force." Qi, which flows along the pathways or meridians of the body, from head to toe, is Energy that can be stimulated or sedated as the need dictates. The acupuncture points are Energy vortexes that swirl clockwise, as do whirlpools and tornados. The speed of the swirl can also be increased or decreased by needling technique. Acupuncture is relatively painless. The ears are slightly more sensitive to the prick of the needle than other, more well-padded parts of the body. But, many do not even feel the prick of the tiny, hair thin needles. Acupressure press beads are often applied to a couple of the points, so the individual can do self-treatment at home.

When there is any type of imbalance—mental, spiritual, emotional, or physical, it is because of blockage along the meridian pathway. By manipulating the flow of the acupuncture point, change is created energetically. This energetic movement is analogous to a stream that flows merrily along until the water comes upon a boulder or beaver dam, slowing or blocking the rhythm. By removing the blockage, i.e. boulder or dam, the stream flows smoothly, again.

In terms of Oriental Medicine, the "corporeal and the ethereal soul" are affected. Addictions affect the Shen (Spirit) and the Qi (Life Force). In Oriental Medicine theory, the spirit resides in the heart. Addiction blocks the pathway to the heart, and this prevents the residing spirit from communicating with the heavenly influences (or intuition). When an individual uses substance of any type, as a way to cope, spiritual growth and the intuitive process come to a standstill. The addict becomes the addiction, losing him- or herself within the cycle of numbing the emotional pain, then experiencing the pain of being addicted.

Oriental Medicine uses a holistic perspective of addiction. This allows a compassionate approach which results in greater success, leading to healing beyond the scope of superficial symptoms. Clients can then release tightly held beliefs of old familiarities of their addictions, which perpetuates denial and pain, and offer them a choice of a healthier future.

The acupuncture points on the ear, which are the main areas for addiction treatment, have individual functions. These points are said to innervate to various parts of the brain that regulate that particular point's function, e.g. sedation or calming, strengtheing the lungs or liver, etc. Blockages or "stuck Qi" in correlating points are going to release with needling. "Feel good" or calming hormones will release and spill into the body and calm the mind and spirit. The result is more focus and less distraction. Patients typically feel better, mentally and spiritually after a treatment, and of course, this leads to increased self-care.

This modality also helps with pain relief, hormonal imbalances, hypertension, detoxing, immune strengthening, and most other illnesses for which individuals use allopathic medicine (drugs and/or some surgeries).

Individuals tend to choose this modality to avoid the side affects of drugs and the risks of surgery.

It is recommended that the individual participate in 6-12 acupuncture sessions. Even those few that stop the substance abuse upon the first treatment should complete the recommended series to stabilize the effect. Relaxation and a sense of "centeredness" occurs during treatment. Depending upon any additional acupuncture points used during treatment, there is sometimes a "purge" of blocked emotions, which then allows the individual to become more centered. This sense of well-being lingers after the treatment, especially if the appropriate herbal remedy is prescribed. These remedies prolong the sense of calm without being addictive and carry the individual through to the next enforcing treatment.

Volunteerism
Allison E. Oja

Kindness and compassion know no boundaries. Love is exponential. Find something you're passionate about and give of yourself.

Volunteering is an act of kindness and compassion people provide when they selflessly give of their time and talent for the benefit of others without the expectation of tangible benefit in return. As a volunteer for most of my life, and a volunteer coordinator for half of it, I have worked with a diverse variety of people who have chosen to share of themselves through volunteering. Just as each individual is unique, each person's reason for volunteering is also different; but, one thing I see over and over again is how people use their volunteer experience to help heal wounds—spiritual, emotional and physical.

For example, I have worked with cancer survivors and diabetics who want to "give back." Volunteering provides them emotional and spiritual closure when they help and/or support others who are going through the same painful journey they themselves have made or are still making. I meet people who have lost loved ones, who use volunteering as a constructive outlet to deal with the grieving process, helping themselves heal through helping others. I see people recovering from addictions and physical ailments, unable to find a job and emotionally spent, coming to volunteer so they can build back their physical stamina, learn new job skills, regain confidence and feel a sense of fulfillment in giving back.

One can volunteer regardless of age, socio-economic status, sex, race or religion. Volunteering should be an activity in your schedule you look forward to. If you wake up in the morning and think, "Ughh, I have to volunteer today... wonder how I can get out of it..." you are not giving your time and talent to something you love, and you need to reconsider why you have chosen to volunteer for that particular cause or organization. If it's not something that gives you joy and makes you feel good, then it is probably not a good fit. It is okay to move on. Sometimes it's simply a matter of time management. Feeling pressured to make time you feel you don't have to volunteer, even for a cause you believe in, can make the process of volunteering less enjoyable, as well. Choose a volunteer opportunity that fits not only with your beliefs, but also with your lifestyle and availability. You should feel comfortable in the environment and enjoy the people with whom you volunteer. Take the time to explore multiple opportunities before making a long-term commitment. Maybe short-term or project-based volunteering is more appealing. Find the right fit for you.

Choosing to volunteer is a gift—to others and yourself. By giving back and helping a cause or organization you believe in, you give yourself the opportunity to learn, grow and find a sense of gratitude and fulfillment that can be hard to find elsewhere. Personally, volunteering has led to discover new talents, exciting career opportunities, new friends, spiritual and emotional growth. Through helping others, I have learned to appreciate the many blessings in my life, and the pleasure of truly making a difference in someone else's. Volunteering can help put your life in perspective, and in the process, motivate you to take the necessary steps to work through issues, make changes, release negative behaviors and discover new aspects of your personality. Look for a cause or organization you are passionate about, expand your horizons, and give of yourself—your time, your talent. Volunteering can be one of the most challenging, rewarding, and life-changing experiences you will ever encounter.

Appendix A
Contributing Authors' Contact Information

Cindy Bann
Crystals and Rocks
Healing Breath
Mindful Meditation for Depression
clbann@q.com

Dr. Louise Cash, D.C., C.A.C
Chiropractic Physician
www.redhathealing.com
redhatchiro@gilanet.com, 575-519-2724

Eric Christopher, MSMFT, CHT
Hypnosis and Hypnotherapy
Past Life Regression
Life Between Lives Hypnotherapy
www.ericjchristopher.com, 651-649-1952

Maggie Christopher, CHNC
Health/Life Coaching
www.maggiechristopher.com, 651.231.1360

Tracye J. Eppler, LBLt, MHt, CHt
Empowerment through Meditation
www.wisdomfromangels.com

Paula Geisler, Feng-Shui Practitioner
Feng-Shui
www.paulageisler.com, 575-534-2087

Jill Hendrickson, MHt, specializing in Past Life Regression
Hypnotherapy and Tarotpy®.
Healing with Cards
Past Life Regression
www.natureshealingroom.com

Sherri and Steve Ingvarsson – Journey of Possibilities
Reiki
singvarsson@frontiernet.net, 612-991-6497

Karen J Lauseng - K J Artworks
Art/Creativity
www.kjartworks.com
karen@kjartworks.net, 575-313-4291

Valerie Lis, MA, EFT-CERT-II, EFT-ADV
Emotional Freedom Technique (EFT)
www.coursesforlife.com, 763-315-0086

Victoria Lucas, LEST, MT, CHT, RM
Wellness Practitioner, Massage
handsofheeling@hotmail.com, 651-338-4869

MarVeena Meek and Ghost Queen Communications
Hypnosis and Hypnotherapy
Mediumship
Soul Clearing
www.MarVeena.com, marveenameek@aol.com, 972-564-0753

Allison Oja, CHt
Jounaling
Volunteerism
allisonoja@gmail.com

Cassandra Roberson, L.Ac, OMD
Traditional Chinese Medicine - Acupuncture
shakticlinic@msn.com, 763-536-9350

Rosemary Rohach, CHt, Certified Life Coach, Holistic Living and Life Strategies, Meditation teacher, Certified Qi Gong instructor
Numerology
rmrohach@yahoo.com, 763-537-5591

Lori Shin, CHT, CR
Integrative Coaching
Reflexology
lshin101@comcast.net

Mary Stoffel
Shamanism
mlstoffel@innovatord.com, 763-444-8146

Sandee Traeger
Energetic Resonance Encoding
Wisdom & Wings Light Center, Avon, MN
spiritgirl343@yahoo.com

Donna Clayton Walter
Writer, editor, nonprofit resource director
Silver Iguana Publishing
Silver City, NM 88061
donnatheiguana@gmail.com

Prof. Debra L. Yeager
Yeager Consulting, LLC
Sensory Science Specialist, Author, Teacher, Political Consultant
Chakra Clearing, Past life regression, Channeler, Future predictions, Energy reads on people and places of residence, Medical reviews, Alien contact, Spirit life connection – lesson plans, Walk Ins, also working with multiple souls in one body.
Park Hill, Oklahoma
Century30@aol.com, 918-718-4077

Appendix B
Original Creations for Sale

- *Be In Love* Oracle Deck
- *Audio/CD Version of Oracle Deck*
- *I AM WOWED*™ Program Workbook
- Self-Hypnosis and Meditation CDs (listed on web site)

Book and Book on CD:
- Becoming Multisensory: A Guide to Discovering and Trusting Your Inner Spirit
- Booklet: Letting Go of Fear

Certifications, Seminars & Classes

Certifications:
- Transpersonal Hypnotherapy Certification – Level 1
- Masters Hypnotherapy Certification – Level 2
- Between Lives Spiritual Regression Certification – Level 3
- I AM WOWED™ Facilitator Training Certification

Seminars/Workshops
- Becoming Multisensory (1 day)
- Hands-on Healing (1 day)
- I AM WOWED™ Classes (4-24 weeks)
- Guided Meditation (4 weeks)
- Group Past Life Regression (3 hrs)
- Birth, Death and the Afterlife: Remembering Who You Really Are

(2 hour intro with 6 hour workshop the following day) Also can be designed as the topic for any speaking engagement.

For a complete listing and description of her products, services, and certification programs, please go to: www.madonnakettler.com

About the Author

Madonna J. Kettler, PhD, is an award winning Master Hypnotherapist and Hypnotherapy Trainer, author (*Becoming Multisensory: A Guide to Discovering and Trusting your Inner Spirit*), Certified Past Life and Life Between Lives Regression Therapist, intuitive, and spiritual teacher. She is the founding president of Golden Visions Center, a nonprofit organization dedicated to offering alternative approaches to physical and spiritual healing, empowering individuals and communities through education and personal transformation. She facilitates lectures and workshops around the country where she empowers people to transform their lives, gain insight into their life's purpose, and remember who they REALLY are. Madonna has created a variety of self-hypnosis and meditation CDs as well as the ground-breaking I AM WOWED™ Program (I Am Worthy Of Whatever Empowerment Desired). She is degreed through American Holistic University and certified as a hypnotherapist and trainer through the National Association of Transpersonal Hypnotherapists. She is a long-time supporter of the ARE (Edgar Cayce Foundation), a member of the National Association for Transpersonal Hypnotherapy (NATH), the National Guild of Hypnotists (NGH), the International Association for Research and Regression Therapists (IARRT), and the Newton Institute for Life-Between-Lives Spiritual Regression (TNI). Madonna travels extensively—speaking, facilitating workshops, trainings, and private sessions. She resides in Silver City, New Mexico.

CPSIA information can be obtained at www.ICGtesting.com
Printed in the USA
LVOW081611250113

317285LV00005B/793/P

9 781452 558981